Threshing Hour

Also by Graeme Carlé and published by Emmaus Road Publishing

Eating Sacred Cows
A Closer Look at Tithing

Because of the Angels
Unveiling 1 Corinthians 11:2-16

The Red Heifer's Ashes
The Ultimate Messianic Prophecy

Born of the Spirit
A Study Guide for New Believers

The Revelation series:

1. Dancing in the Dragon's Jaws
The Mystery of Israel's Survival

2. Slouching Towards Bethlehem
The Rise of the Antichrists

3. Gotta Serve Somebody
The Mystery of the Marks & 666

4. Silencing the Witnesses
Jerusalem & the Ascent of Secularism

5. Threshing Hour
Armageddon & Babylon the Great

6. Back in 7
The Seven Seals, Trumpets & Bowls

Last in the series coming soon:
7. Kingdom Come
Justice For All

Threshing Hour

Armageddon & Babylon the Great

Graeme Carlé

All proceeds from the sale of this book are used for the further publication of this and similar work by Emmaus Road Publishing.

© 2023 Graeme Carlé
All rights reserved including the right of reproduction in whole or in part in any form. The moral rights of the author have been asserted.

Book cover, design and production by Olivia Carlé
Author photo by Samantha Ives

ISBN 978-1-7385820-0-6
Epub ISBN 978-1-7385820-1-3

Unless otherwise stated, all Scripture quoted is from the
NEW AMERICAN STANDARD BIBLE®,
Copyright ©1995 The Lockman Foundation.
Used with permission.

Emmaus Road Publishing
PO Box 38 823, Howick, Auckland 2014, New Zealand
www.emmausroad.org.nz

Contents

Foreword 9

1. The Unholy Trio 11
   Mortally Wounded

2. In Dreams 27
   End of Empires

3. Inciting Armageddon 39
   The Frogs

4. Armageddon 48
   At Har-Magedon

5. Israel's Time 64
   In the Son

6. "But What About...?" 77
   Jacob's Trouble

7. Mystery Babylon 94
   "Is She...?"

8. Babylon the Great 109
   She Is...

9. Two Women 118
   Two Cities

10. The Scarlet Beast 130
    Her Steed

11. The Ten Horns 147
    United They Fall

12. The Apostasy 163
    And the Antichrist

13. "One Hour" 185
    And It's Over

14. God's Eternal Purpose 200
    Back to Eden

Epilogue 208
Appendix A - *Seven, Ten & Seventy* 209
Appendix B - *3½ Years Tribulation?* 225
Appendix C - *Seduction to Apostasy* 236
Bibliography 242
Index 250
Other books by Graeme Carlé 257

Illustrations

Figure (i)   Albrecht Durer's woodcut - first beast 22
Figure (ii) Threshing in Galilee 33
Figure (iii) Winnowing 34
Figure (iv) Map of the Jezreel Valley 49
Figure (v) Daniel's 70th Week 231

Photo (i) Vespasian sestertius coin 137
Photo (ii) Bust of Nero 140

Attributions

Fig (ii) http://commons.wikimedia.org/w/index.php?curid=893101

Fig (iii) http://commons.wikimedia.org/w/index.php?curid=8121480

Photo (i) © The Trustees of the British Museum. Museum number: 1872,0709.477 C&M catalogue number: RE2 (187) (744) (187) Curator's comments: This bucolic reverse scene suggests post-war Rome in a state of relaxed peace after the 'Year of the Four Emperors', AD 69.

Photo (ii) http://commons.wikimedia.org/w/index.php?curid=1814923

"The ten kings… receive authority with the beast for *one hour*." (Rev 17:12)

"Woe, woe, the great city, Babylon… For in *one hour* your judgment has come." (Rev 18:10)

Dedication

To Olivia,
who worked as hard as I did on this book

Thanks

To my friends for their love, support, and feedback:

Arthur Amon, Joanna Bain, Chris & Dianne Bryan, Dmitry & Linda Gafiyatulin, Dale & Donna Gifford, Mohan & Amy Herath, Mike & Jill Meyer, Ben & Dolly Pan, Chris Pan, Shane & Melissa Pope, Murray Powell, Heidi Roussell, Elizabeth Rowe, Peter & Susan Ridley, and Simone Varney

Foreword

In the epilogue to Book 4, I wrote that Book 5 would cover Revelation's last seven chapters, 16 to 22. However, that was overly ambitious and it quickly became three books.[1]

This book therefore covers just Revelation 16:13 to 19:21, i.e. the mysteries of Armageddon, Babylon the Great, New Jerusalem the Bride, and the judgement of the two beasts.

I have two main aims. The first is to dispel some common fears and misconceptions about the Battle of Har-Magedon by showing it will be very brief and Israel's finest hour. Equally misunderstood is Babylon the Great, despite her taking up one eighth of the Book of Revelation. My second aim is therefore to establish that she is not the Roman Catholic Church as the Reformers taught but much older, much larger, and much closer to home for all of us.

In Book 6, *Back In 7*, I will explain the seven seals, trumpets, and bowls, and I have left it to Book 7, *Kingdom Come: Justice for All*, to cover Revelation Chapters 20-22, i.e. the millennium, Satan's end, the resurrection, the judgement of the living and the dead, and Heaven and Hell.

It is easy to become overwhelmed with the details of John's extraordinary Revelation so here is the big picture - it is like a drama with just seven main characters: one Lamb/Lion, three women, one dragon/snake and two beasts. Obviously, the Lamb/Lion is Jesus (Rev 5:5-13) and the dragon/snake is Satan (Rev 12:9) but the three women and two beasts are not so obvious.

In Book 1, I showed that the first woman (Rev 12:1) is Israel 'according to the flesh'; in this book, I establish the identity of the second woman, Babylon the Great, and contrast her

---

[1] A fourth, a stand-alone book called *The Pearl in Plain Sight: Kingdom, Christendom & Colonisation* will look at the Kingdom of God from beginning to end on this old earth.

with the third woman, the Bride.

In Books 2, 3, and 4, I established the identities of the two beasts as the feral state and the spirit of antichrist but, as we will see in this book, it is easy to lose sight of them both.

This is because the first beast briefly appears in Revelation 11,[2] reappears in Revelation 13, 16, and 17[3] only to completely disappear in John's time[4] but is to reappear in the future! As for the second beast, it no longer looks like a lamb but has become 'the false prophet'. This spirit which has created innumerable tyrants over thousands of years will reside in one mortal man, the Antichrist, and both will be judged when Jesus returns.

Threshing Hour

The title of this book comes from the most common metaphor in the Bible for God's judgement. In Chapter 2, we look at this ancient process of separating grain from straw and chaff. Israel's wisest king, Solomon, used it as a metaphor:

> A wise king winnows the wicked,
> And drives the threshing wheel over them. (Prov 20:26)

Our 'wise king', Jesus Christ, will thresh and winnow the greatest empires and powers on earth until, as Daniel saw:

> [They] became like chaff from the summer threshing floors; and the wind carried them away so that not a trace of them was found. (Dan 2:35)

And the events described in Revelation 16-19 will take place in just "one hour".

---

[2] Revelation 11:7.
[3] Revelation 13:1-10, 16:13, and 17:3.
[4] Revelation 17:11.

1
The Unholy Trio
Mortally Wounded

Our opening text of Revelation 16:13 features three of the seven main characters in the drama of Revelation: the dragon/snake of Revelation 12 and the two beasts of Revelation 13. It is wonderful to see that their ravaging of mankind over the millennia will end, but this unholy trio will not go quietly – they have a message and a particular demonic anointing:

> 13. And I saw coming out of the mouth of *the dragon* and out of the mouth of *the beast* and out of the mouth of *the false prophet*, three unclean spirits like frogs
> 14. for they are spirits of demons, performing signs, which go out to the kings of the whole world, to gather them together for the war of the great day of God, the Almighty...
> 16. ... to the place which in Hebrew is called Har-Magedon. (Rev 16:13-16*)[5]

The trio will gather as many 'kings of the whole world' as they can to Har-Magedon, or Armageddon as the *King James Version* translates it. However, this will not be the World War III expected by many - it will be very localised, very brief, and an overwhelming victory for all who love Jesus *and for Israel*, 90% of whom will be trusting in Him before it starts, as I showed in Book 4.[6]

While the dragon/snake is obviously Satan (Rev 12:9), the identities of the beast and the false prophet have been so much debated over the last 2,000 years as to make Revelation unintelligible for most Christians. If, however, you are confident in what I have established about them so far, you can skip this chapter. For anyone not so confident, let me recap.

---

[5] I use asterisks throughout to signify 'emphasis added'.
[6] *Silencing the Witnesses: Jerusalem & the Ascent of Secularism*, pp. 280-302.

The Unsealed Scroll

In this series, I have been using a simple key to unlock Revelation, taking what I call the 1st Century Jewish Teenager's Approach, based on what John was commanded:

> "*Do not seal up* the words of the prophecy of this book, for the time is near" (Rev 22:10*)

Compare this to Daniel being commanded in the 6th century BC to "conceal these words and *seal up* the book", i.e. scroll (Dan 12:4). No-one was to understand his Messianic prophecies until Jesus came to fulfill them, as I showed in Book 1[7] and will briefly in the next chapter. John's revelation, however, was to remain unsealed, i.e. to be understood by his 1st century audience. An on-line encyclopaedia summarises our dilemma today:

> The apocalyptic symbols of Revelation are derived from prophetic books of the Old Testament and from the common Christian tradition. No doubt the earliest readers of the book understood its visions and imagery, but in the centuries since Revelation was written, the key to the original meaning of its symbolism was lost. Efforts to recover it have produced widely divergent systems of interpretation but no general recognition of any one system as nearest to the author's meaning.[8]

As they say, there is 'no doubt the earliest readers of the book understood its visions and imagery' and many indeed believe that 'the key to the original meaning of its symbolism was lost'. However, as the writer also notes, the 'symbols... are derived from prophetic books of the Old Testament and from the common Christian tradition'. This truly is the key but it has *never been lost* – we still have the 'prophetic books of the Old Testament' and all essential 'common Christian

---

[7] *Dancing in the Dragon's Jaws: The Mystery of Israel's Survival,* pp. 93-116, 177-179, 192-193.
[8] Article on Revelation, *Encarta 96.*

tradition' was recorded for us in the New Testament. The key has simply not been recognised or applied sufficiently.

Revelation is a Jewish book, written by a Jew, John, to Jews and to Gentiles in Asia Minor who had come to faith in Jesus through Jewish evangelists and teachers, Paul and Barnabas. Paul had taught in Ephesus for two years until 'all who lived in Asia heard the word of the Lord, both Jews and Greeks' (Acts 19:10). They were familiar with John's allusions, symbols, and metaphors which is why Revelation was an open book to them.

Paul explained this to the Romans, writing that the 1st century Jewish disciples had an 'advantage… great in every respect' (Rom 3:1-2) because of their history. Entrusted with the Scriptures (Rom 3:2), the inspired record of those 1,500 years, they had *lived* in 'the covenants, the Law, the temple service, and the promises' (Rom 9:4).

A 1st century Jewish teenager would have experienced first-hand a dozen cycles of their annual feasts and fasts which re-enact their unique nation's escapes from annihilation and foreshadow the Messiah's coming and His work. Paul therefore urged Gentile disciples to catch up by learning from Israel's history and their many past experiences of God at work in their midst (Rom 15:4, 1 Cor 10:1-11).

In this series, all I am doing is recognising what they already knew. So what did they know of the dragon and the two beasts?

The Unholy Trio

John tells us 'the dragon' is 'the serpent of old who is called the devil and Satan' (Rev 12:9). This was not a new idea to his Jewish audience - eight hundred years earlier, Isaiah had prophesied about the dragon (Isa 27:1) who had attacked them in Egypt (Isa 51:9-10) through the Pharaoh.

(i) 'The dragon' is Satan

Building on that, in Book 1[9] I showed that the dragon's seven heads with their seven diadems (Rev 12:3) reveal Satan's inspiration of the next six Gentile empires to attack Israel, initially 'that he might devour her child' (Rev 12:4). Not knowing when Jesus would be born, Satan inspired Pharaoh's attempt in c. 1526 BC to kill every Hebrew baby boy (Ex 1:16 & 22) and until Herod's slaughter of the baby boys born near Bethlehem in c. 5 BC, Satan was trying to *prevent* Jesus' birth.[10]

He failed but has spent the 2,000 years since then 'persecuting the woman who gave birth to the male child' (Rev 12:13), i.e. Israel 'according to the flesh... from whom is the Christ according to the flesh' (Rom 9:3-5). Today, Satan is gathering forces for his seventh great attempt to annihilate Israel but he is heading into 'the great day of God, the Almighty' - this will be his last.

As for the dragon sweeping away 'a third of the stars of heaven' (Rev 12:4), many think this refers to angels following Satan in his rebellion because stars can symbolise angels (Rev 1:20). However, they can also symbolise Abraham's descendants (Gen 15:5) and there have been at least three fulfilments in the last thousand years when a third were killed during the 12th century Crusades,[11] 19th century Russian pogroms,[12] and Hitler's 20th century Holocaust.[13]

---

9 *Dancing in the Dragon's Jaws*.
10 In between, Satan attacked her using the Assyrian, Babylonian, Medo-Persian, and Greek empires.
11 *Jerusalem & the Ascent of Secularism*, footnote 14, p. 5.
12 *Dancing in the Dragon's Jaws*, p. 154.
13 Ibid, p. 35.

(ii) 'The beast' is the self-exalting State

In Book 2,[14] I showed that 'the beast', the first beast of Revelation 13, is not an individual as is often taught[15] but the invisible 'principality and power'[16] behind the visible human 'princes' or emperors of these seven Gentile empires.

This is a major key to understanding Revelation: the beast's seven 'heads' were the seven Gentile empires that *had ruled* and *would rule over Israel*. In his day, "five have fallen" (Egypt, Assyria, Babylon, Medo-Persia, and Greece), "one is" (Rome), and "the other has not yet come" (Rev 17:10).[17]

In John's day, the time of its sixth head, the beast was manifest in the Roman Empire. Instead of 'bearing the sword' to uphold justice as a 'servant' of God and man (Rom 13:4), Rome was accepting worship as *Dea Roma*, the goddess personifying Rome, with its first temple dedicated in Smyrna in 195 BC.[18]

None of this would have been a surprise to a 1st century Jewish teenager. Every year, every Jewish family celebrated their nation's escapes from annihilation by these empires:

(a) Passover, from Egypt in the 15th century BC.

(b) Purim, from Medo-Persia in the 5th century BC.

(c) Hanukkah, from the Greeks in the 2nd century BC.

Two thousand years later, Jewish people are still celebrating these festivals, joking: "They tried to kill us. They failed. Let's eat!"

---

14 *Slouching Towards Bethlehem: The Rise of the Antichrists*.
15 E.g. by Dispensationalist writers such as Hal Lindsay, John F. Walvoord, and David Jeremiah.
16 The term describes both human and angelic power structures, 'visible and invisible, whether thrones or dominions or rulers or authorities' (Col 1:16).
17 We will look at the beast's seventh head in Chapters 10 and 11.
18 Tacitus, *Annals* 4:56.

They also had annual fasts (Zech 8:19). The most important, of course, is the Day of Atonement but the second is Tisha B'Av (lit. the ninth day of the fifth month) to mourn two major national disasters that occurred on that day:

(d) The razing of the First Temple by the Babylonians in 586 BC.

(e) The razing of the Second Temple by the Romans in 70 AD.[19]

To this day, Jewish weddings include the bridegroom smashing a glass to mark the destruction of the Temple.[20]

We see here how the great Jewish advantage worked for them - no Jewish teenager in John's audience in 95 AD would have had the slightest doubt as to who were the five Gentile empires that had "fallen": Egypt, Assyria, Babylon, Medo-Persia, and Greece. To see which "one is", they had only to look out the window at the Romans. They would be learning, however, that one last great Gentile empire "has not yet come".

John was also revealing to his 1st century audience that this persecution would continue throughout "the times of the Gentiles",[21] which brings us up to today.

(iii) The 'false prophet' is the Antichrist

John had earlier warned them that before the Antichrist came, there would be 'many antichrists' (1 John 2:18), inspired by the 'spirit of antichrist' (1 John 4:3). Today, we often assume 'anti' means 'opposed to' but this Greek prefix actually

---

19 Mishnah Ta'anit 4.6, www.sefaria.org/Mishnah_Taanit.4.6?lang=bi, 2 Feb, 2022.
20 www.jewfaq.org/marriage.htm#Ceremony, 2 Feb, 2022.
21 I showed in Book 1 that the metaphorical 'forty-two months' (also '1,260 days', 'three years and six months', and 'a time, times, and half a time') was the period from 30 AD until 1967 *Dancing in the Dragon's Jaws*, pp. 93-124.

means 'in place of', to denote a replacement or equivalent' of Christ.[22] As I showed in Book 2,[23] this spirit is the second beast of Revelation 13 which looks like 'a lamb' but speaks as 'a dragon' (Rev 13:11). It has a very particular task:

> 12. ...he makes the earth and those who dwell in it *to worship the first beast...*
> 14. And he deceives those who dwell on the earth... telling [them] to make *an image to the beast...*
> 15. And it was given to him to *give breath to the image* of the beast, so that the image of the beast would even speak and cause as many as do not worship the image of the beast to be killed. (Rev 13:14-15*)

'Worship' comes from an old English word 'worth-ship'; 'to worship' means to give ultimate worth to something, even money as in Jesus' references to Mammon, or wealth (Matt 6:24). We see then this spirit deceives humans into exalting not only *the self-exalting State* but also *a living image of it*.

This may sound very strange to modern ears. Nevertheless, we need to learn what Jewish teenagers in 1st century Asia Minor would have already known, especially in Smyrna (Rev 2:8-11) where they worshipped *Dea Roma,* as mentioned earlier, and in Pergamum (Rev 2:12-17). Pergamum became famous in 29 BC as the first city in the Roman Empire to dedicate a temple to *Dea Roma et Augustus,*[24] i.e. the goddess who is Rome *and* Augustus Caesar, i.e. the living image of Rome. This is why the Lord describes Pergamum as being "where Satan's throne is" and "where Satan dwells" (Rev 2:13) – worship of the emperor *created a place for Satan to dwell and reign*:

---

22 Kittel, *Theological Dictionary of the New Testament*, p. 61.
23 See *Slouching Towards Bethlehem*, pp. 92-102.
24 *Slouching Towards Bethlehem*, pp. 97-101. In particular, they worshipped the emperor's *genius* (Latin for the life spirit and/or guardian spirit of his family) which in Greek is *daemon*, i.e. demon. Pompeii had its own Temple of the *Genius Augusti* until Mt Vesuvius erupted. http://pompeiisites.org/en/archaeological-site/temple-of-genius-augusti/, 3 Feb, 2022.

> ...the cult of the ruler in Asia Minor attained a new intensity [when Augustus came to power] ... a plethora of temples and altars were constructed to honor the emperor and *Dea Roma*... The cities which possessed such an official temple to the emperor were permitted to call themselves *neokoros*, which means roughly "guardian of the temple". The achievement of this title played a significant role in the competition for fame among the cities of Asia Minor.[25]

We see too why John called it the spirit of antichrist. We are called to worship Christ because:

> **He is the image of the invisible God (Col 1:15)**

Instead, the Romans were worshipping an antichrist as the image of the invisible State and they continued doing so until Constantine ended the practice in the 4th century.

The spirit of antichrist, however, never ceased its deadly work among "all the nations". As shown in Book 2,[26] for the next thousand years it flourished in the Holy Roman Empire and the Roman Catholic Church, inspiring murderous persecution of dissenters through inquisitions and crusades. 14th century theologians such as John Wycliff[27] and Jan Hus[28] and 16th century Protestant Reformers Martin Luther[29] and John Calvin[30] recognised its effect on the popes, labelling them antichrists. However, they were slow to recognise the Biblical antidote of separating church and state,[31] Calvin executing dissenters in Geneva. It took until the 17th

---

25 https://mappinghistory.uoregon.edu/english/EU/EU10-04.html, 23 Mar, 2022.
26 *Slouching Towards Bethlehem*, pp. 58-63.
27 John Wycliffe (1328-1384), English scholar, theologian, Bible translator, reformer, Catholic priest, and seminary professor at Oxford University.
28 Jan Hus (1370-1415), Czech priest theologian, philosopher, and reformer.
29 Martin Luther (1483-1546), German priest, theologian, author, hymn writer, professor, and reformer.
30 John Calvin (1509-1564), French theologian, pastor, and reformer in Switzerland.
31 *Slouching Towards Bethlehem*, pp. 239-241.

century for the Pilgrims to finally apply it in New World.

In the 20th century, the spirit of antichrist surpassed itself in the regimes of Stalin, Hirohito, Mussolini, Hitler, Mao Zedong, Kim Il Sung, and Pol Pot et al. While many of the nations they controlled then have since become liberal democracies, we still need to keep our eyes on Russia, China, and the Muslim world as new totalitarian rulers emerge.[32] Recent events in China reveal that Xi Jinping has indeed become another antichrist in the People's Republic of China:

> After President Xi Jinping's directive to "sinicize"[33] religion, in 2018 the state issued regulations requiring houses of worship to uphold CCP dictates… thousands of churches, some registered and others underground, have been shut… Christian leaders refusing to comply with CCP directives are put under various forms of confinement, including prison, house arrest, and secret detention centers called "black jails."[34]

As John wrote, 'many antichrists have appeared' but we are to watch for the coming of *the* Antichrist (1 John 2:18). He will be the final manifestation of the spirit of antichrist, 'the false prophet' (Rev 16:13) who will be slain by Jesus when He returns (2 Thess 2:8).

There will not be two men but one – the 'false prophet' is the Antichrist. I believe, as I said in Book 2,[35] that the Antichrist will be a Muslim leader because the Islamic Empire already has possession of the Temple Mount and their eschatology already calls for the annihilation of Israel and the Jews. Muslim or not, this coming charismatic political leader will be the ultimate ravenous wolf in sheep's clothing (Matt 7:15).

---

32 Ibid, pp. 188-189.
33 Coined from Late Latin, *sinae*, meaning to make Chinese.
34 www.nationalreview.com/magazine/2021/08/02/christians-under-xi/#slide-1, 30 Jul, 2021.
35 *Slouching Towards Bethlehem*, pp. 153-172.

Death Throes

Even though the dragon and the beast's seventh head will manifest in a final assault on Israel, as dreadful and catastrophic as that may seem, the worst is over for Israel.

As I will show, the Battle of Har-Magedon/Armageddon will be an astonishing, final victory for them, with God directly intervening to destroy all of their enemies. And immediately beforehand, as I showed in Book 1[36] from the second coming of 'Elijah' and in Book 4[37] from Revelation 11, there will be a spectacular and unprecedented revival of faith among them and they will turn to Jesus as their Messiah.

This resounding victory was foreshadowed and made inevitable by Jesus severely wounding the dragon and the two beasts at the Cross. Let us look again at these wounds.

(i) The dragon's bruised head

The 'serpent of old' fulfilled the oldest of Messianic prophecies when he 'bruised the heel' of the Seed of the woman by crucifying Him but, through that very act, Jesus 'bruised' Satan's head (Gen 3:15) - Satan's headship over the human race has been dwindling ever since. One by one, Satan's subjects have been leaving his kingdom for God's as their sins are forgiven and they are born again. Jesus described this effect of evangelism in the spiritual realm:

> The seventy returned with joy, saying, "Lord, even the demons are subject to us in Your name." And He said to them, "I was watching Satan *fall from heaven like lightning*." (Luke 10:17-18*)

Every time an individual believed the seventy's message of God's kingdom (Luke 10:9), Satan fell from his rule over

---

36 *Dancing in the Dragon's Jaws*, pp. 135-145.
37 Ibid, pp. 280-302.

them. Today, by one count[38] Christians amount to a third of the world's population and, as we will see, Satan will have one final massive but futile attack on Israel before being crushed (Rom 16:20).

(ii) The beast's mortal wound

As I showed in Book 2,[39] this fatal wound to 'one of his heads' (Rev 13:3) was also inflicted by Jesus' crucifixion in 30 AD, in the time of its sixth head, the Roman Empire. The wound was healed and He allowed the beast to live on for the "forty-two months" (Rev 13:5) of "the times of the Gentiles", i.e. the last 2,000 years, but when it manifests in its seventh and last head, He will destroy it.

(iii) The false prophet

The spirit of antichrist will also be in its last manifestation as the Antichrist and, unable to exist without the beast, will be destroyed with it.

Seventh Head with Ten Horns

Over the centuries, there has also been much confusion over where the ten horns are located on the seven heads as well as their identity. Since their identity hinges on their location and the time when they appear, let me restate what I have so far established so there is no room for doubt.

Famous artistic depictions by Albrecht Dürer (1471-1528), Peter Paul Rubens (1577-1640), and William Blake (1757-1827) show one horn on four heads and two on three, as you can see on the next page.

---

[38] https://worldpopulationreview.com/country-rankings/most-christian-countries, 26 May, 2021.
[39] *Slouching Towards Bethlehem*, pp. 49-55.

Figure (i) Albrecht Dürer's woodcut of the first beast

Some Biblical scholars today cannot even imagine it:

> One can imagine seven crowns on seven heads – but ten horns? How do you arrange ten horns on seven heads? It is grotesque.[40]

---

40 Laurie Guy, *Unlocking Revelation*, p. 114.

However, there is no need for any confusion, nor to imagine or arrange the horns. Just look at their timing:

> "The ten horns which you saw are *ten kings* who have *not yet received a kingdom*, but they receive authority as kings with the beast for one hour. (Rev 17:12*)

John's day was the time of Rome, the sixth head ("five have fallen, one *is*"), and the seventh head had "not yet come" (Rev 17:10) so the ten horns have to be on the seventh - they too 'have not yet received a kingdom'.[41] When they do, it will be only for 'one hour' (v. 12) before the Lord's return, i.e. in the future:

> "These [the ten horns] will wage war against the Lamb, and the Lamb will overcome them, because He is Lord of lords and King of kings, and those who are with Him are the called and chosen and faithful." (Rev 17:14)

During that 'hour', the 'ten horns' will also be destroying Babylon the Great (Rev 17:16) so, again, they have to all be on the seventh head.

Kings or Kingdoms?

There has also been much confusion over the identity of the "ten kings", as to whether they are individuals or kingdoms. F. F. Bruce, for example:

> The seven heads are seven successive emperors; the ten horns are subordinate rulers who were to attack and destroy the city [of Rome].[42]

He then admits he cannot identify the seven successive emperors as he had to leave out three[43] and he does not try with the ten 'subordinate rulers'.

---

41 Also noted by Michael Wilcock, *The Message of Revelation*, p. 164; Leon Morris, *Revelation*, p. 211.
42 F. F. Bruce, *Answers to Questions*, p. 141.
43 Ibid.

Others, recognising that the Scriptures sometimes use 'kings' to describe 'kingdoms' (e.g. Dan 8:21), struggle to find which kingdoms have formed, can form, or will form this confederacy of ten. If future, will it be Europe or the G10 countries?

The *New Oxford Annotated Bible* takes a less literal approach:

> Ten horns *represent* subordinate or client rulers [of the Roman emperors][44]

N.T. Wright likewise:

> It is far more likely that the 'ten kings'... are different ruling elites within the larger Roman Empire - kings and princes from the far-flung corners of the Western world...[45]

However, they do not explain the metaphor. Others simply ignore the ten kings[46] or give up altogether:

> A more helpful way to read the text is to recognize that John uses evocative imagery that resists decoding.[47]

> ...we shall never be able to fully explain John's picture language by a translation into plain language.[48]

In other words, their approach makes John's 'revelation' inexplicable. Happily, there is a much better approach which would have been well known by John's 1st century Jewish audience.

Ten Means 'All'

As I showed in Book 2, 'ten' often has a metaphorical meaning in the Scriptures, signifying 'numerous, all, every, complete,

---

[44] *TNOAB*, 3rd Edition, p. 442 New Testament, italics added.
[45] N.T. Wright, *Revelation for Everyone*, p. 156.
[46] E.g. Michael Wilcock, *The Message of Revelation*, pp. 164-165.
[47] Craig R. Koester, *Revelation and the End of All Things*, p. 160.
[48] Laurie Guy, *Making Sense of the Book of Revelation*, p. 142.

the whole or the fullness'.[49] Zechariah's use of this metaphor is particularly relevant:

> Thus says the LORD of hosts, "In those days *ten men* from *all the nations*[50] will grasp the garment of a Jew, saying, 'Let us go with you, for we have heard that God is with you.'" (Zech 8:23*)

'Ten men' here signify 'all the nations'. In the same way, the "ten kings" signify all the rulers of all the nations. This is why John elsewhere refers to them as 'the kings of the whole world' (Rev 16:14).

We see then that when "all the nations" come against Israel, that will be the beast manifesting in its seventh head with its ten horns.

This connection to Israel also explains why the beast was allowed to live on after its fatal wound in 30 AD - Israel lived on, exiled among all the nations from 70 AD until its re-emergence as a sovereign nation in 1948. As the Gentile principality and power allowed to rule over Israel, the beast will be allowed to respond in one last futile attempt to annihilate this unique and extraordinary nation.

This combination of seven and ten is also significant. As I detail in Appendix A – *Seven, Ten and Seventy*, it means that Jesus will be "finally, completely, perfectly, justly" judging "all the kingdoms under the whole heaven" (Dan 7:27).

---

49 *Slouching Towards Bethlehem*, pp. 36-45.
50 Lit. "languages of the nations". This Messianic prophecy reveals God always intended to reunite all the nations in Jesus when He 'confused the language of the whole earth, and… scattered them abroad over the face of the whole earth' from Babel (Gen 11:9).

Summary

(i) 'The dragon' is Satan. Its seven diademed heads reveal that he inspired six empires' past murderous attacks on Israel, trying to prevent the birth of Jesus, and is today working on the seventh head of "all the nations".

(ii) 'The beast', John's first, is the political principality and power consisting of the seven Gentile empires that ruled over the nation of Israel from the 16th century BC until the 20th century AD: Egypt, Assyria, Babylon, Medo-Persia, Greece, Rome, and "all the nations", or Gentiles.

(iii) Even teenagers in John's 1st century Jewish audience would have easily understood this because of their festivals and fasts, teaching them their unique history. Today, we need to catch up with them, as in the 1st century Jewish Teenager's Approach.

(iv) 'The false prophet' is the Antichrist, the final manifestation of the spirit of antichrist, i.e. John's second beast.

(v) This unholy trio of 'the dragon', 'the beast', and 'the false prophet' are living on borrowed time because the dragon and the beast are mortally wounded. John lived in the time of the beast's sixth head, Rome; I believe we are living in the time of the seventh head with its ten horns when "all the nations" are finally uniting, as we will consider in Chapter 11. This is their last hour.

2
In Dreams
End of Empires

John was not the first to see the ten kings and predict their end. Seven hundred years earlier, a Babylonian king, Nebuchadnezzar, and a Jewish prophet, Daniel, also saw in dreams how it would all play out. I covered these in Book 2,[51] so if you are confident in my exposition there, you can skip this chapter too. However, for those not convinced or wanting a reminder, let me recap.

Bear in mind that John refers to all seven Gentile empires because he starts from 15th century BC and therefore includes Egypt and Assyria;[52] Daniel refers to just the last five because the dreams he records begin with Babylon in 6th century BC.

Nebuchadnezzar's Dream

In 604 BC (Dan 2:1), Nebuchadnezzar had an extraordinary dream. He could not go back to sleep and he could not understand it so he ordered his wise men to interpret it. The catch was, in order to be sure that he was not being deceived by them, Nebuchadnezzar refused to recount the dream.

None could answer him except Daniel who soon after had the same dream and was given the interpretation:

> "...there is a God in heaven who reveals mysteries, and He has made known to King Nebuchadnezzar what will take place in the latter days. This was your dream and the visions in your mind while on your bed." (Dan 2:28)

---

51 *Slouching Towards Bethlehem*, pp. 28-41, 69-73.
52 Followed by Babylon, Medo-Persia, Greece, Rome, and "all the nations".

The dream was of a great statue being pulverised by a stone which grew to fill the whole earth. The statue's head was made of gold, its breast and arms were silver, its belly and thighs were bronze, and its legs were iron, with feet and toes of iron and pottery (Dan 2:31-36).

Daniel's inspired interpretation was that the metals symbolised five successive Gentile empires, beginning with Babylon:

> 38. "You, O king, ... You are the head of gold.
> 39. "And after you there will arise *another* kingdom inferior to you, then another *third* kingdom of bronze, which will rule over all the earth.
> 40. "Then there will be a *fourth* kingdom as strong as iron... it will crush and break all these in pieces.
> 41. "And in that you saw *the feet and toes*, partly of potter's clay and partly of iron, it will be a divided kingdom...
> 42. ...some of the kingdom will be strong and part of it will be brittle." (Dan 2:38-41*)

It is easy to overlook the fifth because it is not numbered; all we know is that it is composed of the iron of the fourth but weakened by "potter's clay" (v. 41), i.e. "brittle" pottery (v. 42).[53] Somehow the fourth becomes "part" of the fifth.

Daniel only names the first - the gold is Babylon (v. 38) - but his Jewish audience in the 6th century BC would have seen the rise of the second - the silver is Medo-Persia.[54] John's 1st century AD Jewish audience, however, looked back on them and with particular interest because these were the empires that had *ruled over Israel*. The third and bronze kingdom (v. 39) was the Greek Empire of

---

53 This is the origin of today's idiom 'feet of clay', used to describe a hidden weakness or character flaw in a greatly admired or respected person.
54 Daniel saw the Medes and Persians as one empire (Dan 8:20) ruled by "*the* law of the Medes and Persians" (Dan 6:8), despite some today trying to count them as two for their interpretation e.g. *The New Oxford Annotated Bible*, p. 1258 Hebrew Bible.

Alexander the Great, and the fourth kingdom, Rome, was the iron that crushed and broke "all these in pieces" (v. 40).

What then of the fifth?

The answer lies in its ten toes. Like the ten horns that John saw, the statue's ten toes signify "all the nations", i.e. all the Gentiles/non-Jews, which, of course, includes the Roman Empire. This is confirmed by Jesus in His prediction that the Roman rule would not end with Israel's freedom and restored sovereignty but with *another exile*:

> "...they will fall by the edge of the sword, and will be led captive into *all the nations*" (Luke 21:24*)

From 70 AD until 1948, "all the nations" ruled over Israel in exile. They did so, however, as *individual nations* – they had not yet united or received their "authority as kings with the beast for one hour" (Rev 17:12).

The Stone

Nebuchadnezzar and Daniel then saw the end of the fifth empire:

> 34. "You continued looking until a stone was cut out without hands, and it struck the statue *on its feet of iron and clay* and crushed them.
> 35. Then the iron, the clay, the bronze, the silver and the gold were crushed all at the same time and became like chaff from the summer threshing floors; and the wind carried them away so that not a trace of them was found. But the stone that struck the statue became a great mountain and filled the whole earth." (Dan 2:34-35*)

All of these great empires, formed and highly valued by mankind, will be crushed and replaced by the one least valued, a stone. However, "a stone cut out without hands"[55]

---

[55] Israel's altars were likewise never to be made by stones and shaped by their hands (Ex 20:25).

means this kingdom is not man-made but heavenly, as Daniel explained to Nebuchadnezzar:

> "In the days of those kings the God of heaven will set up a kingdom which will never be destroyed, and that kingdom will not be left for another people; it will crush and put an end to all these kingdoms, but it will itself endure forever." (Dan 2:44)

In other words, during the time that the people of Israel are being ruled over by not just one Gentile empire but by "all the nations", scattered even to the ends of the earth, God will be setting up His kingdom of stone that will "put an end to all" empires. This heavenly kingdom starts small, with a single stone, but its growth is irresistible:

> "...a stone... became a great mountain and filled the whole earth." (Dan 2:34-35)

We do not have to guess at what this means because Jesus explained it all.

The Kingdom of God

Six hundred years after Daniel, Jesus made it abundantly clear to 'the chief priests and the elders' of Israel (Matt 21:23) that He was introducing this kingdom, warning each of them to not reject Him:

> 42. Jesus said to them, "Did you never read in the Scriptures, 'THE STONE WHICH THE BUILDERS REJECTED, THIS BECAME THE CHIEF CORNER stone; THIS CAME ABOUT FROM THE LORD, AND IT IS MARVELOUS IN OUR EYES'?
> 43. "Therefore I say to you, *the kingdom of God* will be taken away from you and given to a people, producing the fruit of it.
> 44. "And he who falls on *this stone* will be broken to pieces; but on whomever it falls, it will *scatter him like dust.*"
> (Matt 21:42-44*)

Quoting Psalm 118:22-23 regarding Himself as the chief corner stone, He spells out that His kingdom of stone will, as Daniel predicted, fall on all opposition until they are "like dust".

With Jesus as its first citizen, the stone kingdom has indeed grown and spread as individual after individual has been born again over the last 2,000 years, from Jerusalem to the uttermost parts of the earth, reaching New Zealand in 1814.

This kingdom will become the only power on earth at the last trumpet:

> Then the seventh angel sounded; and there were loud voices in heaven, saying, "The kingdom of the world has become the kingdom of our Lord and of His Christ; and He will reign forever and ever." (Rev 11:15)

In the meantime, like the leaven[56] hidden in the flour (Matt 13:33), it is the hidden kingdom that has been creating liberal democracy,[57] the freest form of human government ever possible in a sinful world, as explained in Books 2[58] and 4[59] and in my forthcoming *The Pearl in Plain Sight*. Today, over half the nations of the earth are liberal democracies.[60]

---

56 Some insist that leaven always symbolises evil e.g. false teaching (Matt 16:6), hypocrisy (Luke 12:1), malice and wickedness (1 Cor 5:8). However, it does not in this parable. In all of those examples, 'leaven' refers to leavened *bread* which is eaten (Matt 16:7 & 12, 1 Cor 5:8). Here, Jesus is referring to the action of the *yeast* on the flour and that is not inherently evil e.g. in the first fruits offering (Lev 23:17).
57 A 'liberal democracy' is a country or state based on the liberty and equal rights of all citizens and governed by elected representatives.
58 *Slouching Towards Bethlehem*, pp. 228-238.
59 Ibid, pp. 240-243.
60 Pew Research report '96 out of 167 countries with populations of at least 500,000 (57%) were democracies of some kind, and only 21 (13%) were autocracies. Nearly four dozen other countries – 46, or 28% – exhibited elements of both democracy and autocracy.' www.pewresearch.org/fact-tank/2019/05/14/more-than-half-of-countries-are-democratic/, 15 Sep, 2020.

Threshed & Winnowed

Nebuchadnezzar's dream predicts that all the great empires will be threshed and winnowed:

> "[They] were crushed all at the same time and became like chaff from the summer threshing floors; and the wind carried them away so that not a trace of them was found..." (Dan 2:35)

Threshing and winnowing are two stages in the process of harvesting grain and are often used in the Scriptures as graphic metaphors for God's judgement:

> The wicked are... like chaff which the wind drives away. Therefore the wicked will not stand in the judgment, Nor sinners in the assembly of the righteous (Psa 1:4-5)

Solomon urged every king to likewise sort out, sift, and act justly:

> A wise king winnows the wicked,
> And drives the threshing wheel over them. (Prov 20:26)

I have loved this imagery since I first learned of it in the 70s while working with students at a New Zealand university which specialises in agriculture. Noticing their very crude student magazine was called *Chaff*, I went to their library to learn about chaff and was introduced, to my delight, to the process of threshing and winnowing. Consequently, we put out a gospel broadsheet called *Wheat*, opening with a headline, "The trouble with chaff is that it's lifeless..."

(i) Threshing

Wheat and barley have heads of edible grain on long stems. At harvest time in Biblical days, the plants were cut and stacked to dry before being gathered onto a threshing floor – a piece of hard ground, sometimes paved or exposed bedrock surrounded by a low wall, often located outside a village on a high place exposed to the wind. The villagers then separated the grain from the straw by trampling the piled harvest with oxen or a sledge or cartwheels (Isa 28:27-28). Deuteronomy 25:4 commanded them:

"You shall not muzzle the ox while he is threshing."

This was because ancient cultures used to bind the mouths of oxen to stop them eating the straw until after all the grain had been removed.

Figure (ii) Threshing in Galilee

Today in Nepal, as I saw for myself, croppers still do this, although their crops are often spread out on busy roads to be driven over by the traffic.

The Law, however, allowed the oxen a portion of the grain as they worked.[61] The straw was then gathered up for brick-making, bedding, or animal fodder.

---

[61] In New Testament times, Paul explained the typological meaning of this generous command to encourage financial support of Christian workers (1 Cor 9:9, 1 Tim 5:18).

(ii) Winnowing

This left the threshing floor covered in a mixture of grain and chaff, i.e. the dry husks that surround the grain. Inedible to humans, the chaff was removed by throwing the mixture up into the air on a windy day. The lighter chaff blew away over the low wall of the threshing floor and the heavier grain fell back onto the floor to be stored. The resulting heap of chaff was then used as fuel for the fire, hence John the Baptist's prediction of the work of Messiah:

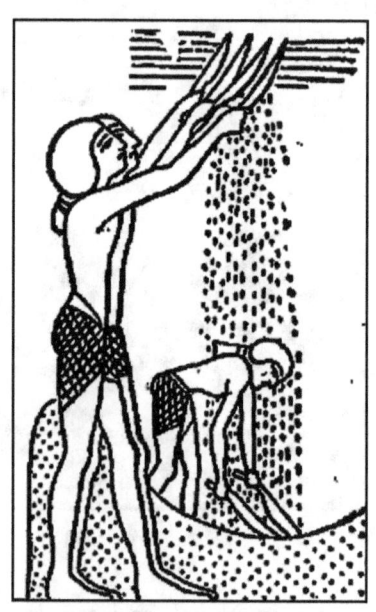

"His winnowing fork is in His hand to thoroughly clear His threshing floor, and to gather the wheat into His barn; but He will burn up the chaff with unquenchable fire" (Luke 3:17)

Figure (iii) Tomb of Nakht: men using winnowing forks

Nebuchadnezzar's dream, therefore, predicted not only the coming of the kingdom of stone but the coming of its King, to judge all the nations, all the great empires, of the earth. And the wind in his dream did not just deposit the chaff in a heap over the wall but was so violent "that not a trace of them was found" (Dan 2:35).

"A Divided Kingdom"

As covered in Book 2,[62] Daniel also saw why the ten would never unite before their last hour:

> 41. "In that you saw the feet and toes, partly of potter's clay and partly of iron, it will be *a divided kingdom*; but it will have in it the toughness of iron, inasmuch as you saw the iron mixed with common clay.
> 42. "As *the toes* of the feet were partly of iron and partly of pottery, so some of the kingdom will be strong and part of it will be brittle. (Dan 2:41-42*)

The statue's ten toes not only greatly differ in strength but, being different material, they also cannot combine despite their best attempts, including royal inter-marriage:

> 43. "And in that you saw the iron mixed with common clay, they will combine with one another in the seed of men; but *they will not adhere to one another*, even as iron does not combine with pottery." (Dan 2:43*)

Marriage has always been seen as an important way to create and maintain alliances and prevent wars. Israel's King Solomon tried to safeguard his kingdom by marrying the daughters of the kings of Egypt, Moab, Ammon, Edom, Sidon, and the Hittites (1 Kin 11:1) but, within a generation or so, they were back at war. The royal houses of Europe - the Habsburgs, Hanoverians, Bourbons, and Romanovs - also tried but ultimately failed to prevent what became World War I. Accordingly, since World War II, "all the nations" have been trying another way - the mediating forum of the United Nations.

What John sees, then, is remarkable. He sees the ten finally uniting just before the end and he sees why:

> "These have one purpose, and they give their power and authority to the beast." (Rev 17:13)

---

62 *Slouching Towards Bethlehem*, pp. 27-33.

Again, this is clearly in the time of its seventh head. We will look soon at the beast's unifying purpose and how, in that hour, they will also destroy Babylon the Great (Rev 17:16) before being threshed and winnowed like chaff. However, there is more for us to learn from another of Daniel's dreams.

Daniel's Ten-Horns Dream

In 553 BC (Dan 7:1), fifty-one years after the statue dream, Daniel had another dream in which he saw the same five empires but this time, as four bizarre wild beasts from which the fifth empire grows as ten horns (Dan 7:2-27). Again, the fifth appearing in this way makes perfect sense if the ten horns are indeed all the kingdoms of the Gentiles because the fourth empire is necessarily included.

As covered in Book 2,[63] Daniel's beasts are also key to understanding John's first beast which is a composite of them (Rev 13:2). This time, however, the empires are not brought to an end by a growing stone but by 'one like a son of man' who is given 'everlasting dominion' (Dan 7:13-14).

This title was clearly Jesus' favourite - the gospels contain eighty-one references to Him using it. At His trial Jesus quotes Daniel 7:13, making it clear that He will judge "all the nations" when He returns:

> 63. ...the high priest said to Him, "I adjure You by the living God, that You tell us whether You are the Christ, the Son of God."
> 64. Jesus said to him, "You have said it yourself; nevertheless I tell you, hereafter you will see THE SON OF MAN SITTING AT THE RIGHT HAND OF POWER, and COMING ON THE CLOUDS OF HEAVEN." (Matt 26:63-64, capitals are quotation)

It is this claim that causes the high priest and the nation's leaders, the Sanhedrin, to condemn Him for blasphemy (Matt 26:65-66). Jesus is also assuring Caiaphas, a Sadducee

---
63 Ibid, pp. 9-17.

who did not believe in resurrection, that He will be coming back from the dead.

The Son of Man

Daniel's prophecy continues:

> "And to Him [the one like a son of man[64]] was given dominion,
> Glory and a kingdom,
> That all the peoples, nations and men of every language
> Might serve Him.
> His dominion is an everlasting dominion
> Which will not pass away;
> And His kingdom is one
> Which will not be destroyed." (Dan 7:14)

It was a short-cut to this that Satan offered Jesus at the beginning of His ministry:

> 8. Again, the devil took Him to a very high mountain and showed Him *all the kingdoms of the world* and *their glory*; 9. and he said to Him, "All these things I will give You, if You fall down and worship me." (Matt 4:8-9*)

This was an all-too-real temptation because it is Satan's to give but *in its fallen state.* Jesus could have avoided His suffering and death but instead chose to pay every cost to redeem us and all of Creation; when He returns, He will judge 'all the kingdoms of the world and their glory'.

We will look at the ten horns in more detail when we come back to this dream in Chapter 11. In the next chapter, however, we will consider the unholy trio's message and mission to gather 'the kings of the whole world… for the war of the great day of God, the Almighty' (Rev 16:14).

---

[64] Jesus also fulfilled Daniel's further prophecy that "the sovereignty, the dominion and the greatness of all the kingdoms under the whole heaven will be given to *the people* of the saints of the Highest One" (Dan 7:27), saying: "Do not be afraid, little flock, for your Father has chosen gladly to give you the kingdom" (Luke 12:32).

Summary

(i) Nebuchadnezzar and Daniel's dreams of the multi-metal statue in 604 BC reveal the principality and power behind the Gentile empires' domination of Israel and predict the rise and fall of the last five of John's seven Gentile empires i.e. Babylon, Medo-Persia, Greece, Rome, and "all the nations".

(ii) They saw it being struck by a heavenly kingdom of stone until it is ground to dust and blown away like the chaff from threshing floors. This was to happen "in the days" of the feet and toes of iron and brittle pottery and Jesus began setting up this kingdom in "all the nations" in 30 AD.

(iii) The statue's ten toes/kings/kingdoms have always existed as separate entities: "all the nations" ruled over the scattered exiles of Israel from 70 AD until 1948. As Nebuchadnezzar saw and Daniel explained, the Gentiles are like iron and pottery, too different to unite until, as John sees, they commit to "one purpose" with the beast for "one hour".

(iv) Daniel's dream in 553 BC portrays the five empires as four bizarre wild beasts from which arises the fifth comprising ten horns which again symbolise "all the nations". He saw them destroyed and their kingdoms given to 'one like a son of man', Jesus' favourite name for Himself.

3
Inciting Armageddon
The Frogs

The dragon, the beast, and the false prophet have a particular message and means of working:

> 13. And I saw coming out of the mouth of the dragon and out of the mouth of the beast and out of the mouth of the false prophet, three *unclean spirits like frogs*
> 14. for they are spirits of demons, performing signs, which go out to the kings of the whole world, to gather them together for the war… (Rev 16:13-14*)

Obviously, they will have a demonic anointing on their words but why frogs?

The Frogs

The Jews in John's 1st century audience would have readily understood this simile because they were taught from childhood every year at Passover to remember the plague of frogs in Egypt before the Exodus. They still are today:

> Since the idea of the [Passover] Seder is to get children interested and involved, the Ten Plagues is a good opportunity to add an experiential, dramatic element to the evening. Plan ahead with some props and you'll see how much fun the Seder can be - for children and adults alike.[65]

The frogs were the second of the Ten Plagues and Moses had warned Pharaoh of a particular effect:

> "The Nile will swarm with frogs, which will come up and go into your house and *into your bedroom* and on your bed" (Ex 8:3*)

---
65 www.aish.com/h/pes/f/48969191.html, 30 Nov, 2019.

The Israelites sang about it in psalms:

> Their land swarmed with frogs, *even in the chambers of their kings* (Ps 105:30*. Also Ps 78:45)

There was no hiding from the frogs anywhere in Egypt, even in Pharaoh's most private living quarters.

That plague prefigured the frogs of Revelation which will seek out all 'the kings of the whole world' and again, there will be no hiding place. Only the godly will be able to recognise and resist their enticement because this deception is for all who 'do not receive the love of the truth so as to be saved' (2 Thess 2:10).

Moses' Miracles

The miraculous signs God used to confront Pharaoh in Egypt foreshadowed Messiah's coming and Judgement Day and, as we can see in Revelation, will be repeated to confront the whole world. Pharaoh's magicians were able to replicate the first three, prefiguring Satan's response.

(i) The staff into a serpent

Moses' first miracle for Pharaoh was to throw Aaron's staff on the ground, turning it into a serpent (Ex 7:9). It is easily missed but this was actually a Messianic prophecy. The staff was an almond branch (Num 17:8) and prefigures Jesus as the Word of God[66] coming to earth to be judged 'in the likeness of sinful flesh' (Rom 8:3). This prefiguring was repeated when the Israelites were healed by looking at the bronze serpent on the

---

66 Jeremiah's vision of a rod of an almond tree [Heb, *shaqed*] is interpreted for him as God "watching over [Heb, *shoqed*] My word to perform it" (Jer 1:11-12) - the Hebrew for watching means 'to be wakeful' and the almond is the first to bloom in the spring, i.e. "wakes up" early. This is why Moses and Aaron were to use 'the staff of God' (Ex 4:20) to "perform [all of] the signs" (Ex 4:17).

pole (Num 21:6-9), bronze being a symbol of God's judgement and the lifting up, to make that judgement known to all:

> "As Moses lifted up the serpent in the wilderness, even so must the Son of Man be lifted up; so that whoever believes will in Him have eternal life. For God so loved the world, that He gave His only begotten Son..." (John 3:14-16)

Pharaoh, however, looked for an alternative supernatural power:[67]

> 11. Then Pharaoh also called for the wise men and the sorcerers, and they also, the magicians of Egypt, did the same with their secret arts.
> 12. For each one threw down his staff and they turned into serpents. But Aaron's staff swallowed up their staffs... (Ex 7:11-12)

The magicians being able to 'do the same with their secret arts' (v. 11) prefigures the coming of the antichrists, as described in Book 2. However, they could not replicate Aaron's becoming a staff again (Ex 4:4), which prefigured Jesus' resurrection, and their serpents were judged (v. 12).

(ii) Water into blood

Moses' second sign, striking the staff on the Nile to curse the water (Ex 7:20), was the first warning plague, killing the fish:

> But the magicians of Egypt did the same with their secret arts; and Pharaoh's heart was hardened, and he did not listen to them, as the LORD had said. (Ex 7:22)

The Egyptians' 'secret arts' could also kill so Pharaoh was unimpressed with Moses and Aaron's. This sign prefigures Revelation's second and third bowls of wrath (Rev 16:3-4).

---

67 Some argue the magicians' miracles only appeared to be so but we are told 'they did *the same* with their secret arts' i.e. occult powers (Ex 7:11, 22; 8:7).

(iii) The plague of frogs

> ... Aaron stretched out his hand over the waters of Egypt, and the frogs came up and covered the land of Egypt. The magicians did the same with their secret arts, making frogs come up on the land of Egypt. (Ex 8:6-7)

In Moses' time, the magicians could replicate the frog plague to deceive Pharaoh. In John's vision, the 'three unclean spirits like frogs... performing signs' (Rev 16:3-4) are breathed out by the dragon, the beast, and the Antichrist, whom Paul describes as:

> 9. ...the one whose coming is in accord with the activity of Satan, *with all power and signs and false wonders,*
> 10. and with all the deception of wickedness for those who perish, because they did not receive the love of the truth so as to be saved. (2 Thess 2:9-10*)

'False wonders' (v. 9), as the *NASB* has it, implies these are not real but a better translation would be 'wonders creating a false impression', or as in the *NIV,* 'wonders that serve the lie'. The supernatural signs performed by the Antichrist and the frogs will attest to lies.

Paul explains this is one of God's judgements:

> 11. For this reason God will send upon them a deluding influence so that they will believe what is false,
> 12. in order that they all may be judged who did not believe the truth, but took pleasure in wickedness.
> (2 Thess 2:11-12)

If we reject the truth because it is humbling or painful, the only alternative we are left with is delusion. Taking pleasure in what is wrong also makes us extremely susceptible to the lie.

(iv) The dust into gnats or lice[68]

Moses' fourth sign, the third plague, was to 'strike the dust of the earth, that it may become gnats through all the land of Egypt... on man and beast' (Ex 8:16-17):

> The magicians tried with their secret arts to bring forth gnats, but they could not... Then the magicians said to Pharaoh, "This is the finger of God." (Ex 8:18-19)

The magicians had true 'wonders that serve the lie' – they could produce serpents, turn water to blood, and call forth frogs - but they could not create gnats or lice from dust. At this point, they acknowledged that God alone is Creator.

Pharaoh, however, remained unconvinced until the tenth plague[69] killed all the first-born in Egypt, human and animal (Ex 12:29-30). This judgement fell on Pharaoh and the Egyptians, God said, for not freeing "Israel... My son, My first-born" (Ex 4:22-23) and killing the baby boys of the Hebrew slaves (Ex 1:16 & 22). Even after Pharaoh did free them, he tried to recapture them and perished in the sea when it closed up (Ex 14:27-28).

---

68 Heb *ken*, an attaching, stinging insect.
69 The fourth plague, swarms of dog-flies, affected only the Egyptians and spared the Hebrews (Ex 8:21-24); the fifth struck all the Egyptians' livestock in the field but again, not the Hebrews' (Ex 9:3-7); the sixth plague, boils from kiln soot (Ex 9:8-11), prefigure those of the first bowl of wrath which afflict only worshippers of the beast (Rev 16:2); the seventh plague, lethal hail except in Goshen where the Hebrews lived (Ex 9:18-26), prefigures the seventh bowl of wrath (Rev 16:21); the eighth plague, locusts, prefigures the locusts of the fifth trumpet which spare all who have the seal of God (Rev 9:1-11); the ninth plague, thick darkness except in the homes of the Hebrews (Ex 10:21-23) prefigures the fifth bowl of wrath on the beast's kingdom (Rev 16:10-11). All of this, Moses told Pharaoh, was "that you may understand how the LORD makes a distinction between Egypt and Israel" (Ex 11:7); there were also Egyptians who listened to Moses' warnings and saved their livestock (Ex 9:20-21). I will cover these in detail in Book 6, *Back In 7*.

This ended the reign of the beast's first head, Egypt, over the children of Israel and, in the process, prefigured the end of the beast's seventh head and its attempts to destroy Israel.

Gathering for War

1st century Jewish disciples would also have known of Micaiah's prophecy from the time of their wickedest king of Israel, Ahab. Ahab had gathered four hundred prophets to the threshing floor of his capital city of Samaria (1 Kin 22:6 & 10) who were all prophesying victory in an imminent battle (vv. 11-12). The godly king of Judah, Jehoshaphat, was not convinced and insisted on hearing from Micaiah who said:

> 19. ...."I saw the LORD sitting on His throne, and all the host of heaven standing by Him on His right and on His left.
> 20. "The LORD said, 'Who will entice Ahab to go up and fall at Ramoth-gilead?' And one said this while another said that.
> 21. "Then a spirit came forward and stood before the LORD and said, 'I will entice him.'
> 22. "The LORD said to him, 'How?' And he said, "I will go out and be a deceiving spirit in the mouth of all his prophets.' Then He said, 'You are to entice him and also prevail. Go and do so.'
> 23. "Now therefore, behold, the LORD has put a deceiving spirit in the mouth of all these your prophets; and the LORD has proclaimed disaster against you." (1 Kin 22:19-23)

Ahab and Jehoshaphat rejected Micaiah's prophecy and imprisoned him, believing instead the enticing words of the four hundred, and Ahab perished in the battle.

'The kings of the whole world' will likewise reject the word of God and perish in their battle.

'From the Mouths...'

The frogs emerging from the mouth of the dragon reveal that Satan is orchestrating the propaganda as 'the god of this world [who] has blinded the minds of the unbelieving' (2 Cor 4:4).

The frogs from the mouth of the beast signify the political influence of this principality and power on "all the nations" - we will explore this further in Chapter 11, when the ten horns unite.

The frogs from the mouth of the false prophet signify religious preaching. If, as I argue in Book 2,[70] the false prophet will be the Muslims' Mahdi, his work is almost complete already:

> The people of Israel in the land of Israel will always be the prime target of militant Islam. In most reports of Islamist attacks anywhere in the world, there are two recurring stated motivations: to support the Palestinians' struggle against Israel and to strike all who support Israel, usually held to be Christian nations on new crusades. Al-Qaeda's official mission statement[71] is headed, 'Jihad Against Jews and Crusaders'.[72]

Muhammad taught that his followers will fight the Jews until the Day of Resurrection:

> By this time, Muslims would have killed all the Jews but one. This one Jew would hide behind a rock, and the rock would say to the Muslims, "There is a Jew hiding behind me. Come and kill him".[73]

His followers are therefore already primed for whatever an emerging Mahdi may say.

---

70 *Slouching Towards Bethlehem*, pp. 168-172.
71 www.fas.org/irp/world/para/docs/980223-fatwa.htm, 27 Apr, 2021
72 *Slouching Towards Bethlehem*, pp. 167-168.
73 Hadith of al-Bukhari. Mark A. Gabriel, *Islam and the Jews: The Unfinished Battle*, Lake Mary, Florida; FrontLine, 2003, p. 115.

Given the ubiquity of television, global communication devices, and social media today, it is not at all hard for the unholy trio and their frogs to reach 'the kings of the whole world', even in their beds.

> And they gathered them together to the place which in Hebrew is called Har-Magedon.[74] (Rev 16:16)

As frightening as all this may appear to us today, John's original Jewish audience would have found it wonderfully reassuring and encouraging - it promises another Exodus, a wonderful day when God will finally deliver all who trust in Him from these three great powers.

If we know what to listen for, we can hear the croaking of the frogs today.

Summary

(i) All the nations will be enticed to 'the war of the great day of God' by frog-like demons coming from the mouths of 'the dragon', 'the beast', and 'the false prophet', i.e. Satan, "all the nations", and the Antichrist respectively.

(ii) Frogs were a familiar and reassuring image to 1st century Jewish disciples because, as Jewish children were and still are taught every Passover, frogs were the second of the Ten Plagues that God unleashed on Egypt in order to free them from slavery.

(iii) Just as the Egyptian frogs entered the most intimate rooms of Pharaoh's palace, this last days' demonic plague on the whole world will search out and tempt

---

74 The *NASB* has one 'd' (so too *RSV* and *CEV*). Most (e.g. *KJV, NIV*) have Mageddon.

every nation's leaders and there will be no place to hide. Only the godly will recognise and resist the frogs' enticement.

(iv) The Jewish disciples would also have known of Micaiah's prophecy about the deceiving spirit in the mouth of the false prophets enticing Ahab, their wickedest king, into his last battle and doom.

(v) The threefold source of this deception is revealed as Satan, the beast's political power, and the Antichrist's religious power.

4
Armageddon
At Har-Magedon

In 1611, the translators of the *King James Version* transliterated the Hebrew name *Har-Magedon* as Armageddon, which then entered the English language as meaning 'the scene of ultimate or large-scale conflict'.[75] This conflict will be the 'ultimate or large-scale' but very localised – whereas World War II was fought throughout Europe, North Africa, Asia, and the Pacific, Armageddon will focus on only one tiny little nation, Israel. It will be mercifully short – World War II dragged on for six years but Armageddon will barely start and be over in 'one hour' and, despite what many of us have been taught, it will be an overwhelming victory for Israel.

Literal…?

Those taking Har-Magedon as a literal place name believe John was referring to Megiddo[76] in the Valley of Jezreel, today's plain of Esdraelon. The valley, 132 kilometres north of Jerusalem, measures 32 kms by 22 kms and many quote Napoleon Bonaparte in 1799 as saying:

> All the armies of the world could manoeuvre their forces on this vast plain.[77]

---

75 *Concise Oxford Dictionary*, p. 46.
76 Megiddo was a major city in antiquity because it guarded the main pass of the Via Maris or Way of the Sea, the main trade route from Egypt to Mesopotamia. Deborah sang of Israel's victory near 'the waters of Megiddo' (Judg 5:19) c. 1300 BC; Solomon fortified the city c. 1000 BC (1 Kin 9:15); Josiah was killed there in 609 BC (2 Kin 23:29).
77 For example, www.charismamag.com/spirit/spiritual-warfare/49907-3-end-time-wars-armies-gather-at-armageddon, 27 May, 2022.

This battle then would be a repeat of Israel's extraordinary win against overwhelming odds in c. 1190 BC, battling the army of Jabin, king of Canaan. Deborah had prophesied to Barak the promise of God:

> "I will draw out to you Sisera, the commander of Jabin's army, with his chariots and his many troops to the river Kishon, and I will give him into your hand." (Judg 4:7)

Sisera's forces included 'nine hundred iron chariots' (Judg 4:13), the ancient equivalent of today's tanks, whereas Barak had only ten thousand infantry without even spears or shields (Judg 4:6, 14; 5:8). Afterwards, Deborah exulted in song:

> 19. "The kings came and fought;
> Then fought the kings of Canaan
> At Taanach near the waters of Megiddo;
> They took no plunder in silver.
> 20. "The stars fought from heaven,
> From their courses they fought against Sisera.
> 21. "The torrent of Kishon swept them away,
> The ancient torrent, the torrent Kishon.
> O my soul, march on with strength." (Judg 5:19-21)

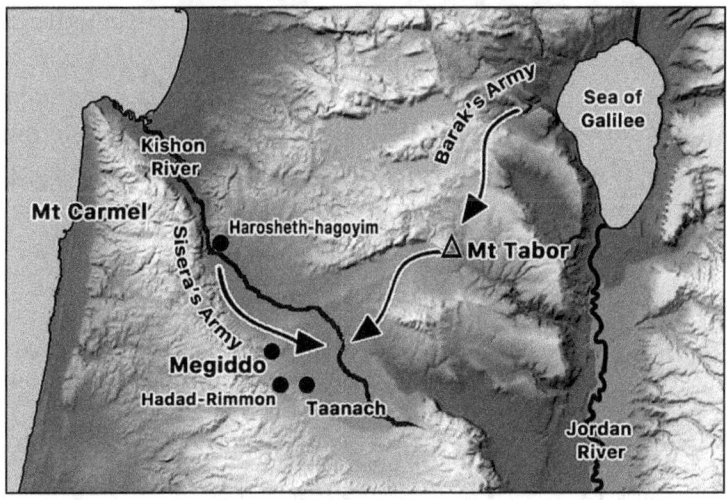

Figure (iv) Map of the Jezreel Valley

We are not told what exactly happened: "the stars fought from heaven" (v. 20) could mean a meteorite shower, huge hail, or angels intervening; torrential rains and a flash flood in the Kishon River seem to have "swept away" Sisera's army, or rendered useless his heavy iron chariots. What is clear, however, is that God intervened to hand an overwhelming victory to His people, as in the Exodus when He swept away the Egyptian chariots (Ex 14:25-27).

Israel still sing of this legendary battle in Psalm 83 when faced with similar threats of annihilation (Psa 83:4-5), praying along with Asaph the psalmist:

> 9. Deal with them as with Midian,
> As with Sisera and Jabin at the torrent of Kishon (Psa 83:9)

...or Metaphorical?

The problem with a literal site is that *Har* means 'Mount', and there is no Mt Megiddo or Mt Magedon.[78] The city famously sat in the middle of a plain, "the Plain of Megiddo' (2 Chron 35:22). Accordingly, Old Testament scholar Meredith Kline argues for Har-Magedon being another name for Jerusalem. He reasons John's Hebrew transliteration of *magedon* comes from *mo'ed*, i.e. assembly, as in Satan's boast that he would "raise [his] throne above the stars of God and sit on the mount of assembly [Heb, *har mo'ed*] in the recesses of the north" (Isa 14:13).[79] He concludes that Har-Magedon is:

> *har mo'ed*, the Lord's Mount of Assembly Mount Zion with its city of Jerusalem, the city of our God.[80]

---

[78] Zechariah refers to the city as Megiddon (lit. Heb, Zech 12:11) and the Septuagint calls it Mageddo (Josh 17:11) and Mageddon (2 Chron 35:22). I stay with John's transliteration, Magedon.
[79] Meredith G. Kline, *God, Heaven, and Har Magedon: A Covenantal Tale of Cosmos and Telos*, Wipf and Stock Publishers, 2006, pp. 49-57. Also Laurie Guy, *Making Sense of Revelation*, p. 135.
[80] Ibid. p. 56.

The Scriptures' first use of *mo'ed* is translated as 'season' or 'sacred time' (Gen 1:14), hence any 'appointed time, place, or meeting',[81] i.e. first appoint the time and place to assemble and then assemble there. There is no doubt that God has appointed the time and the place of Har-Magedon.

However, the *Abarim Publications' Biblical Dictionary* offers another etymological solution:

> Mountain of Invasion… from the noun *har*, mountain, and the verb *gadad*, to cut or invade… Megiddo means Lacerating or Invading [because]… *gadad* denotes an active invasion and the letter *mem* indicates an ongoing action. The name Megiddo means Invading, or Intruding.[82]

In Jeremiah 5:7 and Micah 5:1, *gadad* is translated as 'massing together as troops'.[83] In context, Micah was prophesying to all the nations besieging Jerusalem:

> And now many nations have been assembled against you
> Who say, "Let her be polluted,
> And let our eyes gloat over Zion" (Micah 4:11)

He continues:

> "Now muster [Heb. *gadad*] yourselves in troops…" (Mic 5:1)

The 'Mountain of Invasion' is therefore Zion and, either way, whether the name derives from *mo'ed* or *gadad*, Jerusalem is the location.

Very Different Agenda

Micah adds that the nations will come with one agenda but God has another:

---

81 *NASB Exhaustive Concordance of the Bible*, La Habra, CA; The Lockman Foundation, 1981, p. 1545.
82 www.abarim-publications.com/Meaning/Megiddo.html, 29 Apr, 2021.
83 *Theological Wordbook of the Old Testament*, Harris et al, Chicago; Moody Press, 1980.

> 11. And now *many nations* have been assembled against you
> Who say, "Let her be polluted,
> And let our eyes gloat over Zion".
> 12. But they do not know the thoughts of the LORD,
> And they do not understand *His purpose*;
> For He has *gathered* them like sheaves to the threshing floor...
> 1. Now *muster* yourselves in troops... (Mic 4:11-5:1*)

'Many nations' will 'assemble against' Jerusalem, 'mustering themselves in troops' to 'gloat over Zion' (v. 11) but God's 'purpose' is to 'gather them like sheaves to the threshing floor' (v. 12). Then:

> 13. "Arise and thresh, daughter of Zion,
> For your horn I will make iron
> And your hoofs I will make bronze,
> That you may pulverize many peoples..." (Mic 4:13)

In this metaphor of a threshing ox, Zion's iron horn signifies irresistible authority and her bronze hoofs, the judgement of God.

Micah then goes on into his very familiar prophecy of Jesus' birthplace:

> 2. "But as for you, Bethlehem Ephrathah...
> From you One will go forth for Me to be ruler in Israel.
> His goings forth are from long ago,
> From the days of eternity..." (Mic 5:2)

Jesus came the first time to this little town just south of Jerusalem to save us from sin but when He returns to Jerusalem, it will be threshing time.

The Threshing Floor of Ornan

Har-Magedon as a threshing of grain is also foreshadowed in the site of the Temple. Consider its purchase. David was a remarkable man with his own everlasting covenant with

God, as covered in Book 4.[84] He was also remarkably fallible – his only saving grace was that he knew how to enter the presence of God and repent when he fell. We are not told why David counted his troops, seemingly glorying in his military might,[85] but David knew:

> Now David's heart troubled him after he had numbered the people. So David said to the LORD, "I have sinned greatly in what I have done. But now, O LORD, please take away the iniquity of Your servant, for I have acted very foolishly." (2 Sam 24:10)

However, David was not the only one who had sinned; many of his people had too (2 Sam 24:1) so God was about to judge them all and a great plague broke out for three days in which 70,000 died (2 Sam 24:11-15).

> Then David lifted up his eyes and saw the angel of the LORD standing between earth and heaven, with his drawn sword in his hand stretched out over Jerusalem. Then David and the elders, covered with sackcloth, fell on their faces. (1 Chron 21:16)

The angel was 'standing by the threshing floor of Ornan[86] the Jebusite' (1 Chron 21:15) and David was commanded to erect an altar there (1 Chron 21:18). He quickly obeyed, buying the site from Ornan (1 Chron 21:22-25) and building the altar. However, when he dedicated the site with burnt offerings and peace offerings, there was a spectacular response:

> ... the LORD... answered him with fire from heaven on the altar of burnt offering. The LORD commanded the angel, and he put his sword back in its sheath. (1 Chron 21:26-27)

---

84 *Silencing the Witnesses*, pp. 201-210.
85 His army had more than doubled since the Exodus (1 Chron 21:5-6 cf. Num 2:32).
86 Ornan is the Hebrew form of the Hurrian name Araunah, used in 2 Samuel 24:18, and means lord, or aristocrat (*The Zondervan Pictorial Encyclopedia of the Bible*, Vol 1, pp. 257-258).

Not only was Jerusalem saved and the plague stopped (2 Sam 24:25) but this also began a new era for Israel, the building of a permanent temple in Jerusalem:

> 28. ...when David saw that the LORD had answered him on *the threshing floor of Ornan* the Jebusite, he offered sacrifice there.
> 29. For the tabernacle of the LORD, which Moses had made in the wilderness, and the altar of burnt offering were in the high place at Gibeon at that time...
> 1. Then David said, "This is *the house of the LORD God*, and this is the altar of burnt offering for Israel."
> (1 Chron 21:28-22:1*)

David had already moved the ark of the covenant to Jerusalem but he had left the tabernacle and its altars where they were in Gibeon. Now, recognising what had happened, David planned to build the Temple in Jerusalem.[87]

We learn then that God's judgement of Israel and Jerusalem was moderated by David and the elders' prayers (2 Sam 24:25) which surely consisted of confession, intercession, and rededication at 'the threshing floor of Ornan' where the wheat was separated from the chaff.

Threshing & Winnowing

In Chapter 2, we saw that the dreams of Nebuchadnezzar and Daniel predicting God's judgement of the world's empires end with them blown away like chaff in the wind. I took the time to explain the process of threshing and winnowing because this is the most commonly used metaphor in the Scriptures to describe how God will judge - in the Song of Moses, the psalms of David and Asaph, the prophetic warnings of Isaiah, Jeremiah, Hosea, Micah, Malachi, and

---

[87] He had to pass his plans on to Solomon, however, because he was forbidden to build the Temple due to his being 'a man of war' who had shed blood, including Uriah's (1 Chron 28:3-12).

John the Baptist.[88]

God will have His harvest and everything will be sorted out at the place where He has always offered forgiveness - the Temple was a 'house of prayer for all the nations' (Isa 56:7, Mark 11:17). However, as detailed in Book 4,[89] the Temple was only a shadow, prefiguring the reality of Jesus Himself, in whom 'all the fullness of Deity dwells in bodily form' (Col 2:9). Now Jesus is the only place on earth where we can find forgiveness because of His righteous sacrifice, offered once for all time for every any Jew or Gentile who calls on Him.

We should therefore be quick to respond because when He returns, Jesus will winnow Israel and all the nations, as John the Baptist predicted:

> "His winnowing fork is in His hand to thoroughly clear His threshing floor, and to gather the wheat into His barn; but He will burn up the chaff with unquenchable fire" (Luke 3:17)

This too will take place at His threshing floor in Jerusalem.

Messiah in Zion

To the threshing analogy, God adds the potter and his pottery:

> 6. "But as for Me, I have installed My King upon *Zion*, My holy mountain"...
> 8. "Ask of Me, and I will surely give the nations as Your inheritance,
> And the *very ends of the earth* as Your possession.
> 9. "You shall break them with *a rod of iron*,
> You shall shatter them *like earthenware.*"
> (Psa 2:6-9*)

---

88   Exodus 15:7; Psalms 1:4, 35:5, 83:13; Isaiah 17:13, 21:10, 27:12, 29:5, 41:2, 41:15; Jeremiah 15:7; Hosea 13:3; Micah 4:12; Malachi 4:1; Matthew 3:12; Luke 3:17.
89   *Silencing the Witnesses*, pp. 18-24.

This "rod of iron" to shatter all the nations to the "very ends of the earth" returns us to Revelation 12:5, where the woman's Child was given the rod. Also to Psalm 110:

> 1. The LORD says to my Lord: "Sit at My right hand
> Until I make Your enemies a footstool for Your feet".
> 2. The LORD will stretch forth Your strong scepter
> *from Zion*, saying, "Rule in the midst of Your enemies"...
> 5. The Lord is at Your right hand;
> *He will shatter kings* in the day of His wrath.
> 6. He will judge among the nations... (Psa 110:1-6*)

The "strong scepter" is stretched forth "from Zion" to the nations.

Jesus added a third metaphor, of shepherding:

> "When the Son of Man comes in His glory, and all the angels with Him, then He will sit on His glorious throne. All the nations will be gathered before Him; and He will separate them from one another as the shepherd separates the sheep from the goats..." (Matt 25:31-32. Also John 5:22-29)

We see then these three metaphors describing that day: threshing to separate the wheat from the chaff, the potter shattering pots he does not like, and the shepherd separating his sheep from the goats. When Jesus returns to Jerusalem (Zech 14:4), He will fulfill all three.

All Roads Lead to...

Many other prophecies use other prophetic names for Jerusalem to illustrate that it was always going to be God's place of judgement for both Israel and 'all the nations'. Isaiah calls it Ariel and John says it is 'spiritually called Sodom and Egypt'. It is most commonly called Zion or Mount Zion (over a hundred times) by King David and the prophets Isaiah, Jeremiah, Joel, Amos, Obadiah, and Micah. Ezekiel has a new name for it in the last days: Hamonah.[90] Each of these names is a divine revelation, suitable for its particular time.

(i) Ariel

Some take this name for Jerusalem to mean 'Lion of God', which sounds the same in Hebrew, but when Ezekiel is given the dimensions of a new temple altar (Ezek 43:13-17), 'ariel' clearly means the 'altar hearth' (vv. 15-16). Understanding this better explains Isaiah's prophecy:

> 1. "Woe, O *Ariel, Ariel* the city where David once camped! Add year to year, observe your feasts on schedule.
> 2. "I will bring distress to *Ariel*,
> And she will be a city of lamenting and mourning;
> And she will be like an *Ariel* [i.e. altar hearth] to Me.
> 3. "I will camp against you encircling you,
> And I will set siege-works against you…"
> (Isa 29:1-3*)

Isaiah was not describing Jerusalem as a caged 'lion of God' but instead predicting a truly tragic about turn - David's royal city, where Israel celebrated feasts with sacrifices on the Temple's altar (Deut 16:16), would become instead a place of "lamenting and mourning" for their war dead. The *Jewish Encyclopaedia* explains Isaiah's irony:

> The illustration in verse 2 ("Ariel . . . shall be unto me as Ariel," the city shall reek with blood, like an altar) suggests that the second "Ariel" equals "altar" or… "altar hearth of God"… that is, the place devoted to the worship of God.[91]

Isaiah is predicting that Jerusalem, and thus Israel, will be judged but so will their enemies:

---

90 Ezekiel 39:16. We will look at this in Book 7, *Kingdom Come*, in considering the battle of Gog and Magog in Revelation 20.
91 www.jewishencyclopedia.com/articles/1760-ariel, 6 Dec, 2019.

5. "But the multitude of your enemies will become like fine dust,
And the multitude of the ruthless ones *like the chaff* which blows away;
And it will happen instantly, suddenly...
7. "And the multitude of *all the nations* who wage war against *Ariel*,
Even all who wage war against her and her stronghold [i.e. Zion], and who distress her,
Will be like a dream, a vision of the night."
(Isa 29:5-7*)

The Assyrian siege of Jerusalem in 701 BC when the angel of the Lord struck down 185,000 overnight (Isa 37:36) did not fulfill this prediction, nor did the Roman devastation in 70 AD. Their armies did include mercenaries of other nationalities but not of all the nations so this besieging by "the multitude of all the nations" (v. 7) is yet to occur, as is their being blown away "like the chaff... instantly and suddenly" (v. 5).

(ii) 'Sodom and Egypt'

I established in Book 4[92] that in John's time 'the great city which spiritually is called Sodom and Egypt, where also their Lord was crucified' (Rev 11:8) was Jerusalem, not Rome as is often taught today.[93]

The corruption of Jerusalem's inhabitants in the 1st century AD had reached the same level as in the 6th century BC when:

> "...they all had become to Me like Sodom, and her inhabitants like Gomorrah" (Jer 23:14)

Ezekiel (Ezek 16:2 & 46) and Isaiah also prophesied at that time:

---

92 *Silencing the Witnesses*, pp. 188-190.
93 E.g. N.T. Wright, *Revelation for Everyone*, pp. 99-100.

> "Hear the word of the LORD,
> You rulers of Sodom;
> Give ear to the instruction of our God,
> You people of Gomorrah..."
> How the faithful city has become a harlot,
> She who was full of justice!
> Righteousness once lodged in her,
> But now murderers. (Isa 1:10 & 21)

Seven centuries later, Jesus warned every Jewish city that ignored His messengers:

> "Truly I say to you, it will be more tolerable for the land of Sodom and Gomorrah in the day of judgment than for that city." (Matt 10:15)

In both instances, Jerusalem's "abominations" (Ezek 16:2) reached the tipping point of the infamous cities of Sodom and Gomorrah judged by God in Abraham's time, provoking His anger and the "desolation" of Jerusalem. Daniel refers to their crime as "the transgression that causes horror" (*NASB*) or, as the *NIV* puts it, "the rebellion that causes desolation" (Dan 8:13).

In Book 2,[94] I showed that there have actually been five occasions when Israel's "abominations" caused "desolation" and these were two of them: the people were using the Temple's atonement as an excuse to carry on sinning so in 586 BC the Lord removed the Temple (Jer 7:1-14); in John's time, their rejection of Jesus provoked the desolation of the Second Temple in 70 AD (Matt 21:33-44, 24:2).[95]

Jerusalem was also 'spiritually called Egypt' because 'the present Jerusalem' was not only 'in slavery with her children' (Gal 4:25) but also enslaving (Gal 4:9-10) and persecuting the children born 'according to the Spirit', as 'it is now' (Gal 4:29).[96]

---

94 *Slouching Towards Bethlehem*, pp. 266-270.
95 Ibid, pp. 273-275.
96 *Silencing the Witnesses*, pp. 189-190.

(iii) Zion

Mt Zion was the site of King David's palace (2 Sam 5:6-11) so the name signifies his household and the lineage of Messiah, Jesus of Nazareth (Psa 2:6-12). God's intention was always that the Gentiles would come to Zion, to Messiah, to learn the ways of God and walk in them:

> 2. ...And *all the nations* will stream to it.
> 3. And many peoples will come and say,
> "Come, let us go up to the mountain of the LORD,
> To the house of the God of Jacob;
> That He may teach us concerning His ways
> And that we may walk in His paths".
> For the law will go forth from *Zion*
> And the word of the LORD from *Jerusalem*.
> (Isa 2:2-3*)

The famous plaque outside the United Nations' building in New York quotes only the last four lines of verse 4 of Isaiah's prophecy:

> And they will hammer their swords into ploughshares
> And their spears into pruning hooks.
> Nation will not lift up sword against nation,
> And never again will they learn war. (Isa 2:4)

However, this promise can only ever be fulfilled for those who commit themselves to God as their judge, as in the first two lines:

> 4. And *He will judge* between the nations,
> And will *render decisions* for many peoples;
> And they will hammer their swords into ploughshares...
> (Isa 2:4*)

The writer of Hebrews, however, gives us a spiritual fulfilment for all who have come to Jesus:

> 22. But *you have come to Mount Zion* and to the city of the living God, *the heavenly Jerusalem*, and to myriads of angels,

> 23. to the general assembly and church of the firstborn who are enrolled in heaven, and to *God, the Judge of all*, and to the spirits of the righteous made perfect,
> 24. and *to Jesus*, the mediator of a new covenant, and to the sprinkled blood… (Heb 12:22-24*)

We who are trusting in Jesus have already been judged as guilty, put to death, and buried in baptism (Rom 6:3-4) – raised with Him, we are now citizens of 'the heavenly Jerusalem'.

(iv) 'The present Jerusalem'

Paul contrasts two Jerusalems: 'the present Jerusalem' is 'in slavery with her children' and 'the Jerusalem above' who is free and 'our mother' (Gal 4:25-26).

John describes the latter:

> 1. Then I saw a new heaven and a new earth; for the first heaven and the first earth passed away, and there is no longer any sea.
> 2. And I saw the holy city, *new Jerusalem*, coming down out of heaven from God, made ready as a bride adorned for her husband. (Rev 21:1-2*)

What then of the earthly, 'present' or 'old' Jerusalem?

Many theologians and scholars today are convinced that neither she nor today's nation of Israel have any part left to play in God's plans, having been superseded or replaced, with His promises fulfilled in the church.

However, as I have shown in Books 1 and 4, 'the present Jerusalem' and today's Israel are about to have an extraordinary, starring role on the world stage, very much larger than our current daily news headlines. John sees the last battle as occurring around Jerusalem after Satan is loosed and allowed…:

> … to deceive the nations which are in the four corners of the earth…, to gather them together for the war; the

number of them is like the sand of the seashore. And they... surrounded... *the beloved city* (Rev 20:8-9*)

Biblically, there is only one 'beloved city' on the earth – 'the present Jerusalem'. It is 'the city of our God... the city of the great King' (Psa 48:1-2), as Jesus reaffirmed (Matt 5:35). Although 'trampled underfoot' by Gentiles for almost 2,000 years, Jerusalem seems to have been re-sanctified in 1967,[97] as shown in Book 4.

This battle cannot be around the new heavenly Jerusalem because that will not come down out of heaven to the earth until after John has seen a new heaven and a new earth replace the first earth (Rev 21:1-2).

As for the battle, in marked contrast to previous invasions of Israel when large empires came from the north or south (e.g. Jer 1:13-15, Ezek 38:15, Dan 11), Satan will deceive the nations in every direction, from 'the four corners of the earth', and those deceived will be 'like the sand of the seashore'. Many believe there will be two gatherings of this army of "all the nations", one before the millennium and one after, but, as I will show in my forthcoming Book 7, *Kingdom Come,* there is only one.

---

[97] As I often explain, we cannot be dogmatic about this date because the Israeli army handed back the heart of Jerusalem, the Temple Mount, to the Muslim authorities. On the other hand, they do have sovereignty *Dancing in the Dragon's Jaws,* p. 125; *Slouching Towards Bethlehem,* p. 31; *Silencing the Witnesses,* p. 17.

Summary

(i) Har-Magedon is not in the plain of Meggido or the Valley of Jezreel/Esdraelon because 'Har' means mountain; it is a metaphorical/prophetic name for the city of Jerusalem.

(ii) This name is based on Deborah and Barak's legendary victory at Megiddo. In both battles, Israel face over-whelming enemy forces who have been drawn out by God to be judged.

(iii) All the nations gathering to gloat over Zion will find that they have actually been gathered like sheaves to the threshing floor. This was foreshadowed by the Temple Mount being the threshing floor of Ornan; it is Messiah's work to thresh and winnow all the nations at the place where He earned forgiveness for us all.

(iv) God's pattern of judging 'the Jew first, and then the Greek' is also seen in the other prophetic, typological names for 'the present Jerusalem': Ariel, the altar-hearth of God; 'Sodom and Egypt'; and Zion. We will consider another, Hamonah, in Book 7, *Kingdom Come*, when we consider the battle of Gog and Magog in Revelation 20.

5
Israel's Time
In the Son

We now come to the first of the three women characters in the drama of Revelation: the woman of Revelation 12. Clothed in the sun, moon at her feet, twelve stars crowning her head, she is giving birth to Messiah. In Book 1,[98] I showed that she is Israel "according to the flesh… from whom is the Christ according to the flesh" (Rom 9:1-3). Today, after almost 2,000 years, they again possess the Promised Land.

As surprising as this may seem, the Battle of Har-Magedon will be good for Israel in every way - not only will they overwhelmingly defeat all their enemies but they will also finally welcome their Messiah. For all of those 2,000 years, religious Jews who have rejected Jesus have been waiting for His coming. Maimonides' 12th century creed is still recited today:

> I believe with complete faith in the coming of Messiah. And though he may tarry, I shall wait anticipating his arrival each day.[99]

The good news is that many will find Him before He arrives.

Har-Magedon No Surprise

Israel was reborn and has survived in the face of unending Arab and Muslim belligerence.

---

98 *Dancing in the Dragon's Jaws.*
99 The twelfth of thirteen articles of faith drafted by Moses Maimonides, one of Judaism's greatest sages and considered by many to be a Second Moses. His epitaph reads: "From Moshe [i.e. Moses] to Moshe [i.e. the son of Maimon] there arose none like Moshe." www.chabad.org/library/article_cdo/aid/107769/jewish/The-Rambam.htm, 29 Nov, 2021.

In the 1948 Arab-Israeli War, the armies of Egypt, Lebanon, Syria, Jordan, and Iraq invaded what was then known as Palestine i.e. the remaining 23% of the British Mandate. The other 77% had already been given to the Arabs in 1922 and become the Hashemite Kingdom of Jordan. The Jewish forces kept the Arab armies at bay but were unable to prevent the Egyptians capturing the Gaza Strip and the Jordanians from annexing the West Bank. An uneasy truce followed with the cease-fire lines becoming Israel's de facto boundaries.

Nineteen years later, in May 1967, Egypt's President Nasser assembled his army and expelled UN peace-keepers from the buffer zone between Egypt and Israel, declaring:

> The armies of Egypt, Jordan, Syria and Lebanon are poised on the borders of Israel… to face the challenge, while standing behind us are the armies of Iraq, Algeria, Kuwait, Sudan and the whole Arab nation. This act will astound the world. Today they will know that the Arabs are arranged for battle, the critical hour has arrived. We have reached the stage of serious action and not declarations.[100]

However, Nasser was caught off-guard when Israel struck first. In this Six Day War of June 1967, Israel defeated the armed forces of Egypt, Jordan, Syria, and Iraq, and captured the Sinai Peninsula, the Gaza Strip, the West Bank and Jerusalem, and the Golan Heights.

Six years later, during Yom Kippur in 1973, Egypt and Syria, with the help of Iraqi tanks and infantry and a token Jordanian force, surprised and almost overwhelmed Israel but the Israelis rallied and fought them off.

Since then, sporadic attacks from Hezbollah in Lebanon, the Palestinian Islamic Jihad in Gaza and Syria, and Hamas in Gaza, have kept alive Palestinian and Muslim hopes of

---

100 Gamal Nasser, May, 30, 1967, after signing a defense pact with Jordan's King Hussein. www.jewishvirtuallibrary.org/background-and-overview-six-day-war, 1 May, 2021.

destroying "the Zionist entity" and, of course, Israel faces constant threats of annihilation from Iran and their Quds Brigade.

The Battle of Har-Magedon will therefore be no surprise for Israel but this time, they will have no other nation helping them - their strongest ally, the United States of America, will abandon them to their fate. Their only help will be the God of Abraham, Isaac, and Jacob and He is more than enough.

Zechariah 12

In c. 480 BC, Zechariah also predicted Israel's astonishing victory in their last great battle:

> 2. "Behold, I am going to make *Jerusalem* a cup that causes reeling to all the peoples around; and when the siege is against Jerusalem, it will also be against Judah.
> 3. "And... *all the nations* of the earth will be gathered against it..." (Zech 12:2-3*)

Jerusalem is indisputably the epicentre of this battle. As noted in Book 4,[101] "a cup that causes reeling", or staggering from drunkenness, leads to belligerence and irrationality (Prov 20:1), hallucinations and self-inflicted wounds (Prov 23:29-35). In Book 2,[102] I show the irrationality underlying the Muslim and Arab claims on Jerusalem as their third holiest site which they call al-Quds. Nevertheless, Iran's Quds Force[103] is dedicated to 'liberating' Jerusalem and throughout the Muslim and Arab world, they celebrate International Quds Day on the last Friday of Ramadan.[104]

---

101 *Silencing the Witnesses*, pp. 293-301.
102 *Slouching Towards Bethlehem*, pp. 215-218.
103 One of five branches of their Islamic Revolutionary Guard Corps (IRGC) and under the direct control of Ayatollah Khamenei, the Supreme Leader of Iran.
104 Ramadan is the ninth month of the Islamic calendar, marked by fasting and one of the Five Pillars of the faith.

Jesus was very specific - the Gentiles were only allowed to "trample underfoot" Jerusalem "until the times of the Gentiles are fulfilled" (Luke 21:24). I believe this was fulfilled in 1967 and Jerusalem was re-sanctified as "the holy city" (Rev 11:2), as explained in Book 4.

Zechariah continues:

> 3. "And it will come about in that day that I will make *Jerusalem a heavy stone* for all the peoples; all who lift it will be severely injured. And *all the nations* of the earth will be gathered against it..." (Zech 12:3*)

Jerusalem will become a self-inflicted punishment on wrong-doers: "a heavy stone for all... who lift it will be severely injured". Then God will judge "all the surrounding peoples":

> 6. "In that day I will make the clans of Judah like a firepot among pieces of wood and a flaming torch among sheaves, so they will consume on the right hand and on the left *all the surrounding peoples*..." (Zech 12:6*)

As we saw earlier, Micah predicted "the daughter of Zion" would thresh the sheaves God has gathered to the threshing floor in Jerusalem. Here Zechariah changes the simile to God using the Jewish people as "a flaming torch" among the dry sheaves and nothing will quench His fire. Zechariah continues:

> 8. In that day the LORD will defend the inhabitants of Jerusalem...
> 9. "And it will come about in that day that I will set about to destroy *all the nations that come against Jerusalem.*"
> (Zech 12:8-9*)

Jews for Jesus

The next verse is surely the most wonderful of Zechariah's prophecies:

> 10. "I will pour out on the house of David and on the inhabitants of Jerusalem, the Spirit of grace and of supplication, so that *they will look on Me whom they have pierced* and they will mourn for Him, as one mourns for an only son, and they will weep bitterly over Him like the bitter weeping over a firstborn" (Zech 12:10*)

They will finally understand who Jesus is.

When the people of Israel realise that "all the nations" have turned against them yet again, they will begin to call on the God of Israel. In response, our heavenly Father will "pour out… the Spirit of grace and of supplication" to help them pray properly (Rom 8:26). In other words, God will reveal His triune nature as the Father pours out the Holy Spirit who will glorify the Son - they will at last come to understand the Crucifixion.

Up till now, they have been taught that Jesus cannot be the Messiah because He was executed and cursed of God (Deut 21:23) and therefore must have sinned; now they will see that Jesus died not for His own sin but ours, just as Isaiah prophesied He would:

> 4. Surely our griefs He Himself bore,
> And our sorrows He carried;
> Yet we ourselves esteemed Him stricken,
> Smitten of God, and afflicted.
> 5. But He was *pierced* through *for our transgressions*,
> He was crushed for our iniquities;
> The chastening for our well-being fell upon Him,
> And by His scourging we are healed.
> (Isa 53:4-5*)

Understanding that Jesus is the "only son" and "firstborn" of God, they will mourn with "the bitter weeping" that they would weep for "an only son" and "firstborn" in their own families. In Biblical days, "an only son" was particularly precious because he would carry the family name into the next generation; if he died, the family name would be swallowed up as daughters married into other families.

Mourning in Megiddon

Zechariah then adds that they will also grieve in a very particular way:

> 11. "In that day there will be great mourning in Jerusalem, like the mourning of Hadad-rimmon in the plain of Megiddon." (Zech 12:11, *NASB*, Hebrew spelling)

Hadad and Rimmon were two Syrian deities so some speculate that 'the weeping may be that for Tammuz (Ezekiel 8:14), with whom the old Semitic deity had become confused in the popular mind'.[105] Most, however, take the name as a place (see map on p. 50). The *NKJV*, for example:

> "...like the mourning *at* Hadad Rimmon in the plain of Megiddo."

The *New International Reader's Version* inserts a reason for the grief:

> "At that time there will be a lot of crying in Jerusalem. It will sound like the sobs of the people at Hadad Rimmon *over Josiah's death* in the Valley of Megiddo." (*)

Eastman's *Illustrated Bible Dictionary* explains:

> Hadad-rimmon… is alluded to by… Zechariah in a proverbial expression derived from the lamentation for Josiah, who was mortally wounded near this place… It has been identified with the modern Rummaneh, a village "at the foot of the Megiddo hills, in a notch or valley about an hour and a half south of Tell Metzellim."[106]

---

105 *International Standard Bible Encyclopedia* (1915).
106 Easton M.A., D.D., *Illustrated Bible Dictionary*, Third Edition.

Others added;

> ...it may have been an old Syrian stronghold, and hence Josiah may here have made his last stand in defense of the plain...[107]

We need to catch up with what Zechariah's original audience already knew about Josiah's death.

Good King Josiah

In 609 BC, Josiah had made a tragic error. Ignoring a warning from God, he went to war 'on the plain of Megiddo' (2 Chron 35:22) against Pharaoh Neco, inserting himself into a battle between Egypt and Babylon. Fatally pierced by an arrow (2 Chron 35:23), he was carried home to Jerusalem where he died, aged just thirty-nine.

The mourning of Josiah's death became legendary:

> All Judah and Jerusalem mourned for Josiah. Then Jeremiah chanted a lament for Josiah. And all the male and female singers speak about Josiah in their lamentations to this day. And they made them *an ordinance in Israel*; behold, they are also written in the Lamentations.[108] (2 Chron 35:25*)

'An ordinance in Israel' ensured an annual commemoration of his death. However, Josiah's birth in 648 BC was similarly legendary, having been predicted *by name* some three hundred years earlier. King Jeroboam (r. 930-909 BC) had set up the golden calves to be worshipped in Bethel and Dan and God sent a prophet:

> He cried against the altar by the word of the LORD, and said, "O altar, altar, thus says the LORD, 'Behold, a son shall be born

---

107 McClintock, John. Strong, James, *Cyclopedia of Biblical, Theological and Ecclesiastical Literature*. Harper & Brothers, New York, 1870. www.studylight.org/encyclopedias/eng/tce/h/hadad-rimmon.html.

108 We have Jeremiah's description of Josiah (Jer 22:15-16) but not his lament. However, the fact that he lamented led to the Book of Lamentations being traditionally ascribed to him.

to the house of David, *Josiah by name*; and on you he shall sacrifice the priests of the high places who burn incense on you, and human bones shall be burned on you.'" (1 Kin 13:2*)

Josiah was only eight years old when his father was assassinated in 640 BC and he became king. He was also the only king in all the land of Israel because the northern kingdom had been abolished by the Assyrians in 722 BC.

At age sixteen, Josiah began seeking God and over the next ten years, he not only fulfilled the above prophecy (2 Kin 23:16) but also cleansed the whole land of every kind of idolatry (2 Kin 23:34, 2 Chron 34:33), including the pagan shrines that Solomon had built for his wives in Jerusalem (2 Kin 23:13-14).

At age twenty-six he repaired the Temple, renewed the Mosaic covenant, and restored the Passover:

> There had not been celebrated a Passover like it in Israel since the days of Samuel the prophet; nor had any of the kings of Israel celebrated such a Passover as Josiah did with the priests, the Levites, all Judah and Israel who were present, and the inhabitants of Jerusalem. (2 Chron 35:18)

This brief but golden time ended with his premature death. 'All Judah and Jerusalem mourned' because...:

> *Before him* there was no king like him who turned to the LORD with all his heart and with all his soul and with all his might, according to all the Law of Moses; nor did any like him arise *after him*. (2 Kin 23:25*)

He was the mostly godly of all of Israel's kings.

Parallels with Jesus

We see then what the Jewish disciples in John's audience would have already known – there were extraordinary parallels in the births, lives, and deaths of Josiah and Jesus:

(i) They were truly godly sons of David.

(ii) Their births and deeds were predicted centuries earlier.

(iii) They completely upheld the Law of Moses.

In Book 4, I quoted a remarkable statement issued in 2015 by fifty-four well-known Orthodox rabbis recognising Jesus' faithfulness as Teacher and Sage:

> Jesus brought a double goodness to the world... On the one hand he strengthened the Torah of Moses majestically... and not one of our Sages spoke out more emphatically concerning the immutability of the Torah. On the other hand, he removed idols from the nations...[109]

(iv) They both died young, pierced by their enemies.

We find then one more layer in the name Har-Magedon: just as the entire ancient nation mourned the untimely death of their much-loved and godly young king Josiah, pierced by Egyptian arrows, the entire modern nation will mourn the untimely death of their young Messiah "whom *they* have pierced". When they see all the nations gathering for this battle, "every family" in Israel, from the greatest to the least (Zech 12:11-14), will realise how terribly, tragically wrong they have been to reject Jesus over the last 2,000 years.

Israel's Revival

They will also experience the love, patience, and mercy of God:

> 1. "In that day a fountain will be opened for the house of David and for the inhabitants of Jerusalem, for sin and for impurity.
> 2. "It will come about in that day," declares the LORD of hosts, "that I will cut off the names of the idols from the land, and they will no longer be remembered; and I will

---

[109] *Silencing the Witnesses*, pp. 288-293.

also remove the prophets and the unclean spirit from the land." (Zech 13:1-2)

In Book 4,[110] I showed how this nation-wide repentance was similarly predicted in Revelation 11:13 as 'a great earthquake' in which 'a tenth of the city fell' and 'seven thousand people were killed'.

Many expect this earthquake to be literal and a major disaster but I believe it is metaphorical; the numbers have a symbolic meaning, portraying a complete reversal of past catastrophes in Jewish history. In Amos's time, only a tenth of their soldiers survived the Assyrian invasion (Amos 5:3) and in Isaiah's time, only a tenth remained in the land (Isa 6:11-13). In John's vision, one tenth of the city falling means *nine-tenths will not fall*. Again, this could be literal but consider how it is used as a metaphor:

> "Behold, this Child is appointed for *the fall and rise of many in Israel*, and for a sign to be opposed..." (Luke 2:34*)

Paul also uses 'the present Jerusalem' as a metaphor for the Mosaic Covenant and unbelieving Israel (Gal 4:24-26). Nine-tenths not falling would mean 90% of unbelieving Israel will turn and be saved. Similarly, in Elijah's time, only 7,000 "had not bowed the knee to Baal" (1 Kin 19:18); in John's time, only 7,000 being killed means the rest will live.

This will be an astonishing time of revival in Israel and the Lord will intervene in the battle to destroy "all the nations" coming against them. The Battle of Har-Magedon will be Israel's greatest military victory!

Lastly, God's gathering the nations for this last battle mirrors His promise to Deborah and Barak:

> "I will draw out to you Sisera... with his chariots and his many troops to the river Kishon, and I will give him into your hand." (Judg 4:7*)

---

110 Ibid, pp. 282-287.

And just as God would "sell Sisera into the hands of a woman", Jael, to be killed (Judg 4:9, 17-22), the kings of the earth will be sold into the hands of "the daughter of Zion" to be threshed (Mic 4:13).

Of Narnia & Middle Earth

From my first encounters with C.S. Lewis's *The Chronicles of Narnia*[111] and J.R.R. Tolkien's *Lord of the Rings*,[112] I have loved these books. I read them to my three children for years and we all delighted in the movie adaptations. One of the scenes in the Rings trilogy was shot on a hillside opposite our home in Wellington where we could see the set's lights and we lived in a neighbouring suburb to the WETA Workshop.

I am still astonished at how beautifully Lewis and Tolkien created their make-believe worlds to portray and illustrate profound truths revealed in the Scriptures. It is therefore not easy for me to criticise their works of fiction and allegory but in bringing their masterpieces to climax, they have inadvertently given us a wholly wrong impression of the last days.

In *The Last Battle*, Lewis's last book in the Narnia series has an evil ape, Shift, persuading a naïve donkey called Puzzle to wear a lion's skin to masquerade as Aslan, the great lion and creator of Narnia and the earth. However, immediately prior to Aslan's triumphant return, the Narnian army and its leader Roonwit are all killed in battle. Of course, they are all resurrected so the book ends happily but we are left with the impression of a terrible battle with many heroes as casualties.

---

111 A series of seven fantasy novels written for children and published between 1950 and 1956, *The Chronicles* have sold over 100 million copies in 47 languages.
112 This epic was published in three volumes in 1954 and 1955, translated into 38 languages, and sold over 150 million copies. Its prequel, *The Hobbit*, was written in 1937, sold 100 million copies, and has been adapted for stage, screen, radio, and board and video games.

Similarly, in Tolkien's last book in his series set in Middle Earth, *The Return of the King*, the mysterious Christ-figure Aragorn is crowned as the true King of Gondor but the last battle is long and, again, terrible with many heroes killed.

Of course, these are fantasies and their last battles may have been intended to portray those martyred throughout the last 2,000 years. However, the impression remains of the last battle being vast, drawn out, and deadly to many good characters before they are resurrected. In reality, the Battle of Har-Magedon will not be long and the only casualties will be those who come out to fight against Israel and they will be defeated in a moment.

Summary

(i) The Battle of Har-Magedon will be good for Israel in every way. Immediately beforehand, they will at last find their Messiah and they will finally defeat all who come out against them.

(ii) Since their rebirth as a nation in 1948, the Jews have fought and won wars against their Arab and Muslim neighbours but this time, they will face "all the nations".

(iii) Abandoned by every ally, Israel will know their only help is in the God of Israel. As they call upon Him, He will reveal Himself in all of His triune glory: the Father will first pour out the Holy Spirit who will reveal the Son to His own people.

(iv) This revelation will lead to a nation-wide repentance in "every family", from the greatest to the least. Just as the entire nation of Israel mourned the untimely death of their godly young king Josiah who was mortally wounded at Megiddo in 609 BC, so the entire modern nation of Israel will mourn the untimely death of their young Messiah, Jesus, in 30 AD. They will see that He died for their sins, as for all of ours.

(v) Accordingly, ninety percent of Israel will turn to Jesus and all who assemble to destroy them will be destroyed by the Lord returning in His glory to save them.

6
"But What About…?"
Jacob's Trouble

Some today believe instead that this battle will go very badly for Israel, based on a misunderstanding of prophecies such as Jeremiah's "time of Jacob's trouble" and Zechariah's, that two-thirds of their population will die:

> 8. "It will come about in all the land," declares the LORD,
> "That *two parts* in it will be cut off and perish;
> But *the third* will be left in it.
> 9. "And I will bring the third part through the fire,
> Refine them as silver is refined,
> And test them as gold is tested…" (Zech 13:8-9*)

Some years ago, Mark Alan Siegel, an American Jewish community leader, was asked his thoughts on Christians. He replied:

> The worst possible allies for the Jewish state are the fundamentalist Christians who want Jews to die and convert so they can bring on the second coming of their Lord. It is a false friendship. They are seeking their own ends and not ours… The Christians just want us to be there so we can be slaughtered and converted and bring on the second coming of Jesus Christ…[113]

Mr Siegel's complaint is perfectly understandable and is caused by the widespread promotion of some badly mistaken ideas.

---

113 https://americanvision.org/6370/christians-just-want-jews-slaughtered-and-converted/ 27 Apr, 2021.

Mistaken End Times Ideas

Charles C. Ryrie, for example:

> Jacob's trouble is that coming period of distress described by Jesus as He spoke to His disciples on the Mount of Olives. Jeremiah labelled it 'Jacob's trouble' and said it would be unique in all history (Jer 30:7). Jesus called it a period of unprecedented tribulation (Matt 24:21)... this will be the time of *Israel's greatest bloodbath*.[114]

John F. Walvoord thinks it will happen over three and a half years:

> ...the last seven years or the seventieth week of Daniel's prophecy will immediately precede the second coming of Christ. According to Daniel 9:27 it is divided into two halves: the first 3½ years are a period in which Israel is apparently protected under a covenant with the Gentile world ruler, the prince mentioned in Daniel 9:26. By contrast, however, Daniel indicates that the last 3½ years cover an entirely different situation, one in which there is unprecedented trouble. In this period Israel becomes the object of persecution instead of being protected from her enemies.[115]

He believes the Jewish death toll will be double the Holocaust's:

> ...two thirds of the children of Israel in the land will perish, but the one third that are left will be refined and be awaiting the deliverance of God at the second coming of Christ...[116]

Tim LaHaye agrees:

> Prior to Israel's conversion, Zechariah predicts that two-thirds... of the Jewish people in the land will perish

---

114 Charles Caldwell Ryrie, *The Living End*, Old Tappan, NJ; Revell, 1976, p. 81. Emphasis added.
115 John F. Walvoord, *The Revelation of Jesus Christ*, Chicago, Moody Press, 1966, pp. 131-132.
116 John F. Walvoord, *Israel in Prophecy*, Grand Rapids, MI: Zondervan/ Academie, [1962] 1988, p. 108.

during the tribulation period. Only one third of the Jewish population will survive until Christ comes to establish His kingdom on earth.[117]

How widely are these views shared? Hal Lindsay's *The Late Great Planet Earth* was a publishing phenomenon. The first Christian prophecy book to be published by a secular publisher, Bantam Press, it has sold over 35 million copies and been translated into over 50 languages. In 1979, it was made into a film narrated by Orson Welles.

More recently, Tim LaHaye and his co-author Jerry Jenkins set new records in American multimedia publishing - their sixteen novels in the *Left Behind* series have sold 65 million books and inspired four movie adaptations, an audio drama and a computer game, and twelve more spin-off novels for teenagers.[118]

Conflating Prophecies

These interpretations have conflated five very different predicted times into just one, and all in the future. These are:

(i) "The time of Jacob's trouble".
(ii) Zechariah's "two-thirds" perishing.
(iii) The "three and a half years" of Daniel, Jesus, James, and Revelation.
(iv) Jesus' "great tribulation".
(v) John's "great tribulation".

They are actually five distinct time periods and, thankfully, four of them have already happened and the fifth is almost finished.

I covered (iii), the "three and a half years" prophecies,

---

117 Tim LaHaye, gen. ed., *Prophecy Study Bible,* Chattanooga, TN; AMG Publishers, 2000, p. 991. See also John F. Walvoord, *Israel in Prophecy*, Grand Rapids, MI; Zondervan/Academie, 1988, p. 108.
118 www.tyndale.com/sites/leftbehind/, 27 Apr, 2021.

in Book 1[119] where I show that Daniel's 70th Week does not describe the actions of the Antichrist but the work of "Messiah the Prince" (see Appendix B for a recap).[120] I then showed how the first half of this 'week' of years was literal i.e. the three and half years of Jesus' ministry to Israel between 26 and 30 AD. At the end of that time, i.e. 'in the middle of the week', He introduced the New Covenant and rendered obsolete the animal 'sacrifice and grain offering' (Dan 9:27).

I then showed that the second half was metaphorical, being "the times of the Gentiles".

This should not be considered strange because *all* the literal observances of the Law's festivals, sabbaths, food laws, priests, sacrifices, Tabernacle and Temples became metaphorical/spiritual realities under the New Covenant (1 Cor 5:7-8, Col 2:16-17, 1 Pet 2:5).

The second half of Daniel's 70th Week began in 30 AD when the gospel went out to "all the nations", i.e. Gentiles (Matt 28:19), and lasted until 1967 when Israel regained Jerusalem (Luke 21:24), i.e. almost 2,000 years. This is why Jesus called this time period "the times of the Gentiles".[121]

Let us now consider the other four, beginning with the one most offensive to Mr Siegel.

Two-Thirds Perishing?

As seen above, Zechariah prophesied:

> 8. "It will come about in all the land,"
> Declares the LORD,
> "That two parts in it will be cut off and perish;

---

119 *Dancing in the Dragon's Jaws*, pp. 94-116.
120 See too the commentaries of Albert Barnes, Joseph Benson, John Calvin, Jonathan Edwards, Charles Ellicott, Matthew Poole, the Geneva Study Bible, the Pulpit Commentary, and the Jamieson-Fausset-Brown Bible Commentary. https://biblehub.com/commentaries/daniel/9-27.htm, 26 Jan, 2022.
121 See too Revelation 11:2.

> But the third will be left in it.
> 9. "And I will bring the third part through the fire..."
> (Zech 13:8-9*)

Those quoted above believe this has yet to be fulfilled but they would freely admit that the preceding verse has already been fulfilled:

> 7. "Awake, O sword, against My Shepherd,
> And against the man, My Associate,"
> Declares the LORD of hosts.
> "Strike the Shepherd that the sheep may be scattered;
> And I will turn My hand against the little ones." (Zech 13:7)

"My Shepherd" and "Associate" is obviously Jesus and He said this verse would be fulfilled in 30 AD by His crucifixion (Matt 26:31, Mark 14:27).[122] This was why God said He would "turn *My hand* against the little ones" (v. 7), resulting in two-thirds perishing "in all the land" of Israel (Zech 13:8) - the Father, being the king in Jesus' parable, "sent his armies and destroyed those murderers and set their city on fire" (Matt 22:7).

Recorded History

Flavius Josephus was an eyewitness, travelling with the Roman general Titus. It can be argued that Josephus exaggerated death-tolls but without any other recorded figures that I can find, I start with his and will accept any corrections.

---

[122] Zechariah's prophecies predict both of Jesus' comings and it is easy to confuse which refer to which. I divide them three ways: (i) Obvious first coming: Gentiles trusting in Him (8:23); His humble entrance to Jerusalem on a donkey colt (9:9); being rejected for thirty pieces of silver (11:12-14); being struck as the Shepherd and Jerusalem being judged (13:7-9). (ii) Obvious second coming: rescue of Jerusalem (12:1-13:6, 14:12-15). (iii) If metaphorical, first coming but if literal, second coming: standing on the Mount of Olives, division of the land, endless light, Jerusalem as source of living water, kingdom of God over all the earth (Zech 14:4-9) and celebrating the Feast of Tabernacles (Zech 14:16-21).

Josephus recorded that there were 2,700,200[123] celebrating the Passover in Israel in 70 AD. His figure was calculated from the number of lambs killed for the feast. He went on:

> Now the number of those that were carried captive during this whole war was collected to be ninety-seven thousand, as was the number of those that perished during the whole siege *eleven hundred thousand*, the greater part of whom were indeed of the same nation, but not belonging to the city itself; for they were come up from all the country to the Feast of Unleavened Bread...[124]

This death toll of 1,100,000 in the siege of Jerusalem was the gruesome climax of Titus's campaign but the First Jewish-Roman War had begun four years earlier in 66 AD under Vespasian.

Vespasian began in Galilee and in capturing Gamla, 'the Masada of the north', in 67 AD, his army killed 4,000 while another 5,000 committed suicide rather than surrender. It is estimated 100,000 Jews died or were enslaved in this opening campaign.[125] The First War did not end until they captured Masada in 73 AD. Many others had been killed or died of starvation and disease throughout the land – I assume 200,000.

The Jews rebelled again in North Africa, Cyprus, Mesopotamia, and Judea between 115-117 AD but, after initial successes, were defeated. We are not told Jewish casualties but Dio Cassius records 220,000 Romans and Greeks killed in North Africa and 240,000 in Cyprus.[126] This rebellion came to an end in Lydda in Judea with the capture and execution of its leaders. It is not hard to imagine a comparable number of Jews dying at this time, say 500,000,

---

123 *The* Wars of the Jews, Book 6, Chap 9, para 3. www.gutenberg.org/files/2850/2850-h/2850-h.htm#link62H_4_0001, 18 Apr 2021.
124 Ibid.
125 www.jewishvirtuallibrary.org/the-great-revolt-66-70-ce, 23 Apr, 2021.
126 www.gutenberg.org/files/10890/10890-h/10890-h.htm#a68_32, 18 Apr, 2021.

but let us assume only 100,000 in the land of Israel.

Then in the final Jewish-Roman war, the Bar-Kokhba Revolt (132-136 AD) in Israel, Hadrian's legions killed another 580,000.[127]

These rough estimates would give us a total of 2,080,000 Jewish deaths out of a population of 3,000,000,[128] fulfilling Zechariah's prediction of two thirds "in all the land" perishing (Zech 13:8).[129]

Conclusion

This will not happen again before Jesus returns any more than He will come 'mounted on a donkey, even on a colt, the foal of a donkey' (Zech 9:9). Instead:

> 8. "In that day the LORD will defend the inhabitants of Jerusalem, and the one who is feeble among them in that day will be like David, and the house of David will be like God, like the angel of the LORD before them.
> 9. "And in that day I will set about to destroy *all the nations* that come against Jerusalem." (Zech 12:8-9*)

The terrible time when two-thirds perish is past and will not be repeated – Israel will turn to Jesus as Messiah and win overwhelmingly at Har-Magedon.

"The Great Tribulation"?

The phrase comes from Revelation 7 where, following the numbering of the 144,000, John sees a vast multitude in heaven, clothed in white, and worshipping:

> 13. Then one of the elders [asked] me, "These who are clothed in the white robes, who are they, and where have they come from?"

---

127 www.jewish-history.com/palestine/period1.html, 5 Apr 2021.
128 Josephus had excluded "those that have the leprosy, or the gonorrhea, or… are otherwise polluted".
129 There were another 5-5,500,000 in the Diaspora. Eckstein, Zvi & Botticini, Maristella. 2012. *The Chosen Few: How Education Shaped Jewish History, 70-1492*, Tel Aviv: Tel Aviv University Press, p. 17.

> 14. I said to him, "My lord, you know." And he said to me, "These are the ones who come out of *the great tribulation*, and they have washed their robes and made them white in the blood of the Lamb..." (Rev 7:13-14*)

Four verses earlier, these believers are described as coming from every nation and language group:

> 9. ...I looked, and behold, a great multitude which no one could count, from *every nation and all tribes and peoples and tongues*, standing before the throne and before the Lamb, clothed in white robes, and palm branches were in their hands (Rev 7:9*)

In Book 3,[130] I showed how John's original audience would have been delighted to hear from the last of the Twelve about God's appointing another 12 x 12 x 1,000 apostles to take the gospel "to the remotest part of the earth" (Acts 1:8). This then gives us the timing of this part of John's vision - if the gospel has been successfully preached to "all the nations", John must be seeing *the end of the age* because Jesus taught:

> "This gospel of the kingdom shall be preached in the whole world as a testimony to *all the nations*, and then *the end* will come." (Matt 24:14*)

So when does "the great tribulation" begin?

Tribulation

The New Testament Greek noun, *thlipsis*, comes from the verb to press or squash, literally or figuratively,[131] so is translated as affliction (20 times), anguish (1), distress (2), persecution (1) tribulation (20) and trouble (1). The Scriptures use it in two ways, either generally or of a particular period. We should, for example, expect it at any time:

> "These things I have spoken to you, so that in Me you may

---

130 *Gotta Serve Somebody: The Mystery of the Marks & 666*, pp. 153-187.
131 *Kittel*, pp. 334-335.

> have peace. In the world you have *tribulation*, but take courage; I have overcome the world." (John 16:33*)

> ...but we also exult in our tribulations, knowing that tribulation brings about perseverance (Rom 5:3)

However, Jesus also warned the disciples of a coming period of unsurpassed hardship:

> "For then there will be *a great tribulation*, such as has not occurred since the beginning of the world until now, nor ever will." (Matt 24:21*)

There has been much debate as to when this horrendous time would occur, some arguing for the 1st century AD while others believe it is yet to come. However, I am saying that Jesus and John are describing two very different "great tribulations" and this can be established by considering those affected and their locations.

Locations

Jesus describes an unprecedented and never to be repeated great tribulation – "such as has not occurred since the beginning of the world until now, nor ever will" - squarely in Judea:

> "...then those who are in Judea must flee *to the mountains.*" (Matt 24:16*)

In other words, it could be avoided by leaving Judea. Luke gives us further details:

> 20. "But when you see Jerusalem surrounded by armies, then recognize that her desolation is near.
> 21. "Then those who are *in Judea* must flee to the mountains, and those who are in the midst of the city must leave, and those who are in the country must not enter the city;

22. because these are days of vengeance, so that all things which are written will be fulfilled." (Luke 21:20-22*)

We need to remember that the Lord was warning not only His disciples but also every observant Jew who might be affected:

"...pray that your flight will not be... on a Sabbath." (Matt 24:20)

Luke records that 'a Sabbath's day's journey' from Jerusalem would only get observant Jews to 'the mount called Olivet' (Acts 1:12), i.e. not far enough to escape. However, this would not have been an issue to Jesus' disciples - by 70 AD, they were not under the Law but under the New Covenant. The only ones still under the Law in 70 AD were His Jewish countrymen who had rejected Him and His offer. However, they too could escape before the Roman siege if they would listen to Him.

It was an appalling tribulation for the Jewish people in 70 AD. Jesus called it the "days of vengeance" when "all things which are written will be fulfilled" (Luke 21:22). I detailed in Book 4[132] how this could be seen as a general warning (Lev 26:25-39) but noted that Daniel predicted one would follow the killing of Messiah the Prince:

"...a complete destruction, one that is decreed, is poured out on the one who makes desolate." (Dan 9:27)

"The one who makes desolate" was the nation of Israel; their "abomination" that caused it was the crucifixion. All there who heeded Jesus' warning fled as He urged, to the mountains of today's Jordan. Eusebius was the bishop of Caesarea Maritima in 314 AD and he recorded:

The people of the Church in Jerusalem... [fled to] one of the cities of Perea which they called Pella. To it those who believed on Christ travelled from Jerusalem, so that

---

132 *Silencing the Witnesses*, pp. 94-98.

when holy men had altogether deserted the royal capital of the Jews and the whole land of Judaea…[133]

Epiphanius of Salamis (c. 310-403) wrote similarly:

>…after the exodus from Jerusalem when all the disciples went to live in Pella because Christ had told them to leave Jerusalem and to go away since it would undergo a siege…[134]

As shown above, in the following sixty-five years, the death-toll in Israel was approximately two-thirds of the population in the land. Double the ratio of the Holocaust, this truly was the greatest tribulation Israel has ever endured and, thankfully, ever will, because Jesus promised:

> "For then there will be a great tribulation, such as has not occurred since the beginning of the world until now, *nor ever will.*" (Matt 24:21*)

This then was the time of Zechariah's "two-thirds" prophecy and Israel will never face it again.[135] Although all the nations *will* assemble to retake Jerusalem, Israel will overwhelmingly win their last battle at the Lord's return.

Revelation's "Great Tribulation"

John's vision, however, reveals that those 'who come out of the great tribulation' (Rev 7:14) are 'from every nation and all tribes and peoples and tongues' (Rev 7:9). They are Jesus' martyred disciples from all over the earth, as John is told:

> "…they have washed their robes and made them white in the blood of the Lamb…" (Rev 7:14)

---

133 Eusebius, *Church History*, Book III, 5:3.
134 Epiphanius of Salamis, *Panarion*, Book XXIX, 7:7-8.
135 I have found no death tolls for the Assyrian invasion in the 8th century BC or the Babylonian invasion in the 6th century BC. However, given John's vision of the dragon destroying 'a third of the stars' (Rev 12:4) in Satan's recurring attempts at genocide since the 15th century BC, it may be that the death toll was that high each time. *Dancing in the Dragon's Jaws*, pp. 34-35.

Accordingly, any believer can face this tribulation but we will have His peace:

> "These things I have spoken to you, so that in Me you may have peace. In the world you have *tribulation*, but take courage; I have overcome the world." (John 16:33*)

John certainly endured it:

> I, John, your brother and fellow partaker in *the tribulation*... (Rev 1:9*)

Likewise the Thessalonians:

> You also became imitators of us and of the Lord, having received the word in *much tribulation* with the joy of the Holy Spirit... (1 Thess 1:6*)

Today, Open Doors report that 360,000,000 Christians are being persecuted for their faith in North Korea, Afghanistan, Somalia, Libya, Pakistan, Sudan, Eritrea, Yemen, and India; over 4,000 killed every year, or 11 every day![136]

Conclusion

The Scriptures describe three kinds of tribulation:

(i) General

This is the persecution, affliction, anguish, distress, temptation, and suffering any saint may face simply because of their faith in Jesus.

(ii) The greatest-ever tribulation

Jesus predicted that the 1st century siege of Jerusalem would lead to "a great tribulation" that would never be repeated. In the Roman-Jewish Wars between 66 and 136 AD, two-thirds of the Jews 'in the land' perished, just as Zechariah had also predicted.

---

136 www.opendoorsusa.org/christian-persecution/stories/11-christians-killed-every-day-for-their-decision-to-follow-jesus/, 21 Nov, 2022.

(iii) John's "great tribulation"

The Greek word for great, *megas*, that John uses in Revelation 7:14 means 'big (literally or figuratively, in a very wide application)'.[137] Many have assumed he is referring to its intensity, as in Zechariah's 'two-thirds' prophecy, but he is actually referring to its width and length - it encompasses every kind of persecution, affliction, anguish, distress, temptation, suffering, and martyrdom faced by the saints throughout the world; it began in 30 AD and it will last until Jesus returns.

John's vision was to reassure us, however, that all who hold true in any time will be with the Lord and, Paul adds, will return with Him (1 Thess 4:14).

"Jacob's Trouble"?

The phrase comes from Jeremiah:

> "Alas! for that day is great,
> There is none like it;
> And it is *the time of Jacob's distress* [KJV, trouble],
> But he will be saved from it." (Jer 30:7, *NASB*)

With all prophecies, timing and context really matter so what was Jeremiah's? Jerusalem had been captured by the Babylonians in 597 BC and some ten thousand, including Daniel and Ezekiel, were in exile in Babylon. Jeremiah was prophesying just before Jerusalem was razed in 586 BC (Jer 38:28) and this particular prophecy actually begins with God's promise:

> 3. "For behold, days are coming," declares the LORD, "when I will restore the fortunes of My people Israel and Judah." The LORD says, "I will also bring them *back to the land* that I gave to their forefathers and they shall possess it."
> (Jer 30:3 *)

---

137 G3173, *Strong's Exhaustive Concordance*, p. 1665.

Jeremiah knows this will be after seventy years because he had just prophesied that:

> "For thus says the LORD, 'When seventy years have been completed for Babylon, I will visit you and fulfill My good word to you, to bring you back to this place.'" (Jer 29:10)

However, Jeremiah then begins a new prophecy of a time *after* the restoration:

> 5. "For thus says the LORD, 'I have heard a sound of terror,
> Of dread, and there is no peace.
> 6. 'Ask now, and see
> If a male can give birth.
> Why do I see every man
> With his hands on his loins, as a woman in childbirth?
> And why have all faces turned pale?'" (Jer 30:5-6)

This will be "the time of Jacob's distress" but Jacob will "be saved from it" (v. 7) and the Davidic dynasty will be restored:

> 8. "It shall come about *on that day*," declares the LORD of hosts, "that I will break his yoke from off their neck and will tear off their bonds; and strangers will no longer make them their slaves.
> 9. "But they shall serve the LORD their God and *David their king*, whom I will raise up for them." (Jer 30:8-9*)

"On that day", God will set them free from yokes, bonds, and enslavement to "serve the Lord and David their king", restoring the Davidic lineage. So when is "that day"? Still in the future, or has it already happened? Consider Jewish history from Jeremiah to Jesus.

Jewish History

After the Babylonian exile, in 538 BC Cyrus decreed the Jews could return to the Promised Land (Ezra 1:1) but they remained under Medo-Persian domination. Hear their prayer in c. 430 BC:

36. "Behold, we are slaves today, and as to the land which You gave to our fathers to eat of its fruit and its bounty, Behold, we are slaves in it.
37. "Its abundant produce is for the kings whom You have set over us because of our sins; They also rule over our bodies and over our cattle as they please, So we are in *great distress*." (Neh 9:36-37*)

They were in "great distress" because the Persians still "'rule over our bodies" (v. 37), even drafting them into military service with Xerxes' army when he invaded Greece in 480 BC. Daniel also prophesied of this time:

"So you are to know and discern that from the issuing of a decree to restore and rebuild Jerusalem until Messiah the Prince there will be seven weeks and sixty-two weeks; it will be built again, with plaza and moat, even *in times of distress*." (Dan 9:25*)

Jerusalem and the Temple were rebuilt during these "times of distress".

When the Greeks then defeated the Persians in 331 BC, the Jews became subject to the Greeks, their humiliation completed by Antiochus IV setting up the third[138] 'abomination of desolation' in the Holy Place in 168 BC. After a brief respite due to the Maccabees' Revolt, the Romans invaded Israel in 63 BC and their general Pompeii desecrated the Temple by entering the Holy of Holies.

This then was "the time of Jacob's distress". It began after their restoration to the land, as Jeremiah had predicted, and it lasted over 500 years.

They even knew why - "because of our sins" (Neh 9:37).

Where then was the promised freedom and Davidic restoration? Jesus was offering it to them in 26 AD:

31. So Jesus was saying to those Jews who had believed Him, "If you continue in My word, then you are truly disciples of Mine;

---

138 See *Slouching Towards Bethlehem*, pp. 205-212.

> 32. and you will know the truth, and the truth will make you free."
> 33. They answered Him, "We are Abraham's descendants and have never yet been enslaved to anyone; how is it that You say, 'You will become free'?" (John 8:31-33)

Their thinking of literal slavery ignored not only the previous 500 years but also their very present Roman overlords. However, Jesus had in mind their spiritual slavery:

> 34. Jesus answered them, "Truly, truly, I say to you, everyone who commits sin is the slave of sin.
> 35. "The slave does not remain in the house forever; the son does remain forever.
> 36. "So if the Son makes you free, you will be free indeed." (John 8:34-36)

The promised Son of David was offering them freedom from their sins, to save them, but they had forgotten their sins were the cause of Jacob's distress.

"A Woman in Childbirth"

As quoted above, Jeremiah also prophesied that Israel would be "as a woman in childbirth" (Jer 30:6) *before* the restoration of David's dynasty. The time of Jacob's distress turns out to be *Israel's birth-pangs* in giving birth to Jesus.

Micah also spoke of Israel's birth-pangs in c. 720 BC. Immediately following his famous prophecy regarding Messiah's birthplace, "But as for you, Bethlehem Ephrathah… From you One will go forth for Me to be ruler in Israel" (Mic 5:2), Micah continued:

> 3. Therefore *He will give them up until the time* when *she who is in labor* has borne a child…
> 4. And He will arise and shepherd His flock in the strength of the LORD, in the majesty of the name of the LORD His God… (Mic 5:3-4*)

When and how did God "give them up" (v. 3)? From Micah's time, He gave Israel up to be ruled by the Babylonian, Medo-Persian, Greek, and Roman empires until she gave birth to Jesus, the Son of David and the Good Shepherd.

The time of "Jacob's trouble" was the 500 years between Israel's restoration from Babylon and Jesus' birth. Jeremiah's lamentation, "Alas! for that day is great; there is none like it" was because Israel had lost everything – exiled for 70 years in Babylon, the tiny remnant returned to a desolate Jerusalem and the Temple in ruins. Though restored to the land, they had no Davidic king and were still ruled over by the Medo-Persians, the Greeks, and the Romans. However, these were the birth-pangs before the promised coming of Messiah.

Lastly, John also portrayed Israel as a woman in childbirth in Revelation 12,[139] the first of the three women characters in the drama of the Book of Revelation.

Summary

(i) Many Christians have conflated five very different time periods into just one future time period.

(ii) The prophecies of "Jacob's trouble", "two-thirds" of Israel perishing, the "three and a half years" of Daniel, Jesus, James, and Revelation, and Jesus' "great tribulation" have already been fulfilled while John's "great tribulation" will come to an end when Jesus returns.

---

139 *Dancing in the Dragon's Jaws*, pp. 8-17.

7
Mystery Babylon
"Is She...?"

We now come to the second of the three women in the drama of Revelation. The first, as just mentioned, was Israel "according to the flesh" and the second is Babylon the Great. Before the two beasts are judged (Rev 19:20), they will 'execute God's purpose' by destroying her (Rev 17:16-17), 'the great city' whose downfall will cause the downfall of many cities:

> *The great city* was split into three parts, and *the cities of the nations* fell. *Babylon the great* was remembered before God, to give her the cup of the wine of His fierce wrath. (Rev 16:19*)

The Jews' holy capital Jerusalem is not the only significant city in Revelation (Rev 11:2, 8; 20:9) – there is also Babylon the Great, personified as a mysterious woman. Indeed, about one eighth of Revelation is given to describing her. Some[140] believe Jerusalem is Babylon the Great but as will become clear, there is no possibility of this.

The angel explains to John:

> 1. ..."Come here, I will show you the judgment of the great harlot who sits on many waters..."
> 3. And he carried me away in the Spirit into a wilderness; and I saw a woman sitting on a scarlet beast, full of blasphemous names, having seven heads and ten horns.
> 4. The woman was clothed in purple and scarlet, and adorned with gold and precious stones and pearls, having in her hand a gold cup full of abominations and of the

---

140 E.g. www.revelationrevolution.org/revelation-17-a-preterist-commentary/ 2 May, 2021.

unclean things of her immorality,
5. and on her forehead a name was written, *a mystery*, "BABYLON THE GREAT, THE MOTHER OF HARLOTS AND OF THE ABOMINATIONS OF THE EARTH." (Rev 17:1, 3-5*)

"A Mystery"

Her identity is there to be seen by everyone, written on her forehead, but it is 'a mystery'.

Today, we often use 'mystery' to mean 'a hidden or inexplicable matter',[141] as in, "No one knows – it's a mystery".

We also use it to describe a novel in which the reader 'is invited to try to identify the murderer'[142] from clues in the narrative. Biblical mysteries are more like the latter, always to be understood, but also as explanations of complex issues for receptive hearts:

> … the mystery of God is not capriciously hidden, but is withheld from those who are disposed to reject it anyway.[143]

As Solomon observed, we need to accept our responsibility to seek understanding:

> It is the glory of God to conceal a matter,
> But the glory of kings is to search out a matter. (Prov 25:2)

The parables reveal the mysteries of the kingdom of God are for 'he who has ears to hear', i.e. disciples, rather than for those who can hear but choose not to listen:

> 11. …"To you it has been granted to know the mysteries of the kingdom of heaven, but to them it has not been granted.
> 12. "For whoever has, to him more shall be given, and he will have an abundance; but whoever does not have, even what he has shall be taken away from him.

---

141 *Concise Oxford Dictionary*, p. 669.
142 Ibid.
143 *Zondervan Pictorial Encyclopedia of the Bible*, Vol 4, p. 329.

> 13. "Therefore I speak to them in parables; because while seeing they do not see, and while hearing they do not hear, nor do they understand." (Matt 13:11-13)

Jesus' goal was to prompt a change of heart and a willingness to learn:

> The stress in New Testament is not on the mystery *hidden* from all but a select few initiates, but on the *revelation* of the *formerly* hidden knowledge.[144]

Anyone willing to be a disciple can understand these mysteries and 'Babylon the Great' is no exception. She was readily understood by John and his hearers:

> And the angel said to me, "Why do you wonder? I will tell you the mystery of the woman and of the beast that carries her..." (Rev 17:7)

Biblical mysteries are there for all to see. However, they are often like the last pieces of a jigsaw puzzle, building on what was already known by their original audience. Being Jewish, these mysteries built on what John and any Jew already knew in the 1st century of their nation's history, celebrated in every festival, and recorded in their Scriptures. We 21st century Gentiles simply have to catch up with that audience.

The Woman Is…

The angel's explanation:

> "The woman whom you saw is the great city, which reigns over the kings of the earth." (Rev 17:18)

To Jews, the greatest city on earth is Jerusalem, 'the city of God' (Psa 46:4, 87:3), "the city of the great King" (Psa 48:2, Matt 5:35), and 'the great city' (Rev 11:8). Accordingly, as mentioned above, Preterists[145] believe Babylon the Great is

---

144 Ibid. p. 328, emphasis in original.
145 For example, David Chilton, *The Days of Vengeance*, Ft. Worth; Dominion Press, 1987. The term comes from the Latin *praeter*, meaning past.

Jerusalem and John's prophecy of her fall was fulfilled in 70 AD. They believe Revelation must have been written before then because John was sent to measure the Temple there. However, Irenaeus (c. 130-202) recorded that John wrote it at the end of Domitian's reign (81-96 AD),[146] and Hippolytus of Rome (c. 170-235) confirmed it,[147] giving us the generally accepted date for Revelation of c. 95 AD.

The whole point of John being sent to "measure the temple of God and the altar, and those who worship in it" was *because* the Temple was gone. As I established in Book 4[148] from Ezekiel's and Zechariah's similar visions,[149] measuring was a common Jewish metaphor for comprehending, understanding, and discerning.[150] John was to comprehend, understand, and discern the new spiritual house made of living stones which Paul[151] and Peter[152] had described over thirty years earlier.

Besides, when did Jerusalem ever "reign over the kings of the earth"?

We obviously need to look more closely at Babylon the Great, her location, clothing, and behaviour.

(i) Her location

She is "the great harlot who sits on many waters" (Rev 17:1).

While this may sound odd to modern ears, the metaphor was familiar to John's 1st century Jewish audience; sitting

---

146 'For that (the apocalyptic vision) was seen not a very long time since, but almost in our own day, toward the end of Domitian's reign.' Irenaeus, *Against Heresies*, Book V, Chap 30.
147 'John, again, in Asia, was banished by Domitian the king to the isle of Patmos, in which also he wrote his Gospel and saw the apocalyptic vision…' Hippolytus, *On the Twelve Apostles*, Chap 1, v. 3.
148 *Silencing the Witnesses*, pp. 13-25.
149 Ezek 40:3, Zech 2:1-2.
150 E.g. Job 11:7-9, Eph 3:17-18.
151 Eph 2:21-22.
152 1 Peter 2:5.

"on many waters" was the ideal trading location as coastal cities could tax goods passing through their harbours. They knew Herod the Great had gained vast wealth by building an artificial harbour at Caesarea Maritima in northern Israel.

Isaiah and Ezekiel had similarly described Tyre (Isa 23:2-3, 17; Ezek 27:3, 25) and Jeremiah, Babylon (Jer 51:7, 13). The woman John sees, therefore, is like ancient Tyre and Babylon in their wealth from trading and idolatry, which in Biblical terminology is harlotry (Jer 3:6-9, Ezek 6:9), and in their effect on surrounding nations. In his day, Rome similarly benefitted from her location.

However, the waters of Babylon the Great are also metaphorical:

> "The waters which you saw where the harlot sits, are peoples and multitudes and nations and tongues."
> (Rev 17:15)

Many years earlier, Isaiah had prophesied similarly of Israel's enemies:

> Alas, the uproar of many peoples who roar like the roaring of the seas, and the rumbling of nations
> Who rush on like the rumbling of mighty waters!
> (Isa 17:12)

(ii) Her clothing

Clothed 'in purple and scarlet, and adorned with gold and precious stones and pearls' (Rev 17:4), Babylon the Great is fabulously wealthy. She wears the most expensive jewellery and the costliest materials of the day.

In the ancient world the color purple was a mark of high rank and nobility. This was occasioned by the very high cost of the purple dye used for the clothing of nobles and royalty. A special purple dye was extracted from the murex shellfish found in the eastern Mediterranean...[153]

The 'merchants of the earth' will 'weep and mourn' at her downfall because no one else can afford to buy their opulent cargoes (Rev 18:11-12). They desperately need her custom.

(iii) Her behaviour

She loves to party but her favoured drink is vile:

> ...having in her hand a gold cup full of abominations and of the unclean things of her immorality (Rev 17:4)

Not content with wanton promiscuity, she is intoxicated with a blood-lust:

> 6. And I saw the woman drunk with the blood of the saints, and with the blood of the witnesses of Jesus... (Rev 17:6)

She revels in the murders of Jewish and Christian saints.

"So, Is She...?"

So, if she is not 1st century Jerusalem, is she 5th century Rome?[154] Or the Roman Catholic Church, as taught by the Protestant Reformers such as John Wycliffe, MartinLuther,[155] and John Calvin[156]? Or is she Saddam Hussein's rebuilt

---

153 *Zondervan Pictorial Encyclopedia of the Bible*, Vol 4, p. 960.
154 E.g. Laurie Guy, *Making Sense of the Book of Revelation*, pp. 139-140.
155 Luther believed the Roman Catholic Church is 'nothing else than the kingdom of Babylon and of very Antichrist. For who is the man of sin and the son of perdition, but he who by his teaching and his ordinances increases the sin and perdition of souls in the church; while he yet sits in the church as if he were God? All these conditions have now for many ages been fulfilled by the papal tyranny' (Martin Luther, *First Principles*, pp. 196-197).
156 John Calvin: 'Though it be admitted that Rome was once the mother of all Churches, yet from the time when it began to be the seat of Antichrist it has ceased to be what it was before... I shall briefly show that (Paul's words in II Thess. 2) are not capable of any other interpretation than that which applies them to the Papacy.' (*Institutes of the Christian Religion*, Vol.3, p.149).

city of Babylon in Iraq, as some today believe?[157] Or the Muslims' capital city, Mecca in Saudi Arabia?[158] Or is she the New World Order (NWO), a future totalitarian world government, feared by many Christians today?

It really does matter because we are warned:

> "Come out of her, my people, so that you will not participate in her sins and receive of her plagues..." (Rev 18:4)

How can we heed this call if we do not know who she is?

If Babylon the Great was 1st century Jerusalem or 5th century Rome, there is nothing for us to do except learn from these cities being judged. If she is the Roman Catholic Church today, Protestants have already come out of her but Catholics still need to act. If she is a rebuilt Babylon, we will have to wait until that city is rebuilt and not go there; if Mecca, where only Muslims can go, only Muslims can respond and non-Muslims need do nothing. If, on the other hand, she is the New World Order, what should we do?

Elements of Babylon the Great are indeed to be seen in each of the above, which is why many commentators think the fulfilment is the one they choose, but that also means none of them can be wholly her since she is in the others too. In fact, they are all too young and all too small.

Unique Identifying Features

Besides her name, which we will consider in Chapter 9, let us make sure we understand her unique identifying features as John and 1st century Jewish disciples would have. She has at least seven:

---

[157] Charles H.H. Dwyer, *The Rise of Babylon: Sign of the End Times*; Chicago; 2003, Moody Publishers.
[158] Joel Richardson, *Mystery Babylon: Unlocking the Bible's Greatest Prophetic Mystery*; Leawood, Kansas; 2017, Winepress Media.

(i) Seductress of '*all* the nations' into her adultery (Rev 14:8).

(ii) '*The mother* of prostitutes and of the abominations of the earth' (Rev 17:5).

(iii) She '*reigns* over the kings of the earth' (Rev 17:18)

(iv) "*The* great city" (Rev 18:10, 16, 18, 19).

(v) Home to '*every* unclean spirit' (Rev 18:2).

(vi) Deceiver of '*all* the nations' with 'sorcery' (Rev 18:23).

(vii) The ultimate murderess, responsible for '*all* who have been slain on the earth' (Rev 18:24).

While some read these descriptions ('all', 'every') as hyperbole, what do they reveal if they are not?

(i) Seductress of 'all the nations'

She is first mentioned in Revelation by an angel pronouncing her downfall:

> And another angel, a second one, followed, saying, "Fallen, fallen is Babylon the great, she who has made *all the nations* drink of the wine of the passion of *her immorality.*" (Rev 14:8*)

Her immorality is spiritual immorality, i.e. idolatry. Hosea said of Israel:

> My people consult their wooden idol, and their diviner's wand informs them;
> For a spirit of harlotry has led them astray,
> And they have played *the harlot, departing from their God.*
> (Hos 4:12*)

Isaiah, Jeremiah, Ezekiel, and Micah also condemned Israel's idolatry as harlotry, or prostitution.[159] It was also spiritual

---

[159] Isaiah 1:21; Jeremiah 2:20, 3:6-9; Ezekiel 6:9, 16:17-25; Micah 1:7.

adultery because they were unfaithful to the marriage covenant of God (Jer 31:32) which led to His divorcing of the northern kingdom (Isa 50:1, Jer 3:8).

Preterists are hard pressed to explain how Jerusalem seduced 'all the nations' into idolatry before being destroyed in 70 AD but those who believe Babylon the Great is 5th century Rome have a slightly stronger case. Jerome, living in Bethlehem at the time, wrote of Rome that:

> ...the city which had taken the whole world was itself taken.[160]

It must have seemed like 'the whole world'. But while the Romans did cause many nations to worship the beast (their empire personified as *Dea Roma*), and the living image of the beast (their successive emperors),[161] this was hardly the first taste of idolatry to these nations. Most simply added the emperor to their existing pantheon.

The Reformers make a stronger case for the Roman Catholic Church being Babylon the Great, pointing to its far greater reach which included coercing the peoples of South America into worshipping the beast and the living image of the beast, their popes.[162] The Reformers could also argue that praying to Mary and the saints is idolatrous. But which of the Muslim nations, a third of the earth's, have the Catholic Church seduced into any of this?

Likewise, if Babylon the Great is today's Mecca in Saudi Arabia, or will be the rebuilt city of Babylon in Iraq, can it be said that Islam has seduced the professing Christian nations, whether Catholic or Protestant into honouring their prophet Muhammad? Or the Hindu nations of India and Nepal, the Buddhist nations of Sri Lanka and Thailand, or

---

160 Jerome, *Letter CXXVII. To Principia*, Nicene and Post-Nicene Fathers: Series II/Volume VI/The Letters of St. Jerome/Letter 127, para 12.
161 *Slouching Towards Bethlehem*, pp. 92-101.
162 Ibid, pp. 141-146.

the determinedly secular nations?

This leaves only the New World Order which seems imminent to those expecting it. I believe, however, this possibility is much too young and there is a better fulfilment.

(ii) 'The mother of harlots and of the abominations of the earth'

To be called the father or mother of particular things is Biblically to be the first, the foremost example, the origin, or the originator. Eve, for example, was 'the mother of all the living' (Gen 3:20). In the genealogies, Jabal is described as 'the father of those who dwell in tents and have livestock' (Gen 4:20) and Jubal as 'the father of all those who play the lyre and pipe' (Gen 4:21); Satan is called "the father of lies" (John 8:44).

Each of these was the first or originator.

Babylon the Great being called the mother of harlotry and of the abominations, specifically idolatry, means she was the first, the originator of both. This mysterious entity has therefore been around since the very beginning of mankind's history.

Her motives are also important. In the ancient world, idolatry often included fertility rites with male and female sacral or temple prostitutes (1 Kin 14:24, Hos 4:14); sexual slavery, today's sex-trafficking, was commonplace, as was grinding poverty. Prostitution could therefore include the infamous promiscuity of the Roman empress Messalina (c. 17/20-48 AD),[163] or be coerced. Babylon the Great is depicted as fabulously wealthy (Rev 17:4, 18:16) and wantonly enjoying herself (Rev 18:7) - she is not a slave but a queen (Rev 18:7).

---

163 Wife of Claudius who reigned 41-54 AD.

(iii) She 'reigns over the kings of the earth'

1st century Jerusalem never reigned over any, while 5th century Rome, the Roman Catholic Church, and the Muslims' capital city, Mecca, reigned over some kings for some time, but never over all at any time. As we will see, Babylon the Great has always been reigning over *all* the kings of the earth not in the kingdom of God, and her reign continues today.

(iv) "The great city"

The kings call her "the great city" (Rev 18:10), acknowledging she is supreme; the rich merchants call her "the great city... of such vast wealth" (Rev 18:16-17); "every shipmaster and every passenger and sailor", i.e. those who have travelled the world and seen many cities, cry out:

> "What city is like the great city?" (Rev 18:18)

She is the greatest of all, unique in her power and wealth.

(v) Home to 'every unclean spirit'

> "...She has become a dwelling place of *demons* and a prison of *every unclean spirit*, and a prison of *every unclean and hateful bird*." (Rev 18:2*)

To be the 'dwelling place' and 'prison' of them all, means she houses and retains them all - they all live and act within her borders.

(vi) Deceiver of "all the nations" with "sorcery"

An angel pronounces God's judgement on her:

> "...because all the nations were deceived by your sorcery." (Rev 18:23)

In the Greek, sorcery is *pharmakeia* and describes the use of drugs and/or spells to deceive and control others, often involving evil spirits. Again we see that her effect is universal – she deceives not some but 'all the nations' by occult means. In our day, drug abuse and addictions are common along with the willing adoption of spiritualism, spiritism, witchcraft, and New Age[164] philosophies.

(vii) The ultimate murderess

This is the key identifying feature of Babylon the Great:

> "And in her was found the blood of prophets and of saints and of all who have been slain on the earth." (Rev 18:24)

To find their blood "in her" means that she is responsible for its spilling – she is behind the deaths of not only prophets and saints but of "*all* who have been slain on the earth". That is, every murder. Since the first to ever be slain was Abel, killed by his brother Cain, the mystery of Babylon must have existed then and, as we will see, it includes Cain's hatred.

Jesus warned the scribes and Pharisees:

> 34. "…I am sending you prophets and wise men and scribes; some of them you will kill and crucify, and some of them you will scourge in your synagogues, and persecute from city to city,
> 35. so that upon you may fall the guilt of all the righteous blood shed on earth, from the blood of righteous Abel to the blood of Zechariah, the son of Berechiah,[165] whom you murdered between the temple and the altar."
> (Matt 23:34-35*)

---

164 Michael York says this is 'an umbrella term that includes a great variety of groups and identities… [united by their] expectation of a major and universal change being primarily founded on the individual and collective development of human potential'. Michael York, *The Emerging Network: A Sociology of the New Age and Neo-Pagan Movements*, London: Rowman & Littlefield, 1995, pp. 1-2.

165 There is some controversy, as referenced in the link below, over which of four possible Zechariahs Jesus meant. I believe He was referring to the one whose death is recorded in 2 Chronicles 24:20-22, the last book in the Jewish arrangement of the Hebrew Bible. Abel being the first martyr, as recorded in Genesis, Jesus would therefore have been summing up the whole history of martyrdom in their Scriptures, much as we would say today, 'from Genesis to Revelation'. https://bibletopicexpo.wordpress.com/2015/12/02/zechariah-son-of-berechiah-mt-2335/, 9 Jan, 2022.

Why did He say this and how could they be connected to the murder of Abel? They had been saying:

> "If we had been living in the days of our fathers, we would not have been partners with them in shedding the blood of the prophets." (Matt 23:30)

He was shattering their self-delusion:

> "…you testify against yourselves, that you are sons of those who murdered the prophets. Fill up, then, the measure of the guilt of your fathers. You serpents, you brood of vipers, how will you escape the sentence of hell?" (Matt 23:31-33)

He wants them to recognise a hatred within them that has existed in every generation since Cain killed Abel - if they do not repent, they will be judged as "partners with" their fathers (v. 30), i.e. participants.

Cain's Hatred

John calls us all to watch for this hatred in ourselves and in how others may respond to us when we live God's way:

> 11. For this is the message which you have heard from the beginning, that we should love one another;
> 12. not as Cain, who was of the evil one and slew his brother. And for what reason did he slay him? Because his deeds were evil, and his brother's were righteous.
> 13. Do not be surprised, brethren, if the world hates you.
> (1 John 3:11-13)

Cain hated Abel because he resented Abel's faith and obedience (Gen 4:3-7, Heb 11:4).[166] He indulged this resentment until he became murderous (Gen 4:8). In the

---

[166] Hebrews 11:4 tells us Abel offered his sacrifice 'by faith' and since 'faith comes by hearing', he was obeying what he had *heard* to offer 'the firstlings of his flock and of their fat portions' (Gen 4:4). By virtue of their blood being spilled, Abel's were atonement sacrifices (Lev 4:32-35); Cain's bloodless offerings, however, were not and therefore unacceptable to God (Gen 4:5).

same way, John writes, 'the world' (v. 13) will hate us when we are trusting in Jesus as our atonement sacrifice (1 John 2:2) and trying to live righteously which, as we saw in Book 3, is one of His ownership marks on our forehead and right hand.[167]

Jude likewise warns us that:

> ...ungodly persons who turn the grace of our God into licentiousness... [and] revile the things which they do not understand... have gone *the way of Cain*.
> (Jude 1:4, 10-11*)

Every one of us needs to quickly recognise this hatred of any righteous person if it ever emerges in our hearts because it is a sign we are drifting away from God as the scribes and Pharisees had done.

God did not judge Cain for Abel's murder other than to banish him (Gen 4:11-16) but Abel's blood 'crying out from the earth' for justice became proverbial (Gen 4:10, Heb 12:24); Zechariah the son of Berechiah likewise called for a day of reckoning (2 Chron 24:22).

Jesus therefore warned the scribes and Pharisees in His time:

> "Fill up, then, the measure of the guilt of your fathers..."
> (Matt 23:32)

If they continued to add to it, they would "not escape the sentence of hell" (Matt 23:33).

We see then in John's Revelation that God will judge them as citizens of Babylon the Great unless they did indeed "come out of her". We too must stop participating in her sins lest we receive of her plagues (Rev 18:4) so in the next chapter, we will establish who she is exactly.

---

167 See *Gotta Serve Somebody*, pp. 50-51.

Summary

(i) John's seeing a mystery name, 'Babylon the Great', on the woman's forehead means her identity is there for anyone with 'eyes to see'. Today, however, we need to catch up to what John's 1st century Jewish audience already knew.

(ii) She is like ancient Babylon but also Tyre and Rome, being fabulously wealthy from trade, idolatry, pleasure-seeking, and entertainment. She also revels in the killing of Jews and Christians.

(iii) She has partially manifested in many times and places such as Jerusalem, Rome, the Roman Catholic Church, and Mecca, as noted by many scholars. This means she is older and bigger than all of them.

(iv) Her seven unique identifying features are that she seduces 'all the nations' into idolatry, is 'the mother of prostitutes', reigns over the kings of the earth, is greatest of all in power and wealth, deceives 'all the nations' with her 'sorcery', and is responsible for 'all who have been slain on the earth', i.e. 'Babylon the Great' existed when Cain killed Abel.

(v) Anyone can become responsible for "the guilt of all the righteous blood shed on earth, from the blood of righteous Abel", filling up "the measure of the guilt of [our] fathers", by hating righteousness as Cain did.

(vi) We all need to come out of Babylon the Great so we have to establish who she is exactly.

8
Babylon the Great
She Is...

So what exactly is this spiritual entity, personified as an adulterous woman who seduces all the nations, is the originator of harlotry and of all the abominations of the earth, reigns over the kings of the earth, deceives all the nations with her sorcery, and is horrifyingly murderous, guilty of every murder in history?

Worlds Apart

Babylon the Great is God's name for 'the world'[168] and comes from Nebuchadnezzar's proud boast:

> "Is this not *Babylon the great,* which I myself have built as a royal residence by the might of my power and for the glory of my majesty?" (Dan 4:30*)

His arrogance cost him dearly and he spent seven years in madness before his reason returned to him and he honoured God (Dan 4:31-34). We will look at this more closely in the next chapter.

What then is 'the world'?

The Scriptures use the term in two very different ways. The first, as in "for God so loved the world", refers to people - He loves every human being - but the second, as in 'do not love the world', refers to everything that is bad. These are truly worlds apart.

---

168 See too Michael Wilcock, *The Message of Revelation*, p. 161; Leon Morris, *Revelation*, pp. 202-204. Craig Koester writes, 'the whore is Rome, yet more than Rome... [It] is the Roman imperial world, which in turn represents the world alienated from God.' *Revelation, Anchor Yale Bible 38A,* New Haven, CT; Yale University Press, 2014, pp. 506, 684.

John explains:

> 15. Do not love the world nor the things in the world. If anyone loves the world, the love of the Father is not in him.
> 16. For all that is in the world, *the lust of the flesh and the lust of the eyes and the boastful pride of life*, is not from the Father, but is from the world.
> 17. The world is passing away, and also its lusts; but the one who does the will of God lives forever.
> (1 John 2:15-17*)

We see then this 'passing away' world has two dimensions: the outer material world, which is being constantly eroded by rust, decay, robbery, sickness, and death, and the evil inner-world of humanity – our wrongful desires, values, pleasures, and attitudes. 'The world' also refers to everyone who is rebelling against God, as Jesus warned:

> "If the world hates you, you know that it has hated Me before it hated you. If you were of the world, the world would love its own; but because you are not of the world, but I chose you out of the world, because of this the world hates you." (John 15:18-19)

Babylon's ruler is Satan, as Jesus taught:

> "I will not speak much more with you, for *the ruler of the world* is coming, and he has nothing in Me" (John 14:30*)

The King of Babylon

When Israel was in Babylonian captivity, Isaiah prophesied of the time of their restoration when they would taunt 'the king of Babylon', saying:

> 4. ..."How the oppressor has ceased,
> And how fury has ceased!" (Isa 14:4)

However, Isaiah then began using a metaphor revealing another dimension:

> 12. "How you have fallen from heaven,
> O star of the morning, son of the dawn!
> You have been cut down to the earth,
> You who have weakened the nations!" (Isa 14:12)

The morning star is today's planet Venus. The Hebrew, *heylel* (from the verb *halal*, to shine), means 'light-bearer' but was mistranslated by the *KJV* and *NKJV* as Lucifer, following the Latin Vulgate[169] where Jerome thought this was instead a proper name for Satan. Isaiah was actually predicting the fall of Belshazzar, the king of Babylon, at the hands of Darius the Mede (Dan 5:30-31).

The ancient commentators were correct, however, in recognising the king of Babylon as a type of Satan, just as some Messianic prophecies begin with a king of Israel, often David or Solomon, and foreshadow Jesus.[170] Other Messianic prophecies refer to 'David' becoming king again five hundred years after he died.[171]

The king of Babylon had particular ambitions that offended God:

> 13. "But you said in your heart, 'I will ascend to heaven;
> I will raise my throne above the stars of God,
> And I will sit on the mount of assembly
> In the recesses of the north.
> 14. "I will ascend above the heights of the clouds;
> *I will make myself like the Most High.'*
> (Isa 14:13-14*)

---

169 The 4th century Latin translation of the Hebrew and Greek texts by Jerome of Stridon.
170 E.g. Psalm 2:1-2 (cf. Acts 4:25-27), Psalm 2:7-9 (cf. Acts 13:33, Rev 12:5, 19:15), Psalm 22, Psalm 69:4 (cf. John 15:25), Psalm 69:9 (cf. John 2:17).
171 E.g. Jeremiah 30:9, Ezekiel 34:23-24, 37:24-25.

His arrogance in ruling over Israel[172] and "the mount of assembly"[173] was to usurp God as their king. However, his mortality would become obvious to all:

> 15. "Nevertheless you will be thrust down to Sheol,
> To the recesses of the pit.
> 16. "Those who see you will gaze at you,
> They will ponder over you, saying,
> 'Is this the man who made the earth tremble,
> Who shook kingdoms,
> 17. Who made the world a wilderness,[174]
> And overthrew its cities...?'" (Isa 14:15-17)

This arrogance was also the sin of Satan, 'the serpent of old who is called the devil... who deceives the whole world' (Rev 12:9), beginning with Adam and Eve.

Ezekiel similarly reveals Satan's fall in a rebuke of another typological king, the king of Tyre, who thought he was a god (Ezek 28:2). As I show in *Because of the Angels*,[175] Satan was created sinless and placed in Eden as Adam and Eve's "covering cherub" (Ezek 28:13-15)[176] but he became "lifted up" by his own beauty and splendour and "corrupted" his wisdom (Ezek 28:17).

Paul says he appeared as 'an angel of light' (2 Cor 11:14), betraying both his calling and their trust when he 'deceived Eve by his craftiness' (2 Cor 11:3). She was not fooled by a talking snake but by a beautiful angel.

This was the origin of John the Baptist and Jesus' metaphor for 1st century religious leaders who also appeared outwardly

---

172 As I showed in Book 1, Abraham's descendants are symbolised as "the stars of God" (Gen 15:5). *Dancing in the Dragon's Jaws*, pp. 13, 34.
173 Jerusalem, as established in Chapter 4.
174 As we will see in Chapter 10, Babylon the Great rides her scarlet beast through 'a wilderness' of all the nations (Rev 17:3).
175 *Because of the Angels*, Emmaus Road Publishing, 2002, pp. 53-62.
176 Or guardian angel.

righteous but were inwardly "a brood of vipers" (Matt 3:7, 12:34, 23:33; Luke 3:7), ministering death to their hearers.

From the Beginning

The material world was created by God for us to enjoy, fill, and rule over, as God commanded Adam and Eve:

> "Be fruitful and multiply, and fill the earth, and subdue it; and rule over the fish of the sea and over the birds of the sky and over every living thing that moves on the earth." (Gen 1:28)

Tragically, when they listened to Satan, they created another 'world', in the realm of values and attitudes, which they loved more than God:

> When the woman saw that the tree was good for food, and that it was a delight to the eyes, and that the tree was desirable to make one wise, she took from its fruit and ate; and she gave also to her husband with her, and he ate. (Gen 3:6)

Compare this with John's words:

> For all that is in the world, the lust of the flesh and the lust of the eyes and the boastful pride of life, is not from the Father, but is from the world. (1 John 2:16)

Eve was tempted by her natural appetites for food and beauty but also by 'the boastful pride of life' so she ate and Adam followed suit.[177]

The first murder was similarly due to 'the love of the world' as Cain indulged his worldly desire to stop his brother's righteous presence rebuking his sinfulness (1 John 3:12).

This is why the angel tells John regarding Babylon the Great:

---

[177] As shown in *Because of the Angels*, the sin was Adam's (Rom 5:12) because he deliberately disobeyed God whereas Eve was deceived by an angel (2 Cor 11:3 & 14, 1 Tim 2:14).

> "...in her was found the blood of prophets and of saints and of *all who have been slain on the earth.*" (Rev 18:24*)

Paul described a fellow-worker, Demas, who deserted him as 'having loved this present world' (2 Tim 4:10) and predicted that what we all love will increasingly polarise humanity:

> 1. ...in the last days difficult times will come.
> 2. For men will be *lovers of self, lovers of money*, boastful, arrogant, revilers, disobedient to parents, ungrateful, unholy,
> 3. unloving, irreconcilable, malicious gossips, without self-control, brutal, haters of good,
> 4. treacherous, reckless, conceited, *lovers of pleasure* rather than *lovers of God*... (2 Tim 3:1-4)

It is the ultimate choice for every one of us: are we lovers of self, money, or pleasure, that is the world, or are we lovers of God?

Spiritual Adultery

James wrote that befriending the world is adulterous:

> You *adulteresses*, do you not know that friendship with *the world* is hostility toward God? Therefore whoever wishes to be a friend of the world makes himself an enemy of God. (Jas 4:4*)

It was thinking on this label of adultery that led to my understanding this mystery as a new believer in the 1970s. I found that James was following in the footsteps of Hosea, Isaiah, Jeremiah, Ezekiel, and Micah who, as mentioned earlier, all described Israel's idolatry as harlotry or prostitution. For example:

> My people consult their wooden idol, and their diviner's wand informs them;
> For *a spirit of harlotry* has led them astray,
> And they have played *the harlot, departing from their God.*
> (Hos 4:12*)

Hosea also stayed with his adulterous wife to portray God's love for His people who were spiritually adulterous. As Jeremiah explained, the Mosaic covenant was God's marriage covenant (Jer 31:32) and he identified this adultery as the grounds for God's divorcing the northern kingdom (Jer 3:8). Isaiah did too (Isa 50:1).

John now is revealing that all idolatry, harlotry, and spiritual adultery *began* with Babylon the Great:

> ...and on her forehead a name was written, a mystery, "BABYLON THE GREAT, THE MOTHER OF HARLOTS AND OF THE ABOMINATIONS OF THE EARTH." (Rev 17:5)

Babylon the Great comprises all who are unfaithful to God.

'Two Loves'

Finding I was swimming against the tide of alternative interpretations held by my Christian friends as well as the Protestant Reformers, I was greatly relieved when I discovered that Augustine (354 - 430 AD) had found it too:

> And see ye the names of those two cities, Babylon and Jerusalem. Babylon is interpreted confusion, Jerusalem vision of peace. . . . They are mingled, and from the very beginning of mankind mingled they run on unto the end of the world. . . . *Two loves make up these two cities: love of God makes Jerusalem, love of the world makes Babylon.* Therefore let each one question himself as to what he loves; and he shall find of which he is a citizen...[178]

'Love of the world makes Babylon'. I was also delighted at Augustine's comparing Babylon with Jerusalem because this had been my next breakthrough too. Stepping back to look at the big picture of Revelation, I too had suddenly realised that *all of human history culminates in just these two women.*

---

178 Exposition on Psalm 65, Pt 2. www.ccel.org/ccel/schaff/npnf108.ii.LXV.html, 28 Feb, 2019*.

We will all be found to be citizens of 'new Jerusalem' or 'Babylon the Great', the Bride or the Prostitute, and *there is no third option.*

The good news is, if we find we belong to Babylon, we can leave:

> "Come out of her, my people, so that you will not participate in her sins and receive of her plagues…"
> (Rev 18:4)

How do we do that? Augustine's answer is a simple choice:

> Therefore let each one question himself as to what he loves: and he shall find of which he is a citizen: and if he shall have found himself to be a citizen of Babylon, let him root out cupidity, implant charity: but if he shall have found himself a citizen of Jerusalem, let him endure captivity, hope for liberty.[179]

If we find we are loving the world, his antidote is to 'root out cupidity', i.e. 'greed for money or possessions',[180] and replace it with 'charity', i.e. loving generosity.

I then found that more recently, Merrill C. Tenney had taught similarly:

> The description of Babylon as the harlot, sitting on seven mountains (17:9), reminds one sharply of Rome… but the symbolism of chapters 17 and 18 which must interpret this cryptic allusion in chapter 14 transcends the immediate empire of Rome. It stands for the *entire world system of man's rulership*, the acme of a prosperous but faithless culture. The end time will bring it to its fall, and will supplant it with the kingdom of Christ.[181]

---

179 Ibid.
180 *Concise Oxford Dictionary*, p. 232.
181 *Interpreting Revelation*, p. 79*.

Summary

(i) Babylon the Great is 'the world', the fallen world with its wrong desires, values, pleasures, and attitudes, and Jesus said "the ruler of the world" is Satan.

(ii) Isaiah confirms Satan is the metaphorical king of Babylon in his typological prediction of the fall of Belshazzar, the literal king of Babylon. Just as Belshazzar tried to usurp God's reign over Israel, Satan tried to usurp God's reign over Adam and Eve. We see more details in Ezekiel's rebuke of the king of Tyre.

(iii) The material world was created by God as a paradise for our pleasure and dominion; the fallen world was created by Adam and Eve submitting to Satan in wanting their own way rather than God's. The first bloodshed was likewise due to Cain indulging his hatred to get rid of Abel.

(iv) Loving this fallen world makes us idolaters, i.e. spiritual prostitutes and adulteresses, and thus citizens of Babylon the Great; we are not to be lovers of self, money, and pleasure but of God.

(v) This explains how she has seduced 'all the nations' into her immorality, is 'the mother of prostitutes and of the abominations of the earth', 'reigns over the kings of the earth', houses 'every unclean spirit', deceives all the nations with her 'sorcery', and is responsible for all murders on the earth.

(vi) As Augustine phrased it in the 5th century, 'love of the world makes Babylon' and 'love of God makes Jerusalem'.

9
Two Women
Two Cities

The easiest way to recognise and understand Babylon the Great is to compare her with the third woman character in the drama of Revelation: 'new Jerusalem', the Bride of Christ.

> And I saw the holy city, *new Jerusalem*, coming down out of heaven from God, made ready as *a bride* adorned for her husband. (Rev 21:2*)

> "...for the marriage of the Lamb has come and *His bride* has made herself ready." It was given to her to clothe herself in fine linen, bright and clean; for the fine linen is the righteous acts of the saints. (Rev 19:7-8*)

The Bride is a body of people comprising all who love and are faithful to the Bridegroom, i.e. the Lamb of God, Jesus of Nazareth.

This book on Revelation 16:13-19:21 necessarily focusses on His primary enemies but Jesus is the unrivalled star, the first and the last character to appear in the drama of Revelation.

The Book begins, 'The Revelation of Jesus Christ...' (Rev 1:1) and its climax is His return (Rev 22:20). As the coming Bridegroom, He defines the Bride and the Prostitute:

(i) The Bride is the body of people who love and are faithful to the Bridegroom.

(ii) The Prostitute is the body of people who do not love and will not be faithful to Him.

The Prostitute & the Bride

We can therefore distinguish in real time between the two women with three questions: to whom do they submit? Whose spirit fills them? Whom do they glorify?

(i) To whom do they submit?

A prostitute willingly submits to anyone who will give her what she wants[182] – money, fame, status - but the Bride submits only to Jesus, as Paul explained to the Corinthians:

> 2. For I am jealous for you with a godly jealousy; for I betrothed you *to one husband*, so that *to Christ* I might present you as a pure virgin.
> 3. But I am afraid that, as the serpent deceived Eve by his craftiness, your minds will be led astray from the simplicity and purity of devotion to Christ.
> 4. For if one comes and preaches another Jesus whom we have not preached, or you receive a different spirit which you have not received, or a different gospel which you have not accepted, you bear this beautifully. (2 Cor 11:2-4*)

The Corinthians were being duped by some preachers and teachers urging submission to them:

> For you tolerate it if anyone enslaves you, anyone devours you, anyone takes advantage of you, anyone exalts himself, anyone hits you in the face. (2 Cor 11:20)

All the while, these 'false apostles' (2 Cor 11:13) were preaching 'another Jesus' and 'a different gospel', ministering 'a different spirit' (v. 4), and taking their money (v. 20).[183] Paul also warned the Ephesian elders/pastors (Acts 20:17):

> "I know that after my departure savage wolves will come in among you, not sparing the flock; and from among your own selves men will arise, speaking perverse things

---

182 With the obvious exception of those trafficked.
183 These issues are covered in detail in Book 2, *Slouching Towards Bethlehem*, pp. 111-117.

[*NIV*, distorting the truth] to draw away the disciples after them. Therefore be on the alert..." (Acts 20:29-31)

Writing to the Galatians, Paul added they were not even to listen to him if he went astray from the gospel (Gal 1:8). Jesus likewise warns us of 'ravenous wolves' that look like sheep but are false prophets (Matt 7:15), concluding:

> "See to it that *no-one* misleads you." (Matt 24:4*)

Every cult leader, Christian or non-Christian, and everyone who submits to them therefore belong to Babylon.[184] All who belong to the Bride, however, are to be as 'noble-minded' as the Berean Jews:

> ...they received the message with great eagerness and examined the Scriptures every day to see if what Paul said was true. (Act 17:11, *NIV*)

(ii) Whose spirit fills them?

We see of Babylon the Great:

> "She has become a dwelling place of demons and a prison of every unclean spirit" (Rev 18:2)

The Bride, however, is made up of believers in Jesus,[185] regardless of any denominational allegiance, and He said:

> "He who believes in Me, as the Scripture said, 'From his innermost being will flow rivers of living water.'" But this He spoke of the Spirit... (John 7:38-39)

---

184 Learning this helped me as a new believer navigate my way around New Zealand's non-Christian churches, such as the Mormons, Jehovah's Witnesses, The Way International, the Unification Church, and the Christadelphians, as well as Christian cults like Witness Lee's Local Church, the Children of God, and the Shepherding/Discipleship Movement.

185 Detailed in *Slouching Towards Bethlehem*, pp. 110-117.

The Holy Spirit fills and indwells the Bride, guiding and teaching her how to 'abide in Him' (1 John 2:27) and to clothe herself in 'the righteous acts of the saints' (Rev 19:8).

(iii) Whom do they glorify?

To glorify can mean to exalt or praise but it can also mean to reveal what is truly there. When John sees the new Jerusalem, she is, of course, exalting and praising God but she is also revealing what He is like, in His love, grace, and justice:

> He… showed me the holy city, Jerusalem, coming down out of heaven from God, *having the glory of God*.
> (Rev 21:10-11*)

Babylon the Great, however, glorifies/exalts herself by indulging herself, thus revealing her true self:

> "To the degree that she *glorified herself* and *lived sensuously*, to the same degree give her torment and mourning; for she says in her heart, 'I SIT AS A QUEEN AND I AM NOT A WIDOW, and will never see mourning.'
> (Rev 18:7*)

In her 'boastful pride of life', she is quoting the old Babylonian empire, as prophesied by Isaiah:

> 7. "…you said, '*I will be a queen forever*'…
> 8. "Now, then, hear this, you sensual one,
> Who dwells securely,
> Who says in your heart, 'I am, and there is no one besides me.
> *I will not sit as a widow*,
> Nor know loss of children.'
> 9. "But these two things will come on you suddenly
> in one day:
> Loss of children and widowhood.
> They will come on you in full measure
> In spite of your many sorceries,
> In spite of the great power of your spells.
> (Isa 47:7-9*)

Ancient Babylon's boast of never being a widow came from her trust in her gods, Bel and Nebo (Isa 46:1, Jer 50:2, 51:44). 'Bel', derived from the Semitic word *baal*, or Lord, refers to Marduk, as *Encyclopaedia Britannica* explains:

> Marduk, in Mesopotamian religion, the chief god of the city of Babylon and the national god of Babylonia… was eventually called simply Bel, or Lord… All nature, including humanity, owed its existence to him; the destiny of kingdoms and subjects was in his hands.[186]

'Nebo', or Nabu, was his son:

> Marduk… took precedence over him, at least theoretically, in Babylonia. But in popular devotion, it was Nabu, the son, who knows all and sees all, who was chief, especially during the centuries immediately preceding the fall of Babylon.[187]

The Babylonians thought that with Bel and Nebo reigning, their empire would forever be Queen and retain her citizens, or 'children'. They also boasted of their uniqueness:

> 10. "You felt secure in your wickedness and said, 'No one sees me,'
> Your wisdom and your knowledge, they have deluded you;
> For you have said in your heart, '*I am, and there is no one besides me.*' (Isa 47:10*)

Throughout my decades in ministry, I have seen many cults and churches priding themselves on being the only church of God, from the Roman Catholic Church[188] and Witness Lee's

---

186 www.britannica.com, accessed 2 Mar, 2019.
187 Ibid. Nabu was also 'the patron-god of the Babylonian rulers', according to *The Zondervan Pictorial Encyclopaedia of the Bible*, Vol 4, p. 394.
188 Happily, this began to change with the Second Vatican Council (1962-1965) which affirmed that although the church of God 'subsists in the Catholic Church …many elements of sanctification and of truth are found outside its visible confines' (*Lumen Gentium* 8 - *The Mystery of the Church*). Protestants are now considered to be 'separated brethren'. www.vatican.va/archive/hist_councils/ii_vatican_council/documents/vat-ii_decree_19641121_unitatis-redintegratio_en.html, 2 Marc, 2019.

Local Church to the Jehovah's Witnesses, Christadelphians, and the Church of Jesus Christ of Latter Day Saints, commonly known as Mormons. Their claim of uniqueness is actually proof positive they belong to Babylon the Great.

The Bride, however, boasts of the uniqueness of Jesus and relies completely on His words:

> "I am the way, and the truth, and the life; no one comes to the Father but through Me." (John 14:6)

He is and there is *no one besides Him*. Our churches can save no-one but we can all point to Jesus:

> God willed to make known... this mystery among the Gentiles, which is *Christ* in you, the hope of glory. (Col 1:27*)

Wisdom & Folly

In Proverbs, Solomon tells his sons about two other women. Personifications of wisdom and foolishness, they are inviting naïve young men to a feast. Wisdom calls out:

> "Come, eat of my food and drink of the wine I have mixed. Forsake your folly *and live*, and proceed in the way of understanding." (Prov 9:5-6*)

Wisdom urges them to turn from foolishness to really enjoy life. Folly, however, tempts those trying to live righteously (v. 15) to live a secret life with another kind of meal:

> "Stolen water is sweet; And bread eaten in secret is pleasant." (Prov 9:17)

'Stolen water' and 'secret' bread is a metaphor for adultery (Prov 5:15-20) and folly is has another deadly secret:

> But he does not know that the dead are there,
> That her guests are in the depths of Sheol. (Prov 9:18)

Folly is an adulteress who will draw us in to die.

Again, there is no third option - every day we are embracing one and shunning the other. Wisdom and folly also have *an ultimate outcome*. 'The beginning of wisdom' is 'the fear of the LORD' (Prov 9:10) so all who choose wisdom become the Bride, New Jerusalem; all who choose folly become the Prostitute, Babylon the Great.

Why the City Names?

John and his Jewish hearers would have readily understood the significance of the cities' names.

(i) Babylon/Babel

Babylon was the capital city of 'the land of Shinar' (Dan 1:2) and very significant in Jewish thinking as the place of their seventy year exile. To this day, they still know it by its Hebrew name, *Babel*,[189] which reminds English readers of its famous tower but we need to remember its founding:

> Now *the whole earth* used the same language and the same words. It came about as they journeyed east, that they found a plain in *the land of Shinar* and settled there. (Gen 11:1-2*)

Disobeying God's command to spread out and 'fill the earth', given to Adam and his descendants (Gen 1:28) and Noah and his descendants (Gen 9:1), 'the whole earth' decided instead to build a city and a tower:

> "Come, let us build for ourselves a city, and a tower whose top will reach into heaven, and *let us make for ourselves a name*, otherwise *we will be scattered abroad* over the face of the whole earth." (Gen 11:4*)

---

[189] Every time Jewish readers read their Bibles' 283 Hebrew and 16 Aramaic references to what our English Bibles call Babylon, their text says *babel*.

In other words, it was the capital city of 'the whole earth'. The people did not want to be 'scattered abroad'. Disobedient, self-glorifying, and idolatrous, they provoked God's judgement and He confounded their communication:

> 6. The LORD said, "Behold, they are one people, and they all have the same language. And this is what they began to do, and now nothing which they purpose to do will be impossible for them.
> 7. "Come, let Us go down and there confuse their language, so that they will not understand one another's speech."
> 8. So the LORD scattered them abroad from there over the face of the whole earth; and they stopped building the city. (Gen 11:6-8)

Like a school teacher with an unruly group of pupils, God broke up the gang, scattering them abroad so that He could deal with them one by one:

> Therefore its name was called Babel, *because* there the LORD *confused* the language of the whole earth; and from there the LORD scattered them abroad over the face of the whole earth. (Gen 11:9*)

In Akkadian, it was called *bab-ilu*, literally Gate of God (*bab*, gate, *ilu*, god). However, in Hebrew, *babel* is pronounced similarly to *balal* which means 'to mix, confuse',[190] so it is a play on the words.[191]

Unable to communicate en masse, the people were isolated into language groups so they finally did spread out to become "all the nations". Augustine wrote of this:

> And see ye the names of those two cities, Babylon and Jerusalem. Babylon is interpreted confusion, Jerusalem vision of peace.[192]

---

190 *The Zondervan Pictorial Encyclopaedia of the Bible*, Vol 1, p. 438.
191 'Babylon' comes from the Greek rendition of *bab-ilani* (*bab*, gate, *ilani*, gods, i.e. plural of *ilu*).
192 Exposition on Psalm 65, Pt 2. www.ccel.org/ccel/schaff/npnf108.ii.LXV.html, 3 Mar, 2019.

We learn then that, since mankind has never ceased to be disobedient, self-glorifying, and idolatrous, God will destroy the capital city of 'the whole earth' in the last hour and establish His own.

(ii) Babylon the Great

As mentioned in the last chapter, this name comes from Nebuchadnezzar's boast:

> "Is this not *Babylon the great*, which I myself have built as a royal residence by the might of *my* power and for the glory of *my* majesty?" (Dan 4:30*)

God's response was to humble him:

> While the word was in the king's mouth, a voice came from heaven, saying, "King Nebuchadnezzar... sovereignty has been removed from you..." (Dan 4:31)

He lost his mind for the next seven years (4:33-34) and, from thinking himself a god (3:1 ff.), he became like a beast of the field. Daniel had tried to warn him a year earlier (4:29), interpreting Nebuchadnezzar's dream of a great tree being cut down as God's judgement on his self-glorifying arrogance (4:22) and rejection of His kingdom (4:25).

Daniel called on him to break away from his sins, look after the poor (4:27), and honour God (4:25). Instead, he kept sinning and honoured himself. The tipping point came when he uttered the words, "the might of my power... the glory of my majesty" - God cut him down to size.

Now, when the whole world reaches this tipping point, John hears the heavenly warning voice:

> "Come out of her, my people, so that you will not participate in her sins and receive of her plagues."
> (Rev 18:4)

(iii) New Jerusalem

After Babel, God chose one man who would trust Him, Abraham, to create a new nation, Israel, who were to be 'a kingdom of priests' to reach every other nation for Him (Ex 19:5-6). Israel's capital city, Jerusalem, was originally named Salem which means peace (Heb 7:2).

Jerusalem briefly became a city of peace in a kingdom of peace during the reign of Solomon (c. 1000 BC) whose name also means 'peace'[193] but after he died, the nation was torn in two and in 586 BC, Jerusalem was razed by the Babylonians and again in 70 AD by the Romans.

I prefaced Book 4[194] with historian Eric Kline's summary:

> No other city has been more bitterly fought over throughout its history... There have been at least 118 separate conflicts in and for Jerusalem during the past four millennia – conflicts that ranged from local religious struggles to strategic military campaigns and that embraced everything in between. Jerusalem has been destroyed completely at least twice, besieged twenty-three times, attacked an additional fifty-two times, and captured and recaptured forty-four times. It has been the scene of twenty revolts and innumerable riots, has had at least five separate periods of violent terrorist attacks during the past century, and has only changed hands peacefully twice in the last four thousand years.[195]

The city was finally regained by the Jews in 1967 but the Arabs and Muslims will never accept that, calling it *al-Quds*, lit. the Holy One, and claiming it as their third holiest city after Mecca and Medina.[196] Accordingly, 'the present Jerusalem' (Gal 4:25) is still not the city of peace but it will

---

193 From Heb. *shalom*.
194 *Silencing the Witnesses*, p. 2.
195 Eric Cline, *Jerusalem Besieged: From Ancient Canaan to Modern Israel*, Anne Arbor, MI; University of Michigan Press, 2004, pp. 1-2.
196 I refuted this claim in *Slouching Towards Bethlehem*, pp. 215-218 and *Silencing the Witnesses*, pp. 5-6.

be after its last great battle, the Battle of Har-Magedon.

Jesus called Jerusalem "the City of the Great King" (Matt 5:35) and He will completely vindicate her name on the earth before the arrival of New Jerusalem.

"Come…"

The most important decision anyone can ever make is to leave Babylon the Great and enter New Jerusalem by trusting in Jesus. Tragically, many do not realise they are already in Babylon and need to make a decision to leave. It is as if their car has broken down on a railway line and there is a train bearing down on them at great speed – they can either stay in the car or get out… but they are already sitting in one of the only two options.

At the end of John's Revelation, he summarises how every one of us should join with the Holy Spirit in calling our families, friends, neighbours and strangers:

> The Spirit and *the bride* say, "Come." And let the one who hears say, "Come." And let the one who is thirsty come; let the one who wishes take the water of life without cost. (Rev 22:17*)

Summary

(i) Human history will culminate in two metaphorical women named after two cities: Babylon the Great, a prostitute, and New Jerusalem, a bride. We are all participants in one or the other – it is our choice but there is no third option.

(ii) They are most easily recognised by who they submit to, whose spirit fills them, and who they glorify. Babylon's claims to be unique can also be heard in any church or group claiming to be the only true church; Jerusalem, however, glorifies her Bridegroom and His uniqueness.

(iii) Babylon the Great and New Jerusalem are also the ultimate personifications of folly and wisdom as portrayed in the Book of Proverbs.

(iv) The name 'Babylon the Great' comes from Nebuchadnezzar's boast over his capital city regarding his power and glory; its Hebrew name, *Babel*, reminds us that it was once the capital city of 'the whole earth' in rebellion against God. Everyone needs to "come out of her" by leaving all sinful desires, values, pleasures, and attitudes and submitting to Jesus as King in every area of our lives.

(v) Jerusalem's name means peace. 'The present Jerusalem' will ultimately come to peace on earth and New Jerusalem will be the eternal city of peace.

10
The Scarlet Beast
Her Steed

As mentioned earlier, Babylon the Great sitting "on many waters" (Rev 17:1) means she rules over "peoples and multitudes and nations and tongues" (Rev 17:15) but John also saw her riding a beast in a wilderness:

> And he carried me away in the Spirit into a wilderness; and I saw a woman sitting on a scarlet beast, full of blasphemous names, having seven heads and ten horns. (Rev 17:3)

This wilderness is as metaphorical as she is, being the same wilderness that the woman of Revelation 12, Israel, was exiled to in 70 AD. In Book 1,[197] I pointed out that Ezekiel's prophecy regarding Israel's time out of the Promised Land was not to be again in the wilderness of Sinai or Arabia but in:

> "...the wilderness of the peoples" (Ezek 20:35)

The Jewish people's very reason for existence was to be a holy nation of priests[198] in the Holy Land, living according to the Law of Moses, in order to bring forth the Messiah. However, when exiled among Gentiles with different laws, beliefs, morals, values, customs, and languages, they were as utterly isolated as if they were in a wilderness. Their food laws cut them off from even eating with Gentiles, isolating them socially.

Babylon the Great, however, is utterly at home there. Her scarlet steed is as 'full of blasphemous names' (v. 3) as she is and carries her wherever she wants to go.

---
197 *Dancing in the Dragon's Jaws*, pp. 67-68.
198 Exodus 19:6.

This Beast Is...?

At first glance, the scarlet beast seems to be a new player on the stage. Although it has the same seven heads and ten horns of the first beast of Revelation 13, that beast is a composite of a leopard, a bear, and a lion – with this one, there is no mention of beasts and it is scarlet. However, when the beasts are finally judged, there are only two of them and the second is the second beast of Revelation 13.[199] This one must therefore be the first beast of Revelation 13 and it appears five times.

We know its origin because John tells us that it 'comes up out of the sea' (Rev 13:1). In Biblical days, the sea was considered the den of 'Leviathan the twisted serpent ...the dragon' (Isa 27:1), the abyss or bottomless pit (Grk, *abussos*, bottomless), and the realm of demons (Luke 8:31, Rev 9:2 & 11). 'Many waters' also symbolised the Gentiles: all "peoples and multitudes and nations and tongues" (Rev 17:1 & 15). This beast somehow arises from both.

John had earlier seen it in his vision of Revelation 11 where it 'comes up out of the abyss' (Rev 11:7) to attack and kill the two witnesses, as covered in Book 4.[200] We therefore know its identity but let me recap.

(i) The self-exalting State

The scarlet beast is the 'principality and power' of the State gone feral. In John's day, it was a composite of a lion, a bear, and a leopard (Rev 13:2) because, as I showed in Book 2,[201] it had manifested in the three previous Gentile empires which had ruled over Israel: Babylon, Medo-Persia and Greece (Dan 7:4-6). Ceasing to be domesticated for man's benefit

---

199 It is described as 'the false prophet' when judged (Rev 19:20) because it is the spirit of antichrist in its final manifestation as the Antichrist.
200 *Silencing the Witnesses*, p. 219-221.
201 *Slouching Towards Bethlehem*, pp. 10-17.

(Rom 13:4), it had become a *therion*, Greek for a wild animal or beast.

John's immediate audience were being coerced by the Romans to worship it, personified as the goddess *Roma* – see her on Vespasian's coin in Photo (i) on page 137. They were also being coerced to worship all of their emperors as living images of the State. We saw in Book 3[202] how refusing to offer incense or pour out a libation to the emperors to get the Roman *charagma*, their mark of the beast, meant many followers of Jesus were martyred or forbidden to trade in the marketplaces.

In Book 2, I showed how it manifested in the 20th century in Stalin's Russia, Mussolini's Italy, Hirohito's Japan, Hitler's Germany, Mao Zedong's China, Pol Pot's Cambodia, Kim Il Sung's North Korea, and Ayatollah Khomeini's Iran.[203] Today, and for the last 1,400 years, the beast has been manifesting within jihadist Islam.

In Book 4,[204] I established from Revelation 11 that the beast killing and silencing the two witnesses was the principality and power of the State rising up in 20th century Israel to reject the Law and the Prophets, personified as Moses the Lawgiver and Elijah the Prophet. In 1948, the Jewish people chose, for the first time in their 3,500 year history, to be a secular state. As President Shimon Peres explained it:

> Israel is a secular state. The Orthodox have bargaining power, so everything has to be done by compromise. But Israel is not under religious control: it's not a *halachic*[205] country, it's not a theocracy.[206]

---

202 *Gotta Serve Somebody*.
203 Although these regimes all came to an end, China, North Korea, and Iran are still susceptible.
204 *Silencing the Witnesses* pp. 224-233.
205 Halacha is Orthodox Jewish tradition.
206 http://tabletmag.com/jewish-news-and-politics/81660/raw-deal, 27 Mar, 2022.

On seven previous occasions of Israel being restored,[207] they renewed the Mosaic Covenant but not this time. When they regained their holy city Jerusalem in 1967, they effectively left the dead bodies of Moses and Elijah lying unburied and dishonoured in its main street.

This brings us to the details of Revelation 17 to complete our understanding.

(ii) Why is it scarlet?

In ancient Hebrew thinking,[208] red is the colour of the ground: Adam's name is from *adom*, to be red, like 'the dust from the ground' (Gen 2:7). Esau was likewise called Edom (Heb, *admoni*) because he was 'reddish' (Gen 25:25) and because he sold his birth-right for *ha-adom*, 'the red *stuff*', i.e. red lentil stew (Gen 25:30). This beast being scarlet *and* coming from the abyss therefore identifies and confirms it as both earthly, i.e. man-made, and demonic, just as some wisdom is 'earthly, natural, demonic' (Jas 3:15).[209]

(iii) Why does it mysteriously reappear?

When John sees the scarlet beast in c. 95 AD, it had somehow ceased to exist in his day but would exist sometime in the future, as the angel explains:

> "The beast that you saw was, and *is not*, and is about to come up out of the abyss and go to destruction. And those who dwell on the earth, whose name has not been written in the book of life from the foundation of the world, will wonder when they see the beast, that he was and *is not* and will come." (Rev 17:8*)

---

207 *Silencing the Witnesses*, pp. 231-233.
208 *Dancing in the Dragon's Jaws*, p. 21.
209 Although different Greek words are used to describe the colour of the dragon (*purros*, fiery red, from *pur*, fire) and that of the beast (*kokkinos*, scarlet; the origin of our English word cochineal), the symbolism of earthliness, or manifesting in the earth, is the same.

Its reappearance surprises those "whose name has not been written in the book of life", i.e. unbelievers, just as Israel's reappearance in 1948 was surprising to anyone unfamiliar with the Biblical prophecies we considered in Book 1,[210] believers and scholars alike.

Ceasing to Exist?

The reappearance of this beast[211] *and* Israel is the key to understanding it. As shown in all four previous books in this series, Israel is a primary focus of John's Revelation and his visions can only be understood in relation to the people, the history, the covenants, the rituals, and the land of Israel. In this instance, the interpretation entirely depends on *the state of Israel*, as we will see.

In doing so, let us note that this beast's five appearances in Revelation are not in chronological order:

(i) Revelation 11 - 1967

In Revelation 11, where the focus is on Jerusalem and Israel's fate after 70 AD, the beast kills the two witnesses in Jerusalem *after* 1,260 days (v. 3 & 7), i.e. after "the times of the Gentiles". As I established in Books 1 and 4, this seems to have occurred in 1967[212] when Israel regained Jerusalem, thus ending "the times of the Gentiles" (Luke

---

210 *Dancing in the Dragon's Jaws*.
211 While the first beast of Revelation 13 disappears and reappears, the second beast (the spirit of antichrist) does not. John saw it in Rome in the 1st century AD but it manifests wherever and whenever people worship their leaders, from ancient Egypt, Mesopotamia, China, and Japan, as well as among the Aztecs and Incas, to 20th century Europe. *Slouching Towards Bethlehem*, pp. 94-96, 125-128, 143-146.
212 As explained there, we cannot be dogmatic about this date because Israel immediately handed back the Temple Mount, the very heart of Jerusalem, to the *Waqf*, the Islamic authority, which controls it today *Dancing in the Dragon's Jaws*, p. 124-125; *Silencing the Witnesses*, p. 10.

21:24) - the feral State could be seen in their enthroning secularism rather than God in His own holy city.

(ii) Revelation 13 – the last 2,000 years

In Revelation 13, where the focus is on the Gentiles,[213] the feral State rampages through "all the nations" *for* the 42 months (v. 5), which are "the times of the Gentiles"[214] or the last 2,000 years, culminating in the clash of competing antichrist regimes[215] in the 20th century.

(iii) Revelation 16 – since 1967

In Revelation 16, to incite the last battle at Har-Magedon, the feral State is sending out 'unclean spirits like frogs... which go out to the kings of the whole world, to gather them together for the war...' (Rev 16:13-14) around Jerusalem. This is after "the times of the Gentiles" and Israel's regaining of Jerusalem, i.e. after 1967. We will look at how this is already happening in the next chapter.

(iv) Revelation 17 – the last 3,500 years

In Revelation 17, the feral State is the steed of Babylon the Great (v. 1). She has been riding it from its manifestation in ancient Egypt, when its first head tried to kill all the Hebrew

---

213 *Slouching Towards Bethlehem,* pp. 9ff.
214 In Daniel's vision, on which John's is based, the lion, bear, leopard, and the fourth dreadful beast rising out of the Mediterranean Sea revealed that those four empires would arise on the earth (Dan 7:17) and rule over Israel until Messiah came (Dan 7:13). Daniel was also shown that the lion, the bear, and the leopard empires would be granted "an extension of life... for an appointed period of time" but the fourth beast, the Roman Empire, would be judged and destroyed (Dan 7:12). During this period, "a time, times, and half a time" (Dan 7:25), i.e. during "the times of the Gentiles", the spirit of antichrist would deceive all the nations. John is describing that appointed time after Messiah came.
215 Hirohito's Japan, Mussolini's Italy, Stalin's Russia, Hitler's Germany, Mao's China, et al.

baby boys, and she is still riding it today. However, as we will see next, at the time of the ten horns, it will turn on her and destroy her (Rev 17:16).

(v) Revelation 19 – sometime soon

Finally, John sees this beast/principality and its faithful companion, the second beast of Revelation 13, will be seized at Har-Magedon when the Lord returns, then thrown into the lake of fire (Rev 19:19-20).

When and how then did it cease to exist?

It did not actually cease to exist so much as disappear from sight in Israel – it came back "out of the abyss", where it was unseen by human eye, to again become visible there when the Jews regained Jerusalem and the Temple Mount.

In other words, with Israel's disappearance as a nation in 70 AD, the beast was unable to manifest in Israel; Israel's miraculous re-emergence as a nation in 1948 meant that, for the first time in 2,000 years, the beast could reappear, to kill the two witnesses there. We will see this confirmed when we come to reconsider the scarlet beast's seven heads and ten horns.

Thankfully, John sees the beast will only be around "a little while" (Rev 17:10) after its reappearance and then it "goes to destruction" (Rev 17:11).

"Having Seven Heads…"

The angel continues his explanation of the scarlet beast:

> 9. "Here is the mind which has wisdom. The seven heads are seven mountains on which the woman sits,
> 10. and they are seven kings; five have fallen, one is, the other has not yet come; and when he comes, he must remain a little while.
> 11. "The beast which was and is not, is himself also an eighth and is one of the seven, and he goes to destruction."
> (Rev 17:9-11)

So the beast's seven heads are seven mountains *and* seven kings and the beast's being "an eighth and… of the seven" means it is *a kingdom* that incorporates them.

We are also told we need 'wisdom' to understand this but, as I showed in Book 3,[216] it is not Roman or Greek wisdom – we need Jewish wisdom. Let us consider that, step by step.

"Seven Mountains"

This description was instantly recognisable in the ancient world - the city of Rome was famous for having been founded on seven hills. This coin from the reign of Vespasian (69-79 AD) shows *Roma*,[217] the personification of Rome, reclining on them.

Photo (i) Vespasian sestertius 71 AD
© The Trustees of the British Museum Company Ltd.

This has led many to conclude that Babylon the Great is Rome but, as we have seen, Babylon the Great is much older and larger. She has lasted much longer than the Roman Empire because she is 'the world', the whole realm of man in

---

216 *Gotta Serve Somebody*, pp. 128-137.
217 She was worshipped as such with the emperor as described in Revelation 13, being that time's beast and the living image of the beast. See *Slouching Towards Bethlehem*, pp. 92-102.

rebellion against God. Her ruler is not an emperor but Satan (John 14:30).

John's vision of Babylon the Great seated on Rome's famous hills is instead describing where she is most obviously manifest *in his time*. This is also why Peter refers to the city of Rome as Babylon when he writes from there (1 Pet 5:13).

John is redefining the popular image worshipped by the Romans, from *Roma* their protective mother goddess to a blasphemous prostitute. As we will see, his vision goes on to reveal that, unlike Rome which was razed in 410 AD, she will not come to an end until the Lord returns.

"And… Seven Kings"

The angel continues:

> "…and they are seven kings; five have fallen, one is, the other has not yet come; and when he comes, he must remain a little while." (Rev 17:10)

As noted in Chapter 1, and established in Books 1 and 2, the seven "kings" are not individual kings but kingdoms and empires. In Daniel's vision of the lion, the bear, the leopard, and the "dreadful" beast, he was told:

> "These great beasts, which are four in number, are four *kings* who will arise from the earth." (Dan 7:17*)

These beasts turned out to be the Babylonian, Medo-Persian, Greek, and Roman Empires which ruled over Israel from Daniel's time until the coming of the "Son of Man" (Dan 7:13), i.e. Jesus. The fourth "king" is explicitly called a kingdom:

> "Thus he said: 'The fourth beast will be a fourth *kingdom* on the earth…'" (Dan 7:23*)

Similarly in Daniel's later vision of a ram and a goat, Gabriel explains to him:

> "The ram... represents the *kings* of Media and Persia. The shaggy goat represents the *kingdom* of Greece..." (Dan 8:20-21*)

Accordingly, almost seven hundred years later in c. 95 AD, when John saw "the seven kings", they are not individual kings but kingdoms and empires. "Five have fallen, one is, the other has not yet come" is Jewish history as known by any 1st century Jewish teenager: five Gentile empires had ruled over them and "fallen" – Egypt, Assyria, Babylon, Medo-Persia, and Greece; the one that "is" was Rome; and the seventh with its ten horns was still in future.

The Eighth King

What then of the eighth king?

> 8. "The beast that you saw was, and is not, and is about to come up out of the abyss and go to destruction...
> 11. "The beast which was and is not, is himself also an eighth and is *one* of the seven..." (Rev 17:8 & 11)

This concept can only be understood when we rightly understand the beast's emerging from the abyss to silence the witnesses (Rev 11:7), as explained in Book 4.[218] I will begin with two observations.

(i) It is *not* Nero

The Oxford scholars who take the Roman emperors' path to identify the seven heads assume:

> *The beast* now represents the Emperor Nero, commonly expected to return to life and power.[219]

---

218 *Silencing the Witnesses*, pp. 217-237.
219 *The New Oxford Annotated Bible*, pp. 441-442 *New Testament*.

Photo (ii) Bust of Nero[220]

As detailed in Book 3,[221] after Nero committed suicide in 68 AD, an 'oracle' of the *Sibylline Oracles*[222] dated to about 80 AD predicted he would rise again. Accordingly, these scholars think John may have been referring to this belief in Revelation 13:3.[223]

N.T. Wright notes:

> …it is just possible that… John is writing… about Otho as the seventh, short-lived emperor, who is about to be ousted by the returning Nero, the monster who was and is not and is to come: the eighth, though one of the seven.

---

220 Bibi Saint-Pol, own work, 2007-02-08, Public Domain, http://commons.wikimedia.org/w/index.php?curid=1814923, 2 Feb, 2022.
221 *Gotta Serve Somebody*, pp. 112-113.
222 A collection of apocryphal Jewish writings, written between the 2nd century BC and 3rd century AD, with Book IV, the one being referenced, about 80 AD, following the death of Vespasian. https://sacred-texts.com/cla/sib/sib.pdf, 9 Jan, 2022.
223 *The New Oxford Annotated Bible*, p. 437 *New Testament*. Also Pheme Perkins, *Reading the New Testament*, New York; Paulist Press, 1988, pp. 321-322.

Others like Craig R. Koester see John as merely alluding to this belief:

> Picturing an eighth king as a return of one of the seven seems to play on legends that Nero would return, so that one could say of a future persecution of the people of God: "It is Nero all over again".[224]

However, Augustine was debunking the *Nero redivivus* legends as 'audacious conjecture' in the 5th century:

> ...some suppose that he shall rise again and be Antichrist. Others, again, suppose that he is not even dead, but that he was concealed that he might be supposed to have been killed, and that he now lives in concealment in the vigor of that same age which he had reached when he was believed to have perished, and will live until he is revealed in his own time and restored to his kingdom. But *I wonder that men can be so audacious in their conjectures*.[225]

We do not need to guess at any of this. The beast's fatally wounded head was not a Roman emperor nor a future Fuhrer - Jesus mortally wounded the beast at the Crucifixion, in the time of its sixth head, the Roman Empire.

(ii) Translation issue

The passage is also complicated by a translation issue:

> "The beast which was and is not, is himself also an eighth and is *one* of the seven..." (Rev 17:11)

The *NASB* here has the eighth as "*one* of the seven" but the translators italicised 'one' to show that it is not in the Greek text – it was added to clarify what they believe the phrase means. N.T. Wright also has one of the seven returning in

---

[224] Craig R. Koester, *Revelation and the End of All Things*, p. 161; Leon Morris, *Revelation*, p. 211.
[225] *City of God*, XX 19:3 www.ccel.org/ccel/schaff/npnf102.iv.XX.19.html#iv.XX.19-p6, 18 Feb, 2022.

The Kingdom New Testament.[226]

On the other hand, the *KJV* and *NKJV* translate the phrase more literally:

> "...is himself also the eighth, and is *of the seven*"

The *NIV* has:

> "...an eighth king. He *belongs to the seven*"

So too do the *RSV, NRSV, ESV, CSB*, Phillips' and William Barclay's translations.

Which should it be – is the eighth king one of the seven returning, or is the eighth somehow only 'of the seven"? I believe, the latter. As Henry Alford put it:

> This eighth, the last and worst phase of the beast, is not represented as any one of the beasts, but as being *the beast himself* in actual embodiment. He is *ek ton epta* - not "*one of* the seven" but the successor and result of the seven, following and springing out of them.[227]

The seven heads are the seven Gentile empires who ruled over Israel from her birth as a nation in 15th century BC Egypt to John's 1st century AD Rome ("five have fallen, one is..") through to our day when the seventh has ten horns ("the other has not yet come").

The eighth is therefore not one of the seven returning but *the kingdom of all seven*. The principality and power of the feral State needs the domesticated states to exist before it can usurp and pervert their function so the eighth is 'of the seven' and in all seven rather than 'one of the seven' returning.

---

226 Also in his *Revelation for Everyone*, p. 155.
227 Grk, *ek ton epta*, lit. 'out from among the seven'. Henry Alford, *Greek Testament Critical Exegetical Commentary.*

"Was, and Is Not..."

We considered the beast's mysterious reappearance earlier. Let us now review that in the light of the eighth king:

> 8. "The beast that you saw *was, and is not, and is about to come* up out of the abyss and go to destruction. And [they] will wonder when they see the beast, that he *was and is not and will come...*
> 11. "The beast which *was and is not*, is himself also an eighth and is *of the seven*, and he goes to destruction." (Rev 17:8 & 11*)

Most commentators readily note the parallel with the name of God that John quotes[228] earlier:

> ...from Him who is and who was and who is to come... (Rev 1:4 & 8)

Contrasting the eternity of God with the temporality of the beast, the angel twice adds that the beast rises to "go to destruction" (v. 8); he re-emerges from the abyss and "must remain a little while" (v. 10), as we will consider next, but then he is gone forever (v. 11).

We see then that the beast, itself the eighth king, "was", in that it had manifested in all six of the Gentile empires *when they ruled over Israel*. With the state of Israel destroyed in 70 AD, John described it in c. 95 AD as "is not" - this apparent period of non-existence is specifically *in regard to Israel* and refers to its time back in the abyss, the unseen realm.

When Israel re-emerged from "all the nations" in 1948, as I showed in Book 4,[229] the beast re-emerged in Israel as the secular state. For the first time in their 3,500 year history, the people refused to renew their covenant with God. Moses originally mediated it in 1446 BC and seven times they

---

228 Paraphrasing Exodus 3:14-15.
229 *Silencing the Witnesses*, pp. 223-235.

renewed it after breaking it.[230] They broke it again in 30 AD when they rejected Jesus as their long-promised Messiah and lost everything – their land and nationhood, Jerusalem, the Temple and the sacrifices.

I summarised their extraordinary situation in 1948:

> For 2,000 years, their ancestors had mourned the holy city being "trampled underfoot by the Gentiles", longing and praying for restoration, but when God answered them, instead of renewing His covenant they cast it aside.[231]

The Jews have regained their land and nationhood but for the first time ever, it is not ruled according to the Law and the Prophets. In John's visions predicting the regaining of Jerusalem in 1967 (Rev 11:2), therefore, he sees the two witnesses, i.e. the personifications of the Law and the Prophets, killed by the beast (Rev 11:7) and lying dead and dishonoured in the street (Rev 11:8).

As for the nations, throughout "the times of the Gentiles", while the gospel was reaching to every nation the two beasts were offering their counterfeit, i.e. emperor-worship, to deadly effect. I spelled this out in Book 2.[232]

Today, following the rebirth of Israel, the beast is manifesting in its seventh head with the ten horns so we will consider that next.

---

230 With Joshua in c. 1406 and c. 1381 BC, Jehoiada in 835 BC, Hezekiah in 715 BC, Josiah in 622 BC, Ezra and Nehemiah in 444 BC, and Judas Maccabee in 164 BC.
231 *Silencing the Witnesses*, p. 231.
232 *Slouching Towards Bethlehem*, pp. 92-107.

Summary

(i) Babylon the Great, the horrendous woman who symbolises the God-rejecting world, rides a ferocious beast in 'a wilderness', the same metaphorical wilderness that Israel faced in its exile: Ezekiel's 'wilderness of the peoples', i.e. all the nations.

(ii) Her steed is scarlet, signifying its earthly composition, but rises out of the abyss, signifying its demonic origin. It is the principality and power of the self-exalting State which in Revelation 11 kills the two witnesses in Israel; in Revelation 13 rampages through "all the nations"; in Revelation 16 entices 'the kings of the whole earth' to Har-Magedon/Jerusalem; in Revelation 17 carries then kills the woman, as we will consider soon; and in Revelation 19, it will at last be judged and destroyed.

(iii) Its seven heads have two meanings, one geographical and the other, historical. Geographically, the "seven mountains on which the woman sits" signify Rome. In John's day, 'the world' was enthroned there and the Romans worshipped *Dea Roma*, as in Vespasian's coinage.

(iv) Historically, the seven heads are also the seven successive kingdoms that had ruled, were ruling in the 1st century, and are about to come against Israel. "Five have fallen, one is, the other has not yet come" is Jewish History 101: Egypt, Assyria, Babylon, Medo-Persia, Greece are the five that had "fallen"; in John's time, Rome "is"; the one "not yet come" was waiting for Israel's restoration. This is why the beast seems to temporarily not exist, i.e. it "was, and is not, and is about to come up out of the abyss".

(v) It has always manifested among the Gentile nations but it ceased in the land of Israel in 70 AD when the Jews were sent into exile. Accordingly, in c. 95 AD the angel could say it "was, and is not" but will reemerge from the abyss. It indeed reappeared in Israel when the Jews were restored to the land in 1948 and, instead of renewing the covenant, they chose secularism over God.

(vi) The beast is itself the eighth king, the power within the other seven persecuting Israel.

11
The Ten Horns
United They Fall

In Chapter 1, I showed that the ten horns that John saw in c. 95 AD signify all the kingdoms of "all the nations" and that the horns were located on the seventh head, meaning their power was still in the future for him.

In Chapter 2, we looked at how, seven hundred years earlier in 604 BC, Nebuchadnezzar and Daniel saw this Gentile kingdom too but as ten toes on a multi-metal statue, pulverised by a heavenly stone. They were told that its being iron and pottery meant it would be "a divided kingdom", unable to unite because of its composition. Daniel saw it again, fifty years later in 550 BC, as ten horns which come to an end when "everlasting dominion" is given to "a son of man", Messiah (Dan 7:13-14).

In the last chapter, we saw the ten horns again on the seventh and last head of the scarlet beast ridden by Babylon the Great. Now in their last hour, the ten unite, not because their composition changes but because they have a common purpose. As the angel explained:

> 12. "The ten horns which you saw are ten kings who have not yet received a kingdom, but they receive authority as kings with the beast for *one hour*.
> 13. "These have *one purpose*, and they give their power and authority to the beast.
> 14. "These will wage war against the Lamb, and the Lamb will overcome them…" (Rev 17:12-14*)

Seventh Head, Ten Horns

We also see the significance of the dragon and the first beast having seven heads and ten horns. As I showed in Books 2 and 3 and recap in Appendix A, seven can mean 'justly, completely, or perfectly'[233] while ten is a common metaphor for 'all'.[234] Jesus judging the beast in the time of its seventh head with ten horns, i.e. when the ten "give their kingdom to the beast" (Rev 17:17), means that is when He will finally, completely, perfectly, justly deal with all of the kingdoms of the earth.

This is also the time of the seventh and last trumpet:

> Then the seventh angel sounded; and there were loud voices in heaven, saying, "*The kingdom of the world* has become the kingdom of our Lord and of His Christ; and He will reign forever and ever." (Rev 11:15*)

Daniel also saw this, writing that when the beast finally unites "all the nations"…:

> 26. "…the court will sit for judgment, and his dominion will be taken away, annihilated and destroyed forever.
> 27. "Then the sovereignty, the dominion and the greatness of all the kingdoms under the whole heaven will be given to the people of the saints of the Highest One; His kingdom will be an everlasting kingdom, and all the dominions will serve and obey Him." (Dan 7:26-27*)

It will be Kingdom come.

Notice at this time, Jesus will be annihilating and destroying the beast's dominion forever, as well as that of "all the kingdoms under the whole heaven". He has every right to because:

> …by Him all things were created, both in the heavens and on earth, visible and invisible, whether thrones or

---

233 *Gotta Serve Somebody*, p. 147.
234 *Slouching Towards Bethlehem*, pp. 36-39.

dominions or rulers or authorities - all things have been created through Him and for Him. (Col 1:16)

He created them and when He returns, He will judge all of them, 'both in the heavens and on the earth, visible and invisible'.[235] As Paul explained to the Corinthians:

> ...then comes the end, when He hands over the kingdom to the God and Father, when He has abolished *all rule and all authority and power*. (1 Cor 15:24*)

The United Nations

Today, there is one organisation that comprises all the kingdoms of "all the nations" – the United Nations (UN) with its 193 members. I believe this will be the beast's seventh head with its ten horns.

Let us put it all in context.

Jesus inaugurated Nebuchadnezzar and Daniel's stone kingdom in the 1st century, quoting Daniel 2 to the chief priests and Pharisees as He called them to repentance:

> "Therefore I say to you, *the kingdom of God* will be taken away from you and given to a people, producing the fruit of it. And he who falls on *this stone* will be broken to pieces; but on whomever it falls, it will scatter him like dust." (Matt 21:43-44*)

Contrary to what is often taught, the ten-toes/horns kingdom therefore existed in the 1st century but as individual kingdoms - they had not yet become John's beast's seventh head because they had not yet united into "a kingdom":

> "The ten horns which you saw *are* ten kings who have *not yet* received *a kingdom*, but they receive authority as kings with the beast for *one hour*." (Rev 17:12*)

---

235 We will see how this fits in with the millennium in Book 7, *Kingdom Come*.

The statue's legs of iron, the Roman Empire, continued to fight other empires such as the Parthians, before ultimately losing Rome to the Huns and Visigoths, followed by Constantinople to the Ottomans. As Jesus said, the nations and empires will continue to rise and fall until the end (Matt 24:7).

(i) Israel captive 70 AD

The "ten kings" did, however, take captive the Jewish survivors of Titus's destruction of the nation state of Israel in 70 AD, as Jesus had predicted forty years earlier:

> "...there will be great distress upon the land and wrath to this people; and they will fall by the edge of the sword, and will be *led captive into all the nations*; and Jerusalem will be trampled underfoot by the Gentiles until the times of the Gentiles are fulfilled." (Luke 21:23-24*)

As far as the Romans were concerned, Israel had to be destroyed because they had rebelled against Nero but their armies also fulfilled the purpose and judgement of God (Matt 22:7). As spelled out in Book 4,[236] Moses had warned Israel that they would incur the Law's curse of "a sword which will execute vengeance for the covenant" (Lev 26:25) and be scattered among "the nations" (Lev 26:31-33).[237]

Acting as individual nations, the ten kings then kept Israel "captive in all the nations".

(ii) Israel restored 1948

This was truly momentous. Against all the odds, the Jews had survived this 2,000 years in exile. As detailed in Book 1,[238] some nations had barely tolerated the Jews while others murderously persecuted them, driving them to "the ends of the earth" from their homeland (Deut 30:4).

---

236 *Silencing the Witnesses*, pp. 94-98.
237 The curse of the Law *Silencing the Witnesses*, pp. 147-165.
238 *Dancing in the Dragon's Jaws*, pp. 69-92, 148-153.

Everything changed on 29 November 1947 when the United Nations' General Assembly voted[239] to restore Jewish sovereignty in the land of Israel and on 14 May, 1948, Israel was reborn as a nation. As Isaiah put it:

> "Who has heard such a thing?
> Who has seen such things?
> Can *a land be born in one day*?
> Can a nation be brought forth all at once?
> As soon as Zion travailed, she also brought forth her sons."
> (Isa 66:8*)

Restoration, rebirth, or resurrection, this was miraculous and in 1947, the ten kings served God's purpose in ending Israel's long exile (Lev 26:44-45).

(iii) Stone to mountain

All the while, the kingdom Jesus inaugurated kept growing among "all the nations", just as Daniel saw it would:

> ...the stone that struck the statue became a great mountain and filled the whole earth. (Dan 2:35)

This indestructible kingdom began in one divine Man, a "stone... cut out of the mountain without hands" (Dan 2:45), Jesus of Nazareth. Remarkably, Isaiah had earlier predicted that the Lord would be "a stone to strike and a rock to stumble over" (Isa 8:14) i.e. rejected by His own people (1 Pet 2:7-8).

Over the last 2,000 years, His kingdom has grown into a great mountain, reigning today over one third of the earth's population.[240] Soon it will include all but 'a tenth' in Israel (Rev 11:13)[241] and ultimately, it will fill 'the whole earth'.

---

239 Resolution 181 just reached the required two-thirds majority with 33 votes for, 13 against, 10 abstentions and one absent. Ten of those against were Muslim states.
240 Pew Research Center's estimate in 2015. www.pewresearch.org/fact-tank/2017/04/05/christians-remain-worlds-largest-religious-group-but-they-are-declining-in-europe/ 1 Aug, 2019.
241 *Silencing the Witnesses*, pp. 282-285.

(iv) UN's Change of Purpose

Having served God's purpose by restoring Israel as a sovereign state, the United Nations also tried to set aside Jerusalem for themselves as an international entity. They did not seem to mind, however, when the Jordanian army invaded in 1948 and occupied the West Bank and East Jerusalem, which included the Old City and the Temple Mount.

That all changed when Israel drove the Jordanians back across the Jordan River in the Six Day War of 1967 - the Security Council passed Resolution 242, calling on Israel to withdraw. In 1974, after Israel repelled the invading Egyptian and Syrian armies of the 1973 Yom Kippur War, the UN began referring to "occupied Arab Territories" and, from 1982, to "occupied Palestinian Territories".

I believe that the UN's unjust desire to take Jerusalem off Israel is the "one purpose" through which the ten kings will "give their power and authority to the beast" (Rev 17:13). If so, John's vision in c. 95 AD was looking forward to our day - *the ten kings are now manifesting as the first beast's seventh head* and this will be their downfall:

> "For God has put it in their hearts to execute His purpose by having *a common purpose*, and by giving their kingdom to the beast, until the words of God will be fulfilled."
> (Rev 17:17*)

We will look at this more closely soon.

The Eleventh Horn

The last piece of the jigsaw puzzle we need to complete it is found in Daniel 7.

As mentioned in Chapter 2, some fifty years after the vision of the multi-metal statue, Daniel saw the great Gentile empires ruling over Israel as four wild beasts (Dan 7:1-27).

He then watches ten horns/kings/kingdoms arise out of the fourth beast, the Roman Empire, before they are all destroyed and an everlasting kingdom is given to "One like a son of man". The ten horns, like the ten toes, signify "all the nations" acting independently and ruling over Israel from 70 AD until 1948.

However, Daniel also saw an eleventh horn that would subdue three of the ten:

> "While I was contemplating the horns, behold, another horn, a little one, came up among them, and three of the first horns were pulled out by the roots before it; and behold, this horn possessed eyes like the eyes of a man and a mouth uttering great boasts." (Dan 7:8)

The angel explains:

> 24. "As for the ten horns, out of this kingdom [the Roman Empire] ten kings will arise; and another will arise after them, and he will be *different* from the previous ones and will subdue three kings.
> 25. He will speak out against the Most High and wear down the saints of the Highest One, and he will intend to make alterations in times and in law; and they will be given into his hand for *a time, times, and half a time.*"
> (Dan 7:24-25*)

As I established in Book 2,[242] the eleventh horn is "different" because it is a spirit, the spirit of antichrist; his uprooting of three of the ten means he subdues a third of "all the nations". His being allowed to persecute the saints for "a time, times, and half a time" refers to "the times of the Gentiles" which began in 30 AD due to Israel's rejection of Jesus, i.e. the last 2,000 years.

The eleventh horn is the second beast of John's vision (Rev 13:11) – it is the spirit of antichrist.

It works with the first beast for "forty-two months" (Rev

---

242 *Slouching Towards Bethlehem*, pp. 69-73.

13:5), i.e. the last 2,000 years, causing the phenomenon of emperor-worship. Accordingly, in Book 2 we considered not only the Romans of John's day but also the rise and fall of antichrist regimes in the 20th century. Although Italy eventually escaped from Mussolini, Germany from Hitler, Japan from Hirohito, Russia from Stalin, Cambodia from Pol Pot, we still see China and North Korea ruled by antichrist regimes.

I also showed how one empire stands alone in its longevity, size, and influence – Islam.

This ideological empire has been steadily growing since the 7th century, reigning today over 1.8 billion people, or one quarter of the earth's population of 7.3 billion. Even more significantly, there are fifty Muslim-majority countries[243] and the Organization of Islamic Cooperation (OIC) consists of fifty-seven members, including Palestine.[244] This means that of the 193 nations in the United Nations today,[245] 30% are today submitting to Islam.

Historically, this began with Muhammad's conquest of the Arabian Peninsula (622-632 AD), followed by the Rashidun caliphs (632-661) venturing west to capture half of North Africa, north to Syria, and east to today's Iran. The Umayyad caliphs (661-750) went further west to conquer the other half of North Africa, Spain, and Portugal and further east to conquer North India, creating today's Afghanistan, Pakistan, and Bangladesh.

I believe we are seeing the fulfilment of Daniel's dream - the eleventh horn has in our day subdued three of the ten horns through Islam.

---

[243] www.pewresearch.org/fact-tank/2017/04/05/christians-remain-worlds-largest-religious-group-but-they-are-declining-in-europe/ 1 Aug, 2019.
[244] www.oic-oci.org/states/?lan=en, 1 Aug, 2019.
[245] www.un.org/en/member-states/, 1 Aug, 2019.

United by Mission

What then unites the ten horns into the seventh and final head of the beast where intermarriage has failed? Will Islam continue to grow to subdue all ten, as some fear? No, because Islam has already fulfilled its predicted ascension in subduing only a third.

What finally unites the ten in the last hour before the Lord returns is not religion, not economics, as many believe, nor brute force, but their mission:

> 12. "The ten horns which you saw are ten kings who have not yet received a kingdom, but they receive authority as kings with the beast for one hour.
> 13. These have *one purpose*, and they give their power and authority to the beast." (Rev 17:12-13*)

They will be united by "one purpose" because, as the ancient Indian proverb says, 'the enemy of my enemy is my friend'.[246] The ten may disagree on every other issue – forms of government, ideologies and religions, human rights - but, as the angel explains to John:

> 14. "These will *wage war against the Lamb*, and the Lamb will overcome them, because He is Lord of lords and King of kings, and those who are with Him are the called and chosen and faithful." (Rev 17:14*)

Their common enemy will be Jesus of Nazareth, His followers, and His people 'according to the flesh' (Rom 9:5), the earthly nation of Israel, even those not yet following Jesus. Why? Because Israel is still loved by God:

> From the standpoint of the gospel they are enemies for your sake, but from the standpoint of God's choice they are *beloved for the sake of the fathers*; for the gifts and the calling of God are irrevocable. (Rom 11:28-29*)

---

246 Often considered an Arab proverb, it was first recorded in India in 4th century BC in the *Arthashastra*, a Sanskrit treatise on statecraft, economic policy, and military strategy.

God is and will always remain faithful to the covenant He made with Abraham, Isaac, and Jacob (Jer 31:35-37), as detailed in Book 4.[247] This includes the everlasting 'gift' of the Promised Land (Gen 17:8, 48:4).

United Nations' Animus

How could the United Nations reach such a point, and how likely is it to so turn against Israel as to come against it militarily? It is almost there today and conflict seems inevitable. Consider its history.

After recognising Israel's right to exist as a sovereign nation in November 1947, the UN quickly back-tracked.

(i) UN General Assembly

Over the next forty years, 1947-1990, while Israel was fighting three wars for her survival, the General Assembly passed a total of 690 resolutions or part-resolutions concerning her. Of these, 429 (62%) were unfavourable to Israel while only 56 (8%) were against the wishes of the Arab nations – tellingly, 49 of those were to establish peace-keeping forces. In these resolutions, Israel was "condemned," "vigorously condemned," "strongly condemned," "deplored," "strongly deplored", "censured," and "denounced" some 321 times while the Arab nations were not criticised even once.[248] This is surely the croaking of the frogs, as in Chapter 3.

(ii) UN Security Council

The Security Council was no better, despite the USA's veto power. During those forty years, the Security Council devoted 175 of its 605 resolutions (26%) to the Arab/Israeli

---

247 *Silencing the Witnesses*, pp. 319-322.
248 Shai ben-Tekoa. http://christianactionforisrael.org/un/record.html, 24 November, 2010. Also www.unwatch.org/site/apps/nlnet/content2.aspx?c=bdKKISNqEmG&b=1314451&ct=1715019, 25 Nov, 2010.

conflicts. This was bizarre considering the numerous bloody crises during those years: the partition of India, Pakistan, and Bangladesh in which millions were killed and 14 million had to change countries; the Korean and Vietnamese Wars; tens of millions dying in famines in China and Africa; the super-powers' Cold War, including the Cuban nuclear missile confrontation; 1.8 million killed in the Iran-Iraq war; millions more in Sudan, etc.

Of the Council's 175 resolutions regarding the Arab/Israeli conflicts, 74 are neutral or balanced but of the remaining 101, fully 97 were against Israel's interests but only 4 were against those of her Arab opponents.[249] Listen to those frogs!

(iii) Recent resolutions

There has been no improvement since then.

Between 2012 and 2021, the General Assembly passed 251 resolutions criticising individual nations, of which an astonishing 195 (78%) were against Israel,[250] an average of 22 a year.

The United Nations Educational, Scientific and Cultural Organisation (UNESCO) averages 10 resolutions a year - one in 2013 condemned Syria and every other one has condemned Israel. The U.N.'s World Health Organisation (WHO) and International Labour Organisation (ILO) only ever single out Israel.[251]

In December 2021, the General Assembly approved[252] funding for a permanent Commission of Inquiry into Israel's treatment of Palestinians, as recommended by their Human Rights Council.[253] No such open-ended investigation has ever been launched against any other UN member state and

---

249 http://christianactionforisrael.org/stillbirth/, 27 Oct, 2020.
250 www.cufi.org.uk/opinion-analysis/united-nations-and-bias-against-israel-explained/, 3 Nov, 2020. https://unwatch.org/database/, 29 Mar, 2021.
251 Ibid.
252 125 for, 8 opposed, 34 abstentions.
253 www.ohchr.org/EN/HRBodies/HRC/CoIOPT-Israel/Pages/Index.aspx, 27 Jan, 2022.

its staff have a history of anti-Israel rhetoric.[254] They can now be found guilty more often.

(iv) UN Human Rights Council

The most egregious bias in a UN body is found, ironically, in its human rights investigators. Focused on condemning Israel, the Commission on Human Rights (UNCHR) so blatantly ignored the Sudanese genocide of 1.9 million men, women, and children by Omar al-Bashir's National Islamic Front which began in 2003 that it was disbanded in disgrace in 2006. Its replacement, the Human Rights Council (UNHRC) has been no better. Within a year, even the U.N. Secretary-General, Ban-Ki Moon, was speaking out about its plan to scrutinise Israel in every session:

> The Secretary-General is disappointed at the council's decision to single out only one specific regional item given the range and scope of allegations of human rights violations throughout the world.[255]

By 2021, the UNHRC had passed 167 resolutions of which 94 condemn Israel, compared to 73 for the rest of the world *combined*.[256] Meanwhile, the UNHRC had refused to even consider female genital mutilation, child marriages, and the stoning of women, because Islam might be criticised. The deceiving frogs are busy.

(v) Cultural rewrites

In 2016, UNESCO passed a resolution on 'Occupied Palestine' which referred to Jerusalem's Temple Mount by the Islamic and Arabic names of "Al-Aqsa Mosque/Al-Haram Al-Sharif and its surroundings". They also labelled the sacred Jewish sites of the Tomb of Rachel in Bethlehem

---

254 https://israelinstitute.nz/2022/01/new-zealand-votes-to-fund-unprecedented-attack-on-israel/, 27 Jan, 2022.
255 www.un.org/press/en/2007/sgsm11053.doc.htm, 14 Nov, 2020.
256 https://unwatch.org/database/, 7 May, 2021.

and Hebron's Tomb of the Patriarchs - the burial place of Abraham, Isaac, and Jacob - as 'Palestinian sites.' The text 'deeply regrets' Israel's labelling them Jewish heritage sites 'and calls on the Israeli authorities to act in accordance with' UNESCO's decisions.

In 2020, the General Assembly passed a resolution referring to the Temple Mount only by its Islamic name as part of a parcel of seven anti-Israeli resolutions with another twenty planned before Christmas.[257]

Given this momentum in denouncing Israel, it seems inevitable that sooner or later, the UN will be asked to act for the international community to enforce their resolutions on behalf of the Palestinian Muslims.

(vi) Causes

What causes this unrelenting bias in the world's primary representative organisation?

Politically, there are two powerful voting blocs within the UN which are strongly Muslim: the Organisation of Islamic Cooperation (OIC), which has 56 member states, and the Non-Aligned Movement (NAM) with 50 of its 119 members also belonging to the OIC. They guarantee the Islamic nations strongly influence every decision made in the UN and they believe Israel's very existence is an affront to Muhammad's superior 'revelation'. This is why Iran's Ayatollah Khomeini labelled Israel "the Little Satan" and the USA "the Great Satan" for supporting Israel.

Secondly, human corruption. The UN routinely awards positions on their Human Rights Council (UNHRC) to abusive regimes and dictatorships (e.g. in 2020, China, Russia, Cuba, Pakistan, Gabon, and Uzbekistan). These find Israel a convenient scapegoat to divert attention from their own behaviour. Spiritually, however, the main cause is the

---

257 Ibid.

croaking of the frog-like demons coming out of the mouth of the dragon, the beast, and the false prophet. If he is to be a unifying messianic Muslim, the Mahdi, as I argue in Book 2,[258] he can be expected to call for Israel's annihilation.

The Tipping Point?

The primary restraint on the animus against Israel in United Nations is the USA.

For forty-six years, beginning in 1970, the USA used its veto power in the Security Council to thwart resolutions against Israel but there was a dramatic change in 2016.[259]

Outgoing President Obama used his last days in office to organise for my own nation of New Zealand,[260] acting chair of the Council, to sponsor Resolution 2334 which proclaimed East Jerusalem - including the Jews' holiest site, the Temple Mount, as well as the Jewish Quarter, the Western or Wailing Wall, the Hadassah Hospital, and the Hebrew University - to be illegally occupied territory. The US ambassador then abstained from voting against it or using her veto to annul it.

President Obama's expected successor, his Secretary of State Hilary Clinton, would surely have continued on that tack, leaving Israel to stand alone against the will of "*all* the nations". However, the unexpected election of businessman Donald Trump and his strong support for Israel dramatically halted this escalation. He instead recognised Jerusalem as Israel's capital city and cut funding to the Palestinian

---

258 *Slouching Towards Bethlehem*, pp. 171-172, 214, 218.
259 www.middleeasteye.net/news/43-times-us-has-used-veto-power-against-un-resolutions-israel, 4 Nov, 2020.
260 Our Foreign Minister, Murray McCully, acted without cabinet authority in rushing this through (www.scoop.co.nz/stories/PA1704/S00151/mccullys-diplomatic-blunder-on-israel-damaging.htm). New Zealand has its own shameful voting record regarding Israel in the UN. In the last six years, we have voted against Israel 87 times, abstained 24 times, and for Israel, not even once. https://unwatch.org/database/?showCountry=24246, 28 Jan, 2022.

Authority for its awarding of pensions to the families of suicide bombers.

It remains to be seen today in 2023 if or when the Biden-Harris administration will revert to the Obama-Biden administration's doctrine and leave Israel to face "all the nations" alone. In the meantime, they have recommenced financial aid to the Palestinian Authority.

Soon we will see just how quickly everything can come together and come to an end - Babylon and the two beasts will take just "one hour" to fall - but Paul tells us there are two major signs that we are to look for before that happens. First, however, let us summarise this chapter.

Summary

(i) The climax of earth's history comes with the ten horns on the seventh head. This is because 'seven' signifies 'justly, completely, or perfectly' while 'ten' means 'all'. Jesus' return as judge will be to completely, perfectly, justly deal with all of the kingdoms of the earth.

(ii) The ten horns, being "all the nations", existed in the 1st century as the leaders of individual nations but they had "not yet received a kingdom… with the beast" because, like iron and potter's clay, they were too different to "adhere to one another".

(iii) Although they acted independently in keeping Israel in exile for almost 2,000 years from 70 AD, they acted together in the United Nations in 1947 to restore the Jews to their land, and thereby fulfilled God's purposes.

(iv) The eleventh horn, being John's second beast i.e. the spirit of antichrist, has manifested among all the nations over the last 2,000 years and today has one third subdued under Islam.

(v) This has disproportionately affected the United Nations, despite its democratic structure, into singling out Israel for condemnation and setting up the battle of Har-Magedon for the possession of Jerusalem. All that is needed now is for the USA to stop protecting Israel in the Security Council.

12
The Apostasy & The Antichrist

In the last chapter, we saw that Daniel's vision of the eleventh horn subduing three of the ten horns has been fulfilled by the spirit of antichrist in Islam over the last sixteen centuries, and created the blatant bias against Israel in the United Nations today.

In Book 2,[261] I established that John saw this spirit as looking like 'a lamb' but speaking as 'a dragon' (Rev 13:11). However, when he sees it inspiring Har-Maggedon, it is not in the metaphorical form of a horn or a beast in lamb's clothing but in its human form, in its final manifestation as *the* Antichrist, i.e. '*the* false prophet':

> And I saw coming out of the mouth of the dragon and out of the mouth of the beast and out of the mouth of *the false prophet*, three unclean spirits like frogs (Rev 16:13*).

As I wrote in Book 2,[262] I believe the Antichrist will be Islam's expected Mahdi so his emergence will begin the last hour before the Lord returns. However, Paul warned that an apostasy would precede both the Antichrist and the Lord's return:

> 3. Let no one in any way deceive you, for it [the Day of the Lord] will not come unless *the apostasy comes first*, and *the man of lawlessness* is revealed, the son of destruction...
> (2 Thess 2:3-4*)

We therefore need to watch first for 'the apostasy' and then 'the man of lawlessness'.

---
261 See *Slouching Towards Bethlehem*, pp. 92-102.
262 *Slouching Towards Bethlehem*, pp. 171-172.

'The Apostasy'

'Apostasy' means 'a defection... a forsaking... a falling away' from the faith.[263]

There have always been disciples like Judas Iscariot, tempted away by love of money or selfish ambition; others leave offended by something Jesus said (e.g. John 6:66). However, *the* apostasy' is a mass movement which He said would follow intense persecution of His followers:

> 9. "Then they will deliver you to *tribulation*, and will *kill* you, and you will be hated by all nations because of My name.
> 10. "At that time *many will fall away* and will *betray* one another and *hate* one another." (Matt 24:9-10*)

Some therefore refer to it as the Great Apostasy which accompanies the Great Tribulation.

Many of us have been taught that this time of tribulation and apostasy is yet to happen in a short, intense period immediately before the Lord returns but, as I showed in Chapter 6, there have already been two "great tribulations". One was indeed short and intense but it was against Jews in the Roman-Jewish Wars (66-136 AD); the other has been long and sporadic against Christians over the last 2,000 years, and is still ongoing. The latter included the Lord Himself being 'hated', 'betrayed', and 'killed' as well as Paul, Peter, James the brother of John, James the Lord's brother, and innumerable disciples.

The Great Apostasy also began 2,000 years ago. It was most manifest between the 4th and 20th centuries and so pervasive that it was not recognised until Erasmus's Greek New Testament[264] was published in 1516. His *Textus*

---

263 Vine's *Expository Dictionary of New Testament Words*, p. 126.
264 Dutch scholar Erasmus (1466-1536) published the first printed Latin and Greek New Testaments in 1516. In 1520, Spanish scholars published New Testaments in Hebrew, Aramaic, Greek, and Latin. Renaissance writers also popularised writing in the native language of the people instead of the scholars' Latin.

Receptus[265] corrected a number of mistranslations of the Latin Vulgate, allowing European scholars and believers to see for themselves how far the church had deviated from 'the faith delivered once for all to the saints' (Jude 1:3) in the 1st century. This led to the Reformation and its creed of *sola scriptura*, i.e. by Scripture alone, holding up the Bible as the sole infallible source of authority for Christian faith and practice.[266]

Accordingly, Luther, Calvin, and Zwingli[267] proclaimed that the Roman Catholic Church was not only the Great Apostasy but also Babylon the Great.

However, as I showed in Chapter 8, the Roman Catholic Church is not Babylon the Great. It was, though, as I will show in this chapter, the epitome of the institutional apostasy until the 20th century when it seems four popes officially brought it to a close with Cardinal Ratzinger, who became Benedict XVI, playing a major role. I will also note the role of the Eastern Orthodox Church and how the 16th century Reformation took several centuries to leave it behind too.

Apostasy followed tribulation with the persecution coming initially from the Jewish authorities, then the Roman authorities, then from apostate Church authorities in three distinct phases:

(i) Jewish Authorities

Jesus had earlier predicted what the scribes and Pharisees would to do to His disciples:

---

[265] Since then many older manuscripts such as the Dead Sea Scrolls have been found, enabling even better translations. *A Biblical-Theological Introduction to the New Testament: The Gospel Realized*, ed. Michael J. Kruger, Charlotte, NC; Crossway, 2016.

[266] It was also a remarkable repeat of 7th century BC Jewish history, when Hilkiah the high priest rediscovered the Scriptures and animated Josiah's reforms, as described in Chapter 5.

[267] Ulrich Zwingli (1484-1531), Swiss priest, chaplain, and theologian.

> "Therefore, behold, I am sending you prophets and wise men and scribes; some of them you will *kill and crucify*, and some of them you will *scourge in your synagogues*, and persecute from city to city..." (Matt 23:34*)

He distinguishes here between the maximum penalty the Jewish authorities could inflict in "your synagogues" (scourging up to thirty-nine lashes[268]) and that of the Romans (death by crucifixion)[269] – and He was about to receive both from both.

These were the legal punishments for blasphemy (the Jewish charge against Jesus – Matt 26:65-66) and sedition (the Roman charge against Jesus – John 19:12). He was also forewarning His followers that they too would be hated not only by their fellow-Jews but also killed "by all nations" (Matt 24:9) i.e. Gentiles.

(ii) Roman Authorities

When the Romans found that Christians would not worship the Roman emperor, they too began to kill them, denouncing them as unpatriotic and 'atheists', as covered in Book 2.[270] The Roman persecution was sporadic, as Laurie Guy notes:

> In Christianity's first three hundred years of existence, persecution was typically sporadic rather than sustained... The weather pattern was one of scattered showers of persecution rather than a general rain bloodbath... [In those times, many Christians were heroic but] many compromised their faith in the face of threatened death.[271]

---

268 The Law set the cap at forty (Deut 25:3) which became thirty-nine in case of miscounting. Paul received this on five occasions (2 Cor 11:24).
269 The Romans' removal of the death penalty from the Jewish authorities humiliated them because they had to ask the Romans to enforce it. However, in the sovereignty of God, this meant that Jesus died as an innocent victim of both Jews and Gentiles.
270 *Slouching Towards Bethlehem*, pp. 58-60.
271 Laurie Guy, *Introducing Early Christianity*, p. 52.

Then in the 4th century, persecution came from a different direction – it arose from apostate church leaders, just as Jesus warned:

> "At that time many will *fall away* and will *betray* one another and *hate* one another." (Matt 24:10*)

Those who "fall away" will "betray" and "hate" those who do not. The Lord had also warned they will "kill you":

> 1. "These things I have spoken to you so that you may be kept from stumbling.
> 2. "They will make you outcasts from *the synagogue*, but an hour is coming for *everyone who kills you to think that he is offering service to God.*" (John 16:1-2*)

(iii) Church Authorities

The apostasy became institutionalised when church leaders submitted to the spirit of antichrist and began to rule with Caesar, as detailed in Book 2.[272] While Emperor Constantine's conversion in 312 AD seemed to be good because he decriminalised Christianity and abolished crucifixion, in 380 AD, the three co-emperors Theodosius I, Gratian, and Valentinian II made Catholicism the state church of the Roman Empire:

> We authorize the followers of this law to assume the title of Catholic Christians; but as for the others, since, in our judgment they are foolish madmen, we decree that they shall be branded with the ignominious name of heretics, and shall not presume to give to their gatherings the name of churches. They will suffer in the first place the chastisement of the divine condemnation and in the second the punishment of our authority which in accordance with the will of Heaven we shall decide to inflict.[273]

---

272 *Slouching Towards Bethlehem*, pp. 60-65.
273 *The Edict of Thessalonica*, 27 Feb, 380 AD.

The results were disastrous:

> [There was] a massive influx of superficial converts from paganism. This resulted in declining moral standards and the adoption of some pagan and idolatrous practices... *the persecuted church of the martyrs became before long the persecuting state church.* Legal coercion was used at first against Christian groups deviating from the mainstream 'Catholic Church' and later against pagan worship.[274]

'The persecuted church became the persecuting state church.'

Within five years, in 385 AD,[275] a Spanish bishop, Priscillian of Avila, and five of his companions became the first officially executed dissenters or heretics. He had been condemned for being overly ascetic by the Council of Bordeaux, chaired by their bishop, Saint Delphinius, and was executed for sorcery by the emperor, Maximus.

As Lord Acton wrote, and Tolkien's *Lord of the Rings* perfectly illustrated, 'power tends to corrupt, and absolute power corrupts absolutely'.[276]

In Gethsemane, Jesus had commanded Peter:

> "Put your sword back into its place; for all those who take up the sword shall perish by the sword." (Matt 26:52)

As He soon after explained to Pontius Pilate:

> "My kingdom is not of this world. If My kingdom were of this world, then My servants would be fighting so that I would not be handed over to the Jews; but as it is, My kingdom is not of this realm." (John 18:36)

At the Last Supper, Jesus did tell the Twelve they would need swords when they travelled (Luke 22:36), to defend themselves against attack but not for enforcing the faith.

In the 4th century, the Church simply ignored Him and for

---

274 Tony Lane, *The Lion Concise Book of Christian Thought*, Oxford; Lion Hudson Plc, 1996, p. 11*.
275 Laurie Guy, p. 125.
276 Baron Acton (1834–1902), letter to Bishop Mandell Creighton in 1887.

the next 1,200 years, its leaders used the sword to attack and kill dissenters, whether Christians, Jews, Muslims, or pagans.

Taking Up the Sword

As covered in Book 2,[277] some of the most obvious examples are the Crusades,[278] the Inquisitions,[279] the Albigensian/Cathar Crusade,[280] the Huguenot Massacre,[281] and the slaughter of thousands of unarmed Incas by Pizarro and his Conquistadors in 1532 who conquered Peru so that, in his words, "all may come to a knowledge of God and of His Holy Catholic Faith".[282]

Heretics were particularly to be identified and executed, as explained by the Roman church's leading theologian, Thomas Aquinas (1225-1274):

> [They] deserve not only to be separated from the Church by excommunication, but also to be severed from the world by death. For it is a much graver matter to corrupt the faith which quickens the soul, than to forge money, which supports temporal life. Wherefore if forgers of money and other evil-doers are forthwith condemned to death by the secular authority, much more reason is there for heretics, as soon as they are convicted of heresy, to be not only excommunicated but even put to death.[283]

---

277 *Slouching Towards Bethlehem*, pp. 60-63.
278 11th to 13th Centuries. Ibid. pp. 159-161.
279 12th to 19th Centuries. The Medieval Inquisition was instituted in Rome in 1184, followed by the Portuguese Inquisition in 1536, and the Spanish Inquisition in 1478. Its last execution was in 1826.
280 Southern France (1209-1229) in which an estimated 200,000 died. In *Slouching Towards Bethlehem*, p. 62, I quoted the estimated toll at 1,000,000 but that now seems too high.
281 Also in 1572 in France. Catholic Archbishop of Paris and historian, Hardouin de Péréfixe de Beaumont (1606-1671), estimated the death toll at 100,000. G. D. Félice, *History of the Protestants of France*, New York; Edward Walker, 1851, p. 217.
282 *Slouching Towards Bethlehem*, pp. 143.
283 *Summa Theologiae, Second Part of the Second Part*, q.11 a.3. https://aquinas101.thomisticinstitute.org/st-iiaiiae-q-11#SSQ11A3THEP1

The first recorded burning of heretics was in Orléans, France, in 1022 for issues that are unclear today. The issue was very clear, however, when the 'heretics' were arguing for faith in Jesus and the Scriptures: the Church burned Biblical scholars and reformers like Czech theologian Jan Hus in 1415 and the disinterred bones of English translator John Wycliffe in 1428 (he had died in 1384). They famously failed to kill German monk Martin Luther in 1521 and French theologian John Calvin in 1530 but were more successful in England, burning Bishops Nicholas Ridley, and Hugh Latimer in 1555 and the Archbishop of Canterbury, Thomas Cranmer in 1556.

Historian and philosopher Will Durant summarises:

> For a thousand years Europe was ruled by an order of guardians... The *oratores* (clergy), though small in number, monopolized the instruments and opportunities of culture, and ruled with almost unlimited sway half of the most powerful continent on the globe.[284]

Eastern Orthodoxy & the Reformation

In 1054, the church leaders based in Constantinople split from the Catholic Church in Rome to form the Eastern, Greek, and Russian Orthodox Churches. Although the Byzantine[285] authorities did not execute heretics, they blinded, mutilated, castrated, or exiled offenders.[286] Pagans were forced to attend church and be baptised while Jews were barred from receiving dowries or inheritances unless they converted. Constantinople was captured by the Muslims in 1453 but the Orthodox Churches were by then well-established in the capital cities of Eastern Europe.

As for the Protestant reformers, Luther, Calvin, and Zwingli also persecuted and killed dissenters. Luther's infamous pamphlet of 1543, *On the Jews and Their Lies*, was

---

284 *The Story of Philosophy*, New York; Simon & Schuster, 2005, pp. 52-53.
285 Constantinople was originally called Byzantium so the empire was called the Byzantine Empire.
286 https://pubmed.ncbi.nlm.nih.gov/23511276/, 14 Dec, 2022.

still being quoted five hundred years later by Nazi leaders at the Nuremberg trials to justify the Holocaust.[287] Calvin and the leaders of the churches of Geneva, Zurich, Berne, Basle, and Schaffhausen had Michael Servetus burnt at the stake in 1553 for denying the Trinity.[288] Zwingli died in battle in 1531, trying to forcibly convert Catholics.

Earlier, in 1525, they all objected to the Anabaptists' following the Scriptures in baptising only adult believers rather than believers' babies:

> At the Diet of Speyer in 1529, both Catholics and Lutherans agreed to put Anabaptists to death. Martin Luther publicly affirmed the edict in 1531. Around Europe, many were drowned, burned, beheaded.[289]

Their executioners cheerfully dubbed the drownings as the "third baptism".[290] British scholar Bamber Gascoigne records:

> A larger proportion of Anabaptists were martyred for their faith than any other Christian group in history - including even the early Christians on whom they modeled themselves.[291]

The Anabaptists and Pilgrims had also grasped the Biblical revelation of the separation of church and state which we take for granted today but to live it out in the 17th century, they had to emigrate to the New World to avoid persecution by both Catholic and Protestant rulers. Even they, however, had not fully grasped the difference between Old and New Covenants:

---

287 *Dancing in the Dragon's Jaws*, pp. 88-89.
288 *Slouching Towards Bethlehem*, p. 63.
289 James A. Haught, *Holy Horrors: An Illustrated History of Religious Murder and Madness;* Prometheus Books, 2002.
290 If only the first, that of babies, was legitimate, the second, immersion of believing adults, was heretical, so the third, execution, was appropriate.
291 http://churchandstate.org.uk/2022/06/holy-horrors-christian-persecution-of-anabaptists/, 8 Oct, 2022.

It was failing to recognise this distinction that caused the infamous witch-hunts in Christian nations in Europe and North America between the 15th and 17th Centuries...[292]

Although there were always genuine believers both within and outside the institutional churches, this was apostasy on a vast scale, just as Jesus had predicted:

> "...an hour is coming for *everyone who kills you to think that he is offering service to God.*" (John 16:2*)

How these Catholic, Orthodox, and Protestant leaders will be judged is complex but Jesus made it clear in His parable about 'the faithful and sensible steward' (Luke 12:42-48) that He will hold every leader accountable[293] when He returns on the Last Day: some of His stewards will receive 'many lashes' (Luke 12:47), i.e. of great remorse, while others only 'a few' (Luke 12:48). In Paul's parallel metaphor:

> If any man's work is burned up, he will suffer loss; but he himself will be saved, yet so as through fire. (1 Cor 3:15)

However, some unfaithful stewards will be, in Jesus' own words, "cut in pieces, and assigned a place with the unbelievers" (Luke 12:46). Again, I will cover this properly in Book 7, *Kingdom Come*. In the meantime, however, we do know that many will be condemned for their unfaithfulness to Him:

> "*Many* will say to Me on that day, 'Lord, Lord, did we not prophesy in Your name...?'And then I will declare to them,'*I never knew you*; depart from Me, you who practise lawlessness." (Matt 7:22-23*)

Ending the Apostasy?

In the 20th century, remarkable changes took place within Christendom's largest denomination, Roman Catholicism.[294]

---

292 *Silencing the Witnesses*, p. 117.
293 I will cover this properly in Book 7, *Kingdom Come*.
294 Today there are about 1.3 billion Roman Catholics, 900 million Protestants, and 300 million Orthodox believers. www.worlddate.info/

(i) Renouncing the Crown

From the 8th century until 1963, the popes had been crowned with the triregnum crown, signifying that that the pope is 'Father of princes and kings, Ruler of the world, Vicar on earth of our saviour Jesus Christ'. As I showed in Book 2,[295] this was ruling in His place and cooperating with the spirit of antichrist.

However, in 1964 during the Second Vatican Council (1962-1965), Paul VI[296] officially renounced the crown as "human glory and power" and sold it to raise money for the poor.[297] The two subsequent popes, John Paul I[298] and John Paul II,[299] abandoned coronation altogether while Benedict XVI[300] took it a step further in 2005, removing the tiara from his papal coat of arms and replacing it with a bishop's mitre. Benedict, formerly known as Cardinal Joseph Ratzinger, had been one of the most influential theologians at Vatican II and became a close adviser to John Paul II.[301] He declared:

> It was both necessary and good for the Council to put an end to the false forms of the Church's *glorification of self* on earth, and by suppressing her compulsive tendency to defend her past history, to eliminate her false justification of self.[302]

---

religions/christianity.php, 14 Dec, 2022.
295 *Slouching Towards Bethlehem*, pp. 60-62, 141-142.
296 Pope from 1963 to 1978.
297 It was purchased by Catholics to be kept in the Basilica of the National Shrine of the Immaculate Conception in Washington, D.C.
298 He was only 33 days in office in 1978.
299 Pope from 1978 until 2005.
300 Pope from 2005 until 2013.
301 In 1981, John Paul II appointed him Prefect of the Congregation for the Doctrine of the Faith, President of the Biblical Commission and of the Pontifical International Theological Commission where he could steer the church back into the Biblical faith and repentance towards Protestants and Jews.
302 *National Catholic Register*, www.ncregister.com/commentaries/why-vatican-ii-was-necessary, 27 Oct, 2022. Emphasis added.

Vatican II was therefore a major step away from Babylon the Great's self-glorification, as described in Chapter 9.

As for the Inquisition, as noted earlier, it lasted from the 12th century until the 19th. Its last execution was in 1826 when Cayetona Ripoll, a Spanish school teacher, was garrotted for teaching deism;[303] its last outrage was in 1858 in Bologna when Inquisition agents legally removed a 6-year-old Jewish boy, Edgardo Mortara, from his family.[304] However in 1965, as part of the Vatican II reforms, Paul VI renamed it and in 1981, John Paul II appointed Cardinal Ratzinger as its head.[305] In 1998, John Paul II confessed:

> The Inquisition belongs to a tormented phase in the history of the Church, which… Christians [should] examine in a spirit of sincerity and open-mindedness.[306]

(ii) Regarding Dissenters

In 1999, John Paul II travelled to Czechoslovakia to apologise, as described in Book 2, for "the cruel death inflicted on Jan Hus" and the consequent wound imposed on the Bohemian people.[307]

In March 2000, he made a sweeping apology for the last 1,600 years of violence, persecution, and blunders, asking God for forgiveness for sins committed against Jews, heretics, women, Gypsies and native peoples:

> Fighting through trembles and slurrings caused by

---

[303] The belief that 'God created the universe and established rationally comprehensible moral and natural laws but does not intervene in human affairs through miracles or supernatural revelation'. *The American Heritage Dictionary of the English Language*, 5th Ed.

[304] The boy had been secretly baptised by his nursemaid and it was illegal in the Papal States for a Catholic child to be raised by Jews. Pope Pius IX raised him as a Catholic and he went on to become a priest.

[305] See Footnote 302.

[306] Pope John Paul II, *Address to the International Symposium on the Inquisition*, 31 Oct, 1998.

[307] *Slouching Towards Bethlehem*, p. 62.

Parkinson's disease, the Pope electrified ranks of cardinals and bishops by pleading for a future that would not repeat the mistakes. "Never again," he said. Centuries of hate and rivalry could not recur in the third millennium. "We forgive and we ask forgiveness. We are asking pardon for the divisions among Christians, for the use of violence that some have committed in the service of truth, and for attitudes of mistrust and hostility assumed towards followers of other religions."[308]

In 2001, he apologised to the Eastern Orthodox Church for the sacking of Constantinople by Catholic Crusaders in 1204.[309] He also apologised to Muslims for the Crusades at the Umayyad mosque in Damascus.[310]

In 2008, Benedict XVI declared that Luther was right regarding salvation by faith in Jesus:

> Benedict affirmed that Luther had correctly translated Paul's words as 'justified by faith alone' - the well-known *sola fide*... It was disagreement over the doctrine of salvation by faith that sparked the Protestant Reformation in the 16th century, splitting Christianity in Western Europe. Yet, said the Pope, it was indeed biblical to say, as did Luther, that it was the faith of a Christian, not his works that saved him.[311]

(iii) Regarding Jews

For some 1,600 years, the church had persecuted the Jews as "Christ-killers"; in 1998, John Paul II publicly apologised to them for enabling the Nazi persecution and not doing more during the Holocaust. In 2000, he went to the Holocaust Museum, Yad Vashem, in Jerusalem to express his deep sorrow at...:

---

308 www.theguardian.com/world/2000/mar/13/catholicism.religion, 31 Oct, 2022.
309 Address to Holy Synod, Athens, May 4, 2001.
310 www.bbc.co.uk/religion/religions/christianity/pope/johnpaulii_1.shtml, 31 Oct, 2022.
311 www1.cbn.com/ChurchWatch/archive/2009/02/06/pope-benedict-xvi-luther-was-right, 1 Nov, 2022.

>...the hatred, acts of persecution and displays of anti-Semitism directed against the Jews by Christians at any time and in any place.[312]

The effects in Israel have been startling, as I described in Book 4.[313] In 2015, Orthodox rabbis issued a statement saying Vatican II had led them to re-evaluate Jesus and conclude that He had upheld the Torah more than any other Sage in Jewish history and "removed idols from the Gentiles".[314]

I believe this wonderful fruit from the pope's repentance is an essential part of the coming great revival in Israel predicted in Chapter 5.

(iv) Protestant Repentance

By the 18th century, Protestants were rediscovering and practising the Biblical revelation of the separation of church and state championed by the Anabaptists and Pilgrims. However, it took until the 20th century before some attempts were made to put things right.

In 1903, followers of John Calvin erected a memorial acknowledging his horrendous error in executing Michael Servetus as a heretic.[315] In 1984 and 1994, Lutheran leaders apologised to the Jews for their 500 year history of accepting Luther's antisemitism;[316] in 2010, they apologised to the Mennonite Church for persecuting them as Anabaptists in the 16th century.[317]

---

312 www.bbc.co.uk/religion/religions/christianity/pope/johnpaulii_1.shtml, 31 Oct, 2022.
313 *Silencing the Witnesses*, pp. 288-293.
314 Ibid, p. 291.
315 Ibid, p. 117-118.
316 www.tampabay.com/archive/1993/10/16/lutherans-to-apologize-to-jews/, 7 Nov, 2022. www.jewishvirtuallibrary.org/declaration-of-the-evangelical-lutheran-church-in-america-to-the-jewish-community,   7 Nov, 2022.
317 www.dw.com/en/lutherans-reconcile-with-mennonites-500-years-after-bloody-persecution/a-5837683, 7 Nov, 2022.

Asceticism & Licentiousness

Paul also wrote regarding the apostasy:

> 1. But the Spirit explicitly says that in later times[318] *some will fall away from the faith,* paying attention to *deceitful spirits* and *doctrines of demons*...
> 3. men who *forbid marriage* and *advocate abstaining from foods* which God has created to be gratefully shared in by those who believe and know the truth. (1 Tim 4:1 & 3*)

Where coercion failed, seduction often succeeded. Professing Christian leaders went astray off both sides of the narrow way to life: some promoted a false spirituality of extreme self-denial, forbidding marriage and enjoyment of food. By the 4th century, this asceticism was accepted, advocated, and institutionalised by the Desert Fathers, the Catholic Church, and Eastern Orthodoxy.[319]

At the other extreme, Peter warned of apostate prophets and teachers who would practise extreme self-indulgence, predicting they would...:

> ...secretly introduce destructive heresies, even denying the Master who bought them... *Many* will follow their *sensuality*... For speaking out arrogant words of vanity they *entice* by *fleshly desires,* by sensuality... promising them freedom while they themselves are slaves of corruption. (2 Pet 2:1-2, 18-19*)

Jude likewise warned his 1st century audience to:

> ...contend earnestly for the faith which was once for all handed down to the saints. For certain persons have crept in unnoticed..., ungodly persons who *turn the grace of our God into licentiousness* and deny our only Master and Lord, Jesus Christ. (Jude v. 3*)

---

318 The expression 'later times' (v. 1) is often assumed to mean just before the Lord's return but, as Hebrews 1:2 makes clear, 'these last days' began with Jesus' first coming.
319 See Appendix C – Seduction to Apostasy for details.

Graeme Carlé

Others took over the priesthood of all believers, following 'the way of Cain… the error of Balaam, and… the rebellion of Korah' (Jude v. 11).[320]

Happily for us today, the institutionalised asceticism and licentiousness of 'the apostasy' are largely behind us. While marriage is still forbidden to Catholic clergy and Orthodox bishops,[321] their people as well as all Protestants and Pentecostals marry and enjoy the food God gave us.

Summary of the Apostasy

(i) Paul said that before Jesus returns, there would be 'the apostasy', i.e. a falling or turning away from the faith, and 'the appearance of the man of lawlessness', the Antichrist. We should therefore be looking for both.

(ii) When Jesus predicted the apostasy, He said that "many will fall away" due to tribulation and persecution. There have been two "great tribulations": the worst targeted Jews in Israel between 66 and 136 AD in which two-thirds in the land died; the second has targeted innumerable Christians since 30 AD and is on-going.

(iii) Paul predicted the apostasy would include a false spirituality of severe self-denial, forbidding marriage and enjoyment of food. Peter and Jude warned of apostasy through a seduction to immorality and self-indulgence.

(iv) While all of this was occurring in the 1st century, the apostasy became institutionalised in the 4th century when the Church persecuted and executed non-conformists, heretics, and genuine believers while forbidding leaders to marry.

---

320 Details of this are on our website: www.emmausroad.org.nz
321 Orthodox priests have to marry.

(v) In 16th century Europe, the Protestants began regaining 'the faith once for all delivered to the saints'; by the 20th century, so too was the Roman Catholic Church which seems to be the end of 'the apostasy', even though Francis has turned back to the error of indulgences.

'The Man of Lawlessness'

I showed in Book 2 that this man will be the Antichrist and 'the false prophet',[322] the last of all the false prophets in history, the final wolf in sheep's clothing (Matt 7:15). I also showed how God has always allowed false prophets to come with supernatural signs and wonders,[323] in every generation, to test His people:

> "…to find out if you love the LORD your God with all your heart and with all your soul." (Deut 13:3)

I showed in Book 3[324] that passing this test is actually the fourth metaphorical ownership mark that God places on our right hand and forehead for all to see that we really do belong to Him.

Jesus warned the disciples in 30 AD that there would be many antichrists:

> "For many will come in My name, saying, 'I am the Christ,' and will mislead many." (Matt 24:5)

However, we know this man will be the last in the long line because he will be executed by the Lord when He returns:

> Then that lawless one will be revealed whom the Lord will slay with the breath of His mouth and bring to an end by the appearance of His coming… (2 Thess 2:8)

---

[322] Ibid, pp. 194-199. Some teach they are two different men, e.g. John Walvoord (*The Revelation of Jesus Christ*, pp. 210-211) and David Jeremiah (*What in the World is Going On?* pp. 142-143).
[323] Ibid, pp. 79-80.
[324] *Gotta Serve Somebody*, pp. 65-68.

Paul specifically notes the Antichrist will be attested by supernatural signs and wonders:

> ...that is, the one whose coming is in accord with the activity of Satan, with all power and signs and false wonders, and with all the deception of wickedness for those who perish, because they did not receive the love of the truth so as to be saved. (2 Thess 2:9-10)

He is 'the man of lawlessness' (2 Thess 2:3) because he accepts no laws but his own, the ultimate rebel against God; he is 'the son of destruction' (2 Thess 2:3), the term Jesus applied to Judas (John 17:12), because he is willing to destroy anything and everything.

Seated in the Temple

He will not be shy. Paul continues:

> ...who opposes and exalts himself above every so-called god or object of worship, so that he takes his seat in the temple of God, *displaying himself as being God*. (2 Thess 2:4*)

As we often do, we have to decide between a literal or metaphorical reading of this 'temple of God'.

If the Antichrist is to seat himself in a literal one, Israel will first have to build it, their Third.[325] Many are therefore expecting the Antichrist to make a seven-year peace treaty with Israel, allow them to rebuild the temple, and restore the Mosaic sacrificial system. They then expect him to break this treaty after three and a half years and "put a stop to sacrifice and grain offering" (Dan 9:27).[326]

---

325 The First (959-586 BC) was Solomon's; the Second (516 BC-70 AD) was built by the returnees from the Babylonian exile and beautified by Herod the Great.
326 E.g. Dispensationalist teachers such as Dr David Jeremiah, *What in the World is Going On?* p. 157.

However, as I showed in Book 1[327] and recap in Appendix B of this book, Daniel's 70th Week predicts the work of Jesus, not the Antichrist. Accordingly, there is no need for the Third Temple to be built except to fulfill Paul's prophecy to the Thessalonians in a literal temple.

If on the other hand Paul was speaking metaphorically, he could mean the church of God, which Peter called God's 'spiritual house', built of 'living stones' (1 Pet 2:5). This could mean the Antichrist will be a deceptive Christian leader, emerging out of the apostasy. I remain open to that as we wait to see but I believe he will be a Muslim leader[328] - Islam already controls one third of all the nations, claims the Temple Mount as their third holiest site, and has the armies to invade any time.

I believe Paul means the Antichrist will follow in the footsteps of Satan's proud boast:

> 13. "But you said in your heart, 'I will ascend to heaven;
> I will raise *my throne* above the stars of God,
> And *I will sit* on the mount of assembly
> In the recesses of the north.
> 14. 'I will ascend above the heights of the clouds;
> I will make myself like the Most High.'"
> (Isa 14:13-14*)

Satan fulfilled this in the Garden not by literally sitting on God's throne but by persuading Adam and Eve to submit to his tempting rather than obey God's command.[329] Paul applies this metaphor of sitting to us as believers:

> 4. But God, being rich in mercy, because of His great love with which He loved us,
> 5. even when we were dead in our transgressions, made us alive together with Christ...,

---

327 *Dancing in the Dragon's Jaws*, pp. 102-106.
328 Some believe he will emerge from the apostasy but none of the antichrists in the 20th century did.
329 See my *Because of the Angels*, pp. 53-67.

6. and raised us up with Him, and *seated us with Him in the heavenly places* in Christ Jesus… (Eph 2:4-6*)

In case we are in any doubt as to our place, Paul adds 'where Christ is, seated at the right hand of God' (Col 3:1). We are not sitting on the literal throne of God – we are seated with Him metaphorically, reigning with Him as 'royal priests' (1 Pet 2:9) as we carry out His will.

Recapitulating Prophecies

The nearest any Roman leader came to sitting in the Jerusalem Temple was Pompey's entering the Holy of Holies in 63 BC but he neither sat down nor claimed divine status.

However, by 9 BC, from Augustus on,[330] Roman emperors did allow their images to be worshipped. As noted in Book 2,[331] the victorious Roman legions in 70 AD burned incense before standards bearing the image of Vespasian in the courts of the Temple. Some have therefore taken this as fulfilling Jesus' prophecy forty years earlier, where He quoted Daniel:

> "Therefore when you see the ABOMINATION OF DESOLATION which was spoken of through Daniel the prophet, *standing in the holy place* (let the reader understand)…" (Matt 24:15*)

There was and is only one holy place on earth for Jesus' Jewish audience – Jerusalem. Mark phrases it slightly differently for a Gentile audience:

> "…when you see the ABOMINATION OF DESOLATION *standing where it should not be* (let the reader understand)…" (Mark 13:14*)

I believe that 70 AD was indeed a fulfilment but, as I showed in Book 2, there have been five[332] 'abominations of desolation'

---

330 *Slouching Towards Bethlehem*, pp. 114-115.
331 Ibid, pp. 205, 277-278.
332 These were: 1. The misuse of the Ark of the Covenant, causing the desolation of Shiloh (c. 1050 BC); 2. The misuse of the First Temple,

in Israel; I believe the sixth will be the appearance of the Antichrist in Jerusalem, claiming to be the Christ.

We will also see a recapitulation[333] of Jesus' prophecy about the siege of Jerusalem:

> "But when you see Jerusalem surrounded by armies, then recognize that her desolation is near... there will be great distress upon the land and wrath to this people; and they will fall by the edge of the sword, and will be led captive into all the nations... (Luke 21:20, 23-24)

Obviously, this was fulfilled in 66-70 AD but Jerusalem will again be "surrounded by armies" when "all the nations" gather for 'the war of the great day of God, the Almighty', at Har-Magedon. This time, however, there will be an altogether different outcome – this time, as described in Chapter 5, Israel will have our returning Lord Jesus overcoming all. Matthew and Mark inserted 'let the reader understand' to refer the reader to Daniel's prophecies (Dan 9:27, 11:31, 12:11) as predicting the Crucifixion.

However, if Jesus' prophecies of the abomination and the siege are to be fulfilled twice, that would be perfectly consistent with the two comings of the spirit of Elijah, the two comings of Messiah, and the two Days of Judgement, as spelled out in Book 1.[334] This recapitulation of all of these prophecies with very different outcomes each time surely requires the reader to apply themselves to understand it all.

If the Antichrist is the Muslim Mahdi, with the Muslims already controlling the Temple Mount in Jerusalem, he could appear there at any time.

---

causing the desolation of Jerusalem (586 BC); 3. The misuse of the Second Temple, causing its desecration (167 BC); 4. The crucifixion of Jesus, the living Temple of God (30 AD), causing the desolation of Jerusalem (70 AD); 5. The misuse of the Second Temple in 68 AD, also causing the desolation of Jerusalem (70 AD). Ibid, pp. 265-283.
333 Recapitulation is repetition in a pattern or recurring theme and prophecies can have several fulfilments.
334 *Dancing in the Dragon's Jaws*, pp. 129-130.

This, I believe, will begin the last hour and the first casualty will be Babylon the Great.

Summary of the Antichrist

(i) 'The man of lawlessness', the Antichrist, will be the last in the long line of antichrists and will appear just before Jesus returns.

(ii) His taking 'his seat in the temple of God, displaying himself as being God' could be literal, which would require the rebuilding of the Temple in Jerusalem. However, this expression is used as a metaphor in Isaiah's description of Satan's usurping of God's rule over Adam and Eve and in Paul's description of all believers reigning with Jesus.

(iii) Paul's prediction could therefore be fulfilled at any time by the Muslims' Mahdi proclaiming himself on the Temple Mount with supernatural signs and wonders.

13
"One Hour"
And It's Over

We come now to the demise of three of the seven main characters in the drama of Revelation: the two beasts and the woman, Babylon the Great.

John wrote in his first letter:

> Do not love the world nor the things in the world.... For all that is in the world, the lust of the flesh and the lust of the eyes and the boastful pride of life, is not from the Father, but is from the world. *The world is passing away*, and also its lusts; but the one who does the will of God lives forever. (1 John 2:15-17*)

Here in Revelation, he describes that world's 'passing away' like a razed city but also personified as Babylon the Great, devoured and burned.

Babylon's Last Hour

The powerful will mourn her strength going so quickly:

> 9. "And the kings of the earth... will weep and lament over her when they see the smoke of her burning,
> 10. ...saying, 'Woe, woe, the great city, Babylon, *the strong city*! For *in one hour* your judgment has come.'"
> (Rev 18:9-10 *)

The rich merchants of "all things that were luxurious and splendid" (18:14) will mourn so much wealth being destroyed in a moment:

> 15. "The merchants of these things, who became rich from her, ... weeping and mourning,
> 16. saying, 'Woe, woe, the great city, she who was clothed

> in fine linen and purple and scarlet, and adorned with gold and precious stones and pearls;
> 17. for *in one hour* such *great wealth* has been laid waste!'"
> (Rev 18:15-17*)

Every traveller on every sea, who would have seen every great city on every coast, will also marvel at the speed of her destruction:

> 17. "...And every *shipmaster* and every *passenger* and *sailor*...
> 19. ...crying out, weeping and mourning, saying, 'Woe, woe, the great city, in which all who had ships at sea became rich by her wealth, for in *one hour* she has been laid waste!' (Rev 18:17-19*)

Travellers in the ancient world were the only ones who personally experienced other lands and cultures - as they say, travel broadens the mind. The angel Gabriel told Daniel:

> "But as for you, Daniel, conceal these words and seal up the book until the end of time; many will *go back and forth*, and *knowledge will increase*." (Dan 12:4*)

In the 17th and 18th centuries, young upper-class Englishmen completed their education with the Grand Tour of Europe to experience the cultural legacy of classical antiquity, see the masterpieces of art and sculpture, and listen to the music. Rail and steamship eventually made tourism available to all and with today's air travel, most of us have travelled abroad.

All this will be gone in "one hour".[335]

Heaven and all believers, however, will be overjoyed because they know all too well the terrible cost of her extravagance:

> 20. "Rejoice over her, O heaven, and you saints and apostles and prophets, because God has pronounced judgment for you against her."
> 21. Then a strong angel took up a stone like a great

---

[335] All the talents God gave us, being 'gold, silver, and precious stones' (1 Cor 3:12), will be refined and at last properly employed and appreciated in the coming kingdom.

millstone and threw it into the sea, saying, "So will Babylon, the great city, be thrown down with violence, and will not be found any longer." (Rev 18:20-21)

How will it happen?

The Beasts' Last Hour

The Chinese have a proverb that he who rides a tiger can never dismount. Babylon the Great revels in her power and the beast she rides but she vastly overestimates her safety. She is riding a *therion*, a wild and ravaging beast, and John sees that in that hour, it will turn on her:

> 12. "The ten horns which you saw are ten kings who have not yet received a kingdom, but they receive authority as kings with the beast for *one hour*…
> 16. "And the ten horns which you saw, and the beast, these will hate the harlot and will make her desolate and naked, and will *eat her flesh* and will *burn* her up with fire. (Rev 17:12 & 16*)

When the ten kings of the seventh head unite and hand their authority to the beast, it will strip, eat, and burn her.

This judgement on Babylon the Great was not a new metaphor to John's Jewish audience. When Ezekiel prophesied against the kingdoms of Israel and Judah, he described their capital cities, Samaria and Jerusalem, as two women who lusted after and became lovers to the Egyptian, Assyrian, and Babylonian empires (Ezek 23:2-16). God responded to Israel by withdrawing His protection:

> "Therefore, I gave her into the hand of her lovers, into the hand of the Assyrians, after whom she lusted." (Ezek 23:9)

Similarly, with Judah:

> 22. "Behold I will arouse your lovers against you, from whom you were alienated, and I will bring them against you from every side:

> 23. the Babylonians and all the Chaldeans, …and all the Assyrians with them…
> 24. "They will come against you with weapons, chariots and wagons, and with a company of peoples… and *I will commit the judgment to them*, and they will judge you according to their customs." (Ezek 23:22-24*)

Ezekiel describes these 'customs' and 'judgements' of the Assyrians and the Babylonians:

> 26. "'They will also strip you of your clothes and take away your beautiful jewels…
> 29. "They will deal with you in hatred, take all your property, and leave you naked and bare…
> 30. "These things will be done to you because you have played the *harlot with the nations*, because you have defiled yourself with their idols." (Ezek 23:26-30*)

John's vision of the ten horns and the beast in the last hour devouring Babylon the Great would also have reminded the Jewish disciples of Elijah's prophecy against the wicked queen Jezebel – she was thrown down, trampled underfoot, and eaten by dogs (2 Kin 9:33-37).[336]

"Gone With the Wind"

Babylon the Great is also to be "burned up with fire" by the ten kingdoms (Rev 17:16).

It is easy to understand cities like Samaria, Jerusalem, and Rome being destroyed by fire but what about a spiritual city like 'the world'? What exactly will be destroyed?

> 16. For all that is in the world, *the lust of the flesh* and *the lust of the eyes* and *the boastful pride of life*, is not from the Father, but is from the world.
> 17. The world is *passing away*, and also *its lusts*; but the one who does the will of God lives forever. (1 John 2:16-17*)

---

[336] Many years ago I heard Dr Derek Prince teaching that Israel's wickedest king and queen, Ahab and Jezebel, foreshadow the Antichrist and Babylon the Great. The image has never left me.

This world's value systems, treasures, and pleasures will all pass away with the old material world to be replaced by a new heaven and a new earth, which we will consider in Book 7, *Kingdom Come*.

Author Margaret Mitchell (1900-1949) used a similar metaphor in her Pulitzer-prize winning novel about the American Civil War, *Gone with the Wind*. Her heroine Scarlett O'Hara is a southern belle who has lived the high life of society parties in the Old South, dressed and served by slaves. As the war comes to an end, she wonders if her plantation home is still standing or if it has "gone with the wind which had swept through Georgia". Her house has survived but what has gone is her whole way of life. Her friend Ashley Wilkes sums it up:

> I do mind, very much, the loss of the beauty of the old life I loved. Scarlett, before the war, life was beautiful. There was a glamor to it, a perfection and a completeness and a symmetry to it like Grecian art. Maybe it wasn't so to everyone. I know that now… Now, I know that in the old days it was a shadow show I watched. I avoided everything which was not shadowy, people and situations which were too real, too vital. I resented their intrusion.[337]

"The wind" was the victorious Union army; Scarlett and Ashley's swept away world was the value systems, treasures, and pleasures enjoyed only by the white population of the Old South.

"Paradise" Lost?

In 1990, BBC documentary-maker Lawrence Rees asked Wilfred von Oven, a former member of the Nazi Party, for his overall impression of the Third Reich. Mr Rees expected that, with the benefit of fifty years' hindsight…:

---

[337] Margaret Mitchell, *Gone with the Wind*, Penguin, 2020.

...this intelligent and charming man [would refer] to the horrible crimes of the regime – crimes he freely admitted had occurred – and the damage Nazism had wreaked upon the world. "Well", he finally said, "if I was asked to sum up my experience of the Third Reich in one word, that word would be – Paradise".

"Paradise"? That didn't coincide with anything I had read in my history books. Nor did it square with the elegant, sophisticated man who sat in front of me, who did not, come to that, look or talk as I had imagined a former Nazi should. But "Paradise"? How was it possible he could say such a thing? How could any intelligent person think of the Third Reich and its atrocities in such a way?[338]

Mr Rees, however, was overlooking Hitler's achievements which even Winston Churchill, his greatest and bitterest enemy, acknowledged in 1935:

> [Hitler] has succeeded in restoring Germany to the most powerful position in Europe, and not only has he restored the position of his country, but he has even, to a very great extent, reversed the results of the Great War.... When Hitler began, Germany lay prostrate at the feet of the Allies. He may yet see the day when what is left of Europe will be prostrate at the feet of Germany. Whatever else may be thought about these exploits, they are certainly among the most remarkable in the whole history of the world.[339]

David Lloyd George, the British Prime Minister, visited Germany the following year and reported:

> It is not the Germany of the first decade that followed the war - broken, dejected and bowed down with a sense of apprehension and impotence. It is now full of hope and confidence, and of a renewed sense of determination to lead its own life… One man has accomplished this miracle. He is a born leader of men. A magnetic and

---

338 Lawrence Rees, *Auschwitz: The Nazis and the Final Solution*, London; BBC Books, 2005, p. 7.
339 https://winstonchurchill.org/publications/finest-hour/finest-hour-156/the-truth-about-hitler-1935-hitler-and-his-choice-1937/, 25 Mar, 2022.

dynamic personality with a single-minded purpose, a resolute will and a dauntless heart... I have never met a happier people than the Germans and Hitler is one of the greatest men. The old trust him; the young idolise him. It is the worship of a national hero who has saved his country.[340]

Hitler had enacted Keynesian[341] economic theory:

Germany's economic recovery, which was complete by 1936... was caused mainly by lavish expenditure on public works, particularly on motor roads, and this public spending stimulated private spending also, as Keynes had said it would.[342]

General Dwight D. Eisenhower, Supreme Commander of Europe after World War II, was so impressed by the autobahns that when he became president, he replicated them in the USA, creating their first interstate highway system.

Hitler also rebuilt the military and improved conditions for workers, instituting a five-day working week, subsidised international holidays, theatre attendance, and concerts. He set up national health care, unemployment insurance, and education standards, and every citizen was given a radio, the better to hear his propaganda.

For a few years, Nazi Germany was Paradise for many until he led the nation into the catastrophe of World War II and the horror of the Holocaust. His final orders before committing suicide were to 'scorch the earth', to annihilate the entire infrastructure of Germany and punish the German people for failing him.[343]

---

340 David Lloyd George, British Prime Minister, *The Daily Express*, 17 Sep,1936.
341 Named for British economist John Maynard Keynes (1883-1946).
342 A. J. P. Taylor, *From Sarajevo to Potsdam*, Orlando, FA; Harcourt Brace Jovanovich, 1975, p. 140.
343 Hitler's "Scorched Earth" Decree, or Nero Decree (March 19, 1945) and Albert Speer's Response (March 29, 1945). https://ghdi.ghi-dc.org/pdf/eng/English_100.pdf, 25 Mar, 2022.

Burning Babylon the Great

In America's Civil War and Germany's defeat, we see the end of their 'worlds', the values, treasures, and pleasures destroyed by the war brought on by the very leaders who had led them to greatness.

In the same way, when all "the kings of the earth" lead all the nations to war against Israel, they will have achieved an extraordinary unity, a unity of purpose not seen since the Tower of Babel (Gen 11:1-4). They will delight in the self-righteousness of their cause, passed without a single veto in the Security Council of the United Nations, but they will be leading the armies of "all the nations" directly into the wrath of God.

In so doing, all "the kings" who have loved Babylon the Great will actually cause her downfall, initially standing back as if innocent spectators lest they be dragged in:

> 9. "And the kings of the earth, who committed acts of immorality and lived sensuously with her, will weep and lament over her when they see the smoke of her burning, 10. *standing at a distance because of the fear of her torment,* saying, 'Woe, woe, the great city, Babylon, the strong city! For in *one hour* your judgment has come.'" (Rev 18:9-10*)

They do not seem to realise her "one hour" (v. 10) is also theirs and it is they, together with the beast, who are devouring and destroying her with fire before they too are judged.

...But Unforgettable

All who love the world will mourn her passing but John hears a great multitude in heaven shouting for joy because they remember her crimes:

> "Hallelujah! Salvation and glory and power belong to our God because His judgments are true and righteous; for He has judged the great harlot who was corrupting the earth

with her immorality, and He has avenged the blood of His bond-servants on her." (Rev 19:2)

She, her immorality and murderous reign, will never be forgotten:

> And a second time they said, "Hallelujah! *Her smoke* rises up *forever and ever.*" (Rev 19:3*)

This is really important - what smoke? When anything material burns, eventually all that is left is ashes and a last wisp of smoke before that too ceases. Isaiah, however, also prophesied of everlasting smoke after God judges "all the nations" and "utterly destroys all their armies" (Isa 34:2) which, as we saw in Chapter 4 will be the battle of Har-Magedon. He writes of Edom:

> 9. ... its land will become burning pitch.
> 10. It will not be quenched night or day;
> *Its smoke will go up forever.*
> From generation to generation it will be desolate;
> None will pass through it forever and ever.
> (Isa 34:10*)

Smoke that "rises up forever and ever" signifies an everlasting memorial of this fiery judgement, that a great battle has taken place and been forever lost.

We will consider this further in Book 7, *Kingdom Come*, when we come to the lake of fire.

Assembling for War

In executing God's judgement on Babylon the Great, the two beasts also come to the end of their reign at Har-Magedon:

> 19. And I saw the beast and the kings of the earth and their armies assembled to make war against Him who sat on the horse and against His army (Rev 19:19)

The Battle of Har-Magedon will not be long. Zechariah's

awful description of Israel's enemies rotting where they stand (Zech 14:12-15) are thought by some to portray nuclear warfare but I believe supernatural fire more likely, as Paul wrote to the Thessalonians:

> ...the Lord Jesus will be revealed from heaven with His mighty angels in flaming fire, dealing out retribution to those who do not know God... (2 Thess 1:7-8)

John too saw His return:

> 11. And I saw heaven opened, and behold, a white horse, and He who sat on it is called Faithful and True, and in righteousness He judges and wages war.
> 12. His eyes are a flame of fire, and on His head are many diadems...
> 14. And the armies which are in heaven, clothed in fine linen, white and clean, were following Him on white horses. (Rev 19:11-14)

Jesus' only weapon is on His lips, words that created the heavens and the earth:

> 15. From *His mouth comes a sharp sword*, so that with it He may strike down the nations, and He will rule them with a rod of iron; and He treads the wine press of the fierce wrath of God, the Almighty. (Rev 19:15*)

Judging the Beasts

How long will all this take? The battle will be over before it even starts for the two beasts of Revelation 13:

> 20. And *the beast* was seized, and with him *the false prophet* who performed the signs in his presence, by which he deceived those who had received the mark of the beast and those who worshiped his image; these two were thrown alive into the lake of fire which burns with brimstone... (Rev 19:20*)

What exactly will be accomplished in this judgement?

(i) The beast

This is the first beast of Revelation 13 and is the 'principality and power' of the Gentile empires that had, were, and would rule over the people of Israel throughout their many-storied 4,000 year history. It will be judged in its final incarnation of the seventh head with ten horns.

As I showed in Book 3,[344] the number seven as a metaphor means 'justly, completely, perfectly'; in Book 2,[345] I showed that the number ten as a metaphor means 'numerous, all, every, complete, whole, and fullness'. The beast is therefore being judged when it finally consists of "all the nations" uniting for one last futile attack on Israel. We see then that in the Battle of Har-magedon, God will be judging "all the nations", principalities, and powers. We will look at the effect of this in the next chapter and more fully in Book 7, *Kingdom Come*.

Being a principality and power, however, means it is neither a human nor an angelic being but the culmination of 'all rule and all authority and power', as Paul explained to the Corinthians:

> 24. then comes the end, when He hands over the kingdom to the God and Father, when He has abolished *all rule* and *all authority and power*.
> 25. For He must reign until He has put all His enemies under His feet.
> 26. The last enemy that will be abolished is death.
> (1 Cor 15:24-26*)

Only death will be left to be abolished (v. 26), when everyone who has ever died will be raised to life to be judged.

---

344 *Gotta Serve Somebody*, p. 147.
345 *Slouching Towards Bethlehem*, pp. 36-39.

(ii) 'The false prophet'

There are actually two to be judged here, one spirit and one human, i.e. the spirit of antichrist and the Antichrist.

As I showed in Book 2,[346] the second beast of Revelation 13 which looks 'like a lamb' but speaks 'as a dragon' (Rev 13:11) is the spirit of antichrist. Being a spirit, it has been able to deceive its hearers since the 1st century up to the present, enticing them to deify and worship their political and religious leaders instead of Christ. I also showed in Books 2[347] and 3[348] how this phenomenon of 'the false prophet' was allowed by God throughout Israel's long history as the ultimate test of each generation's love for Him, and foreshadowed the fourth mark of the beast.

Here in the last battle, the testing has reached its climax in human history so the spirit can be judged and the phenomenon of 'the false prophet' will come to an end.

As for the Antichrist, the last human to be raised up by the spirit of antichrist, he will die along with the flesh and blood armies:

> And the rest were killed with the sword which came from the mouth of Him who sat on the horse, and all the birds were filled with their flesh. (Rev 19:21)

We see then that while the two beasts are immediately judged and 'thrown alive into the lake of fire' (Rev 19:20), their human allies, including the Antichrist, will be resurrected to be judged with their eternal destiny individually decided (Rev 20:12). We will look at this in Book 7.

Lastly, this is also the judgement that Daniel saw:

> "Then I kept looking because of the sound of the boastful words which the [eleventh] horn was speaking; I kept looking until the beast was slain, and its body was destroyed and given to the burning fire." (Dan 7:11, clarification inserted)

---

346 Ibid, pp. 74-83.
347 Ibid, pp. 78-80.
348 *Gotta Serve Somebody*, pp. 65-68, 86.

As I established in Book 2,[349] Daniel's eleventh horn is John's second beast, the spirit of antichrist, and he too sees both beasts being slain and burned.

Predetermined Plans

When Jesus was arrested in 30 AD, He went willingly, saying to the chief priests, officers, and elders:

> "...this hour and the power of darkness are yours."
> (Luke 22:53*)

He knew the exact time, plan, and purpose of God behind His imminent death. The apostle John recorded numerous references to Jesus' 'hour' (John 2:4, 7:30, 8:20), 12:23, 12:27, 13:1) before He finally prayed at the Last Supper:

> "Father, the hour has come; glorify Your Son, that the Son may glorify You" (John 17:1)

As Peter explained on the Day of Pentecost:

> "Men of Israel, listen to these words: Jesus the Nazarene…, delivered over by *the predetermined plan* and *foreknowledge of God*, you nailed to a cross by the hands of godless men and put Him to death." (Acts 2:22-23*)

No one's freewill was violated because God foreknew and worked with everyone's own sinful agendas, choices, and actions. In Book 2, I wrote of how we all, Jews and Gentiles, had a part in it:

> Peter begins with God's sovereignty. Jesus has always been the Passover Lamb of God, known and slain before the foundation of the world (1 Pet 1:19-20). With His "foreknowledge", God's "predetermined plan" was always to use this terrible sin both of "the men of Israel" (executing Jesus for blasphemy for claiming to be their Messiah) and of the "godless men" (the Roman soldiers) to save us all, if we will accept that He died for us.[350]

---

349 *Slouching Towards Bethlehem*, pp. 69-73.
350 Ibid, p. 275.

This was His 'hidden wisdom', that even today we can still cooperate with His "predetermined plan" by trusting in Jesus as His provision in that 1st century hour:

> 7. ...we speak God's wisdom in a mystery, the hidden wisdom which God predestined before the ages to our glory;
> 8. the wisdom which none of *the rulers of this age* has understood; for if they had understood it they would not have crucified the Lord of glory (1 Cor 2:7-8*)

'The rulers of this age' who crucified Jesus were not just the Roman and Jewish authorities in 30 AD; they included Satan who did not understand that his bruising the woman's Seed on His heel would cause Jesus to bruise his head (Gen 3:15), the oldest Messianic prophecy.

Now here in the last hour, the tables are turned. Now it is the hour for Babylon the Great and the two beasts to be judged, according to "the predetermined plan and foreknowledge of God... by the hands of godless men", and the return of Jesus as Lord of all:

> 13. "...And behold, with the clouds of heaven
> One like a Son of Man was coming,
> And He came up to the Ancient of Days
> And was presented before Him.
> 14. "And to Him was given dominion,
> Glory and a kingdom,
> That all the peoples, nations and men of every language might serve Him.
> His dominion is an everlasting dominion
> Which will not pass away;
> And His kingdom is one
> Which will not be destroyed."
> (Dan 7:13-14)

Summary

(i) The end of 'the world', i.e. Babylon the Great, will come in just "one hour", i.e. a very short time. Those trusting in their own power, riches, education, and knowledge of the world will be astonished and appalled.

(ii) Assembling for Har-Magedon, the ten horns of "all the nations" will not destroy Israel as they intend but instead they will destroy this world ruled by Satan and mankind. However, Babylon the Great will never be forgotten - the smoke of her judgement "rises up forever and ever".

(iii) The two beasts of Revelation 13 – the principality of the feral State and the spirit of antichrist - will be judged immediately but the Antichrist and their armies will die and await judgement.

(iv) The battle will be over before it even starts – the armies simply have to assemble.

(v) Just as the Crucifixion was according to the predetermined plan and foreknowledge of God incorporating the freely chosen plans of men and angels, so too will be the last hour of Babylon the Great, her dreadful steed, and the Antichrist. The Son of Man will receive His everlasting kingdom and usher in the new heavens and new earth, as we will see in Book 7, *Kingdom Come*.

14
God's Eternal Purpose
Back to Eden

We now come to the climax - what was the point of it all? Paul explains it is...:

> 10. so that the *manifold wisdom* of God might now be made known through the church to the rulers and the authorities in the heavenly places.
> 11. This was in accordance with the *eternal purpose* which He carried out in Christ Jesus our Lord... (Eph 3:10-11*)

So much in so few words. What is His 'manifold wisdom' and 'eternal purpose'? Why 'through the church', and why 'to the rulers and the authorities in the heavenly places'? We need to answer the last question first.

(i) 'To the rulers and authorities'

The heavenly rulers and authorities could already see, as we all can, God's invisible power and nature in the visible realm:

> For since the creation of the world His invisible attributes, His *eternal power* and *divine nature*, have been clearly seen, being understood through what has been made... (Rom 1:20*)

However, as Kenneth Wuest points out, ever since Creation the angels:

> ...have been contemplating the majesty and glory of the Godhead... and yet have not learned some things regarding the Creator that the Church can teach them... The angels never had a conception of the *love*, the *grace*, the *humility*, the *self-sacrifice* of God until they saw it in the Church.

There they see Calvary where the Creator died, the Just for the unjust.[351]

(ii) 'Through the church'

The Church reveals His personality, His astonishing humility, selflessness, and kindness:

> There they see the incarnation where the Creator took to Himself the form and limitation of a created being. There they saw the power of God in transforming a sinful human being into the image of God's dear son, manifestation of power far greater than that which operated in the creation of the universe. God spoke a universe into being by uttering a word. *It took Calvary to make possible the Church.* Thus the Church provides a university course for angels. How they watch us. How they wonder at us. Beings lower than angels and the scale of creation, raised in Christ to beings higher than angels, into the family of God.[352]

Peter confirms that salvation is such a great mystery that even the prophets who announced 'the sufferings of Christ and the glories to follow' had to wait patiently:

> It was revealed to them that they were not serving themselves, but you, in these things which now have been announced to you through those who preached the gospel to you by the Holy Spirit sent from heaven - things into which *angels long to look*. (1 Pet 1:12*)

Even if we have not recognised this revelation in our churches, the angelic majesties have seen it and marvelled at it.

(iii) 'Manifold Wisdom'

When Paul first preached in Greece, his Greek audience believed that our primary need is wisdom but he preached

---

351 Kenneth S. Wuest, *Golden Nuggets from the Greek New Testament*, Grand Rapids; Wm. B. Eedermans, 1973, pp. 32-33. Emphasis added.
352 Ibid.*

'God's wisdom', a manifold wisdom:

> 6. Yet we do speak wisdom among those who are mature; a wisdom, however, not of this age nor of the rulers of this age, who are passing away;
> 7. But we speak *God's wisdom* in a mystery, the hidden wisdom…
> 8. …which none of the rulers of this age has understood; for if they had understood it they would not have crucified the Lord of glory. (1 Cor 2:6-8*)

At the time, 'the rulers of this age' were both human and demonic, i.e. the Jewish and Roman authorities and Satan and his angels. None of them understood it then. And why?

> 27. …God has chosen the foolish things of the world to shame the wise, and God has chosen the weak things of the world to shame the things which are strong,
> 28. and the base things of the world and the despised God has chosen, the things that are not, so that He may nullify the things that are,
> 29. so that no man may boast before God. (1 Cor 1:27-29)

God's goal has always been to humble us so He can give us grace.

His extraordinary patience and manifold wisdom is also to be seen in the Church coming out the apostasy to 'the faith which was once for all delivered to the saints' (Jude v. 3), as described in Chapter 12, *and* in Israel coming to accept Jesus as their Messiah too, as described in Chapter 5.

(iv) 'His Eternal Purpose'

Paul explained His purpose to the Romans:

> 28. And we know that God causes all things to work together for good to those who love God, to those who are called according to *His purpose*.
> 29. For those whom He foreknew, He also predestined

> to become *conformed to* the image of *His Son,* so that He would be the firstborn among many brethren (Rom 8:28-29*)

God's purpose has always been and always will be that we are like Jesus, that we are fit to be His children.

'Every Tribe and Tongue'

His love and desire for us to be His children is for 'every tribe and tongue and people and nation' (Rev 5:9). Jesus said He would not return until everyone has been invited into His kingdom:

> "This gospel of the kingdom shall be preached in the whole world as a testimony to *all the nations,* and then the end will come." (Matt 24:14*)

It does seem to have been now. He also gave them a parable that is easily overlooked:

> Then He told them a parable: "Behold *the fig tree* and *all the trees;* as soon as they put forth leaves, you see it and know for yourselves that summer is now near. So you also, when you see these things happening, recognize that the kingdom of God is near. Truly I say to you, this generation will not pass away until all things take place." (Luke 21:29-32*)

This can seem like a simple illustration of spring heralding the coming of summer but, as I established in Book 1,[353] the fig tree can also symbolise Israel 'according to the flesh',[354] just as the olive tree can symbolise spiritual Israel (Rom 11:17). Seen in this light, the fig tree putting forth leaves can be seen as Israel being restored to their land, as it

---

353 *Dancing in the Dragon's Jaws,* pp. 55-61.
354 This explains Jesus' earlier parable of the owner of a fig tree looking for fruit from it after three years and cutting it down in the fourth (Luke 13:6-9) – as the vineyard-keeper, He had been ministering in Israel for three years for very little fruit but wanted one last season. It also explains Jesus' cursing the fruitless fig tree on His way to die in Jerusalem, even though it was 'not the season for figs' (Mark 11:13).

was in 1948 – not spiritual Israel but ethnic Israel, 'according to the flesh' and not yet believing in Jesus. And it is not just the fig tree but "all the trees" which are to "put forth leaves" (vv. 29-30) i.e. "all the nations" as well.

As I see it, this is being fulfilled in Aotearoa-New Zealand by the renaissance of our Maori people's culture and language and in many other countries over the last hundred years. The breaking up of the European empires and the decolonisation that began after World Wars 1 and 2 caused the spread of liberal democracy to over half the nations of the world and a subsequent resurgence of indigenous languages and cultures everywhere. The dismantling of the USSR thirty years ago is bearing similar fruit, despite President Putin's present attempts to overturn that.

We see then that as the gospel penetrates the last corners of the earth until 'the fullness of the Gentiles has come in' (Rom 11:25), as described in Book 1,[355] Jesus will be glorified in every culture and in every language on the earth before He returns:

> And they sang a new song, saying, "Worthy are You to take the book and to break its seals; for You were slain, and purchased for God with Your blood men from *every tribe and tongue and people and nation!*" (Rev 5:9*)

Selah.[356]

Back to the Garden

Revelation 16-19 describes the last hour of Babylon the Great and all the kingdoms of the world – all that is left to be judged is Satan and his angels (Rev 20:10, Matt 25:41) and every single human being, living or dead (Rev 20:11-13), and finally death itself (Rev 20:14).

---

355 *Dancing in the Dragon's Jaws*, pp. 172-177.
356 A Hebrew expression calling for a pause or an interlude for thought.

Everything else will have been judged. As Paul explained the timing:

> 24. then comes the end, when He hands over the kingdom to the God and Father, when He has abolished *all rule and all authority and power*.
> 25. For He must reign until He has put all His enemies under His feet.
> 26. The last enemy that will be abolished is death.
> (1 Cor 15:24-26*)

We have been looking at the end of John's first beast, the feral principality that will soon direct all the nations against Israel, but when Jesus abolishes 'all rule and all authority and power' (v. 24), that includes even those that have remained domesticated and served us well. Liberal democracy, for example, has maximised individual freedom while restraining corruption in our fallen world.[357]

However, when Jesus returns, no 'rule', 'authority' or 'power' of any kind will be necessary. We will have returned to God's original intention in Eden, when Adam and Eve were self-governing.

Paul compared Adam and Jesus, 'the second man':

> 47. The first man is from the earth, earthy; *the second man* is from heaven.
> 48. As is the earthy, so also are those who are earthy; and as is the heavenly, so also are those who are heavenly.
> 49. Just as we have borne the image of the earthy, *we will* also bear the image of the heavenly. (1 Cor 15:47-49*)

Jesus lived His whole life on earth perfectly self-governing in the love and wisdom of God and John assures us:

> Beloved, now we are children of God, and it has not appeared as yet what we will be. We know that when He appears, *we will be like Him*, because we will see Him just as He is. (1 John 3:2*)

---

357 I will cover this properly in *The Pearl in Plain Sight: The Kingdom, Christendom & Colonisation*.

Everything Necessary

Not only will we be like Him but we will know immeasurably more:

> 12. For now we see in a mirror dimly, but then face to face; now I know in part, but then I will know fully just as I also have been fully known.
> 13. But now faith, hope, love, abide these three; but the greatest of these is love. (1 Cor 13:12-13)

All that will be necessary, the three essentials that will 'abide', or remain, as we move into eternity, is faith, hope, and love. Like Adam and Eve at Creation, we will always need all three.

We will, however, all know all too well the consequences of choosing our own way – the smoke of Babylon the Great ascending "forever and ever" will remind us (Rev 19:3). We will all have seen the best and the worst that mankind and angels were ever able to achieve in governing without God.

Like Jesus in the New Creation, we will still have free-will but our choices of faith, hope, and love will be based on seeing Him 'face to face' and, after Judgement Day, on finally seeing fully, knowing fully everything that has ever happened:

> "...for there is nothing concealed that will not be revealed, or hidden that will not be known." (Matt 10:26)

We will consider this further in Book 7, *Kingdom Come*.

Be Ready

In the meantime, we need to be ready and stay ready. As Jesus warned, many will not be:

> 26. "And just as it happened in the days of Noah, so it will be also in the days of the Son of Man:
> 27. they were eating, they were drinking, they were marrying, they were being given in marriage, until the

day that Noah entered the ark, and the flood came and destroyed them all. (Luke 17:26-27)

Ignoring Noah's warnings before the Flood (2 Pet 2:5), they went about their daily lives. So too in Lot's day:

> 28. "It was the same as happened in the days of Lot: they were eating, they were drinking, they were buying, they were selling, they were planting, they were building;
> 29. but on the day that Lot went out from Sodom it rained fire and brimstone from heaven and destroyed them all.
> 30. "It will be just the same on the day that the Son of Man is revealed." (Luke 17:28-29)

We can be certain that Jesus is coming and it will not be long:

> 12. "Behold, I am coming quickly, and My reward is with Me, to render to every man according to what he has done.
> 13. "I am the Alpha and the Omega, the first and the last, the beginning and the end."
> 14. Blessed are those who wash their robes, so that they may have the right to the tree of life, and may enter by the gates into the city. (Rev 22:12-14)

Amen!

Epilogue

Today, Satan understands that he has failed and he does not have much time left because this is the hour of threshing for his two beasts and his dominion, Babylon the Great. In this book covering Revelation 16:13 to 19:21, I have shown that this means:

> (i) The end of the first beast, i.e. the feral principality and power of the self-exalting State.

It will be in its final manifestation as the seventh head when all the kingdoms of the world unite into '*the* kingdom of the world' (Rev 11:15) against Israel to take possession of Jerusalem; its end will be 'when He [Jesus] hands over the kingdom to the God and Father, when He has abolished all rule and all authority and power' (1 Cor 15:24).[358]

> (ii) The end of the second beast, i.e. the spirit of antichrist, in its ultimate manifestation as the Antichrist.

> (iii) The end of 'all that is in the world, the lust of the flesh and the lust of the eyes and the boastful pride of life' (1 John 2:16).

I only touched briefly on Jesus' return as the Commander of the heavenly armies in Chapter 12, commenting that this last battle will be very short. In Book 7, Kingdom Come, we will at last see Him in all His glory, power, and majesty in Revelation 20-22 as we consider the millennium, the Battle of Gog and Magog, Satan's end, the resurrection and judgement of the living and the dead, Hell, and the new heavens and new earth.

---

358 I will explain this in *The Pearl in Plain Sight*

Appendix A
Seven, Ten, and Seventy

One feature of John's Revelation is the number of sevens in the text. Besides the seven heads of the dragon and of the beast, John wrote to seven churches via their seven messengers about seven lamps, seven Spirits of God, and the Lamb with seven horns and seven eyes. He sees seven seals on a divine scroll, hears seven thunders and seven angels blowing seven trumpets, and watches another seven pouring out seven bowls of wrath. In total, there are fifty-four sevens.[359]

Craig R Koester recognises a metaphorical meaning:

> Elsewhere in Revelation, the number seven indicates completeness… Accordingly, identifying the seven heads with seven kings seems to point to the totality of the beast's power.[360]

He is right that this 'seven' is metaphorical but it is not 'the beast's power' that is total, as I will show.

Seven as Metaphor

In Book 3,[361] I pointed out that the metaphor of seven is first used by God Himself:

> So the LORD said to him, "Therefore whoever kills Cain, vengeance will be taken on him *sevenfold*." (Gen 4:15*)

I commented:

> It is important that we recognise this was not a literal, disproportionate response (how was God to punish

---

359 There are 735 mentions of 'seven' in the Scriptures, plus 6 of 'sevenfold' and 119 of 'seventh', totalling 860.
360 Craig R. Koester, *Revelation and the End of All Things*, p. 161.
361 *Gotta Serve Somebody*, p. 147.

anyone who killed Cain? Put them to death seven times by resurrecting them six times?) but rather a metaphorical expression meaning justly, completely, or perfectly. It originates from the seventh day, the Sabbath, when God rested from all His works – He had finished Creation to the state of [absolute] goodness or perfection, i.e. nothing was wrong or lacking (Gen 1:31).[362]

This is why He promised Israel that if they were disobedient and He had to discipline them...:

> "...I, even I, will strike you seven times for your sins." (Lev 26:24. Also 26:18, 21, & 28)

God's striking Israel seven times was to 'justly, completely, perfectly' punish them for their sins. Conversely, the blood of their sin offerings was to be sprinkled seven times[363] to make a just, complete, perfect atonement for their sins.

The seven heads ruling over Israel do not therefore 'point to the totality of the beast's power' as Prof Koester believes – in fact, the beast has sustained a fatal wound and is living on borrowed time (Rev 13:3 & 5). Rather, they are seven literal Gentile empires which have been fulfilling God's *seven strikes* for Israel's sins.[364]

Ten as Metaphor

Ten can symbolise 'all', as I established in Book 2[365] and applied in Chapter 1. When ten is used with seven, the two metaphors create a remarkable application very familiar to ancient Israel in their holiest day, Yom Kippur, the Day of Atonement:

> "On exactly the *tenth* day of this *seventh* month is the day of atonement" (Lev 23:27*)

---

362 Ibid.
363 Leviticus 4:6, 17; 8:11; 14:7, 51; 16:14, 19; Numbers 19:14.
364 This is further evidence that Jesus did not abolish the Law of Moses but will continue to fulfil it "until heaven and earth pass away" (Matt 5:17-18).
365 *Slouching Towards Bethlehem*, pp. 36-45.

This day was to bestow 'just, complete, perfect' forgiveness of 'numerous, every, the whole, or the fullness' of Israel's sins for that year.

In the same way, the seventh head having ten horns is no coincidence. Just as God has used the Gentiles to strike Israel seven times for their sins, in perfect symmetry, He is also judging the Gentiles.

(i) Justice for All

This will be the completion of history as we know it, when *all* the nations gather for this *just, complete,* and *perfect* judgement on Israel and on themselves. There will be justice for all.

Jesus predicted this gathering using a shepherding analogy:

> "...when the Son of Man comes in His glory, and all the angels with Him, then He will sit on His glorious throne. *All the nations* will be gathered before Him; and He will separate them from one another, as the shepherd separates the sheep from the goats..." (Matt 25:31-32*)

Paul explains the logic to the Romans, beginning with God offering His grace first to Israel:

> ...the gospel... is the power of God for salvation to everyone who believes, to *the Jew first* and also to *the Greek* [i.e. Gentile].... (Rom 1:16*)

Every Jew who has rejected His offer will face judgement first:

> There will be tribulation and distress for every soul of man who does evil, of *the Jew first* and also of *the Greek*, but glory and honor and peace to everyone who does good, to *the Jew first* and also to *the Greek*. (Rom 2:9-10*)

(ii) The Climax of Evil

The seventh head manifesting with its ten horns also signifies that at the very time when 'the fullness' of believing Gentiles

(Rom 11:25) and all in Israel who will finally believe (Rom 11:26) come into God's kingdom, His enemies, demonic and human, will come to *the fullness of their opposition*.

Seventy as Metaphor

The number seventy is also used as a metaphor in the Scriptures with two meanings based on events in Jewish history and another as the product of seven *times* ten. So, when Jesus sent out seventy disciples to proclaim the Kingdom (Luke 10:1-16), did He have one of these three in mind?

The Zondervan Pictorial Encyclopedia of the Bible explains the first two:

> The number seventy was symbolic to the Jews. It suggested the number of elders that Moses had chosen to help with the task of leading Israel in the wilderness... It was also the "number" of the nations in the world (see Gen 10, the LXX has seventy-two)... Some have supposed that Jesus foreshadowed the preaching of the Gospel to all the nations.[366]

Consider the elders:

> "Gather for Me *seventy* men from the elders of Israel, whom you know to be the elders of the people and their officers..." (Num 11:16*. Also Ex 24:1)

They were to represent the twelve tribes and He placed the Holy Spirit on these seventy to lead the nation alongside Moses (Num 11:25); their successors became known as the Sanhedrin.[367]

We see this illustrated typologically after the Exodus when God led the new nation to a place of rest:

---

[366] *The Zondervan Pictorial Encyclopedia of the Bible*, Vol 5, p. 363. Genesis 10 lists fourteen nations as descended from Japheth, thirty from Ham and twenty-six from Shem, totalling seventy.
[367] www.chabad.org/library/article_cdo/aid/4100306/jewish/The-Sanhedrin-The-Jewish-Court-System.htm, 16 Jan, 2020.

> Then they came to Elim where there were *twelve* springs of water and *seventy* date palms, and they camped there beside the waters. (Ex 15:27*)

Again, this was no coincidence: there was a spring of life-giving water for each of the twelve tribes and they were to find sustenance and shade in the wisdom of the seventy elders. At the annual Feast of Tabernacles, God required Israel to offer seventy bulls as burnt offerings, symbolising the elders' rededication to God to lead His people for the next year.

This is why, after Jesus sent out the Twelve (Luke 9:1), He sent out the seventy (Luke 10:1). With the Twelve, Jesus was establishing patriarchs for the New Covenant that mirrored Jacob's twelve sons in the Mosaic covenant, hence the twenty-four elders around the throne of God (Rev 4:4) and the names on the twelve gates and twelve foundation stones of the wall of New Jerusalem (Rev 21:12 & 14). With the seventy, Jesus was establishing the pattern for His church to also be led by elders. Paul and Barnabas recognised this and acted accordingly among the Gentiles (Acts 14:23).

What then of the third option, the metaphor of seven *times* ten?

Seven *Times* Ten

The Lord had repeatedly rebuked Israel for breaking the Sabbath through Isaiah (Isa 56:2-6, 58:13), Jeremiah (Jer 17:21-27), and Ezekiel (Ezek 20:12-24, 22:8, 22:26, 23:38, 44:24). When they refused to listen, Jeremiah pronounced God's judgement that they would be exiled to Babylon for seventy years (Jer 25:11, 29:10). The Chronicler explains the reason for that number:

> ... to fulfill the word of the LORD by the mouth of Jeremiah, until the land had enjoyed its *sabbaths*. All the days of its desolation *it kept sabbath* until *seventy years* were complete. (2 Chron 36:21*)

Israel's refusal to keep the weekly sabbaths included the land's sabbath year (Lev 25:2-4) so the seventy years of exile was to allow the land to keep sabbath for ten cycles of sabbath years.

Why ten? They had been in the land from 1406 BC until the Babylonian exile in 586 BC, i.e. 820 years and 117 sabbath years. It is possible they had not kept a literal ten of those but the number ten being a metaphor for 'all' would mean the seventy years was for 'all the sabbaths' Israel had broken.

Seventy *Times* Seven

God then multiplied this keeping of ten sabbath years by another seven.

As we saw in Book 1,[368] in c. 539 BC, when Daniel read Jeremiah's prophecy, he began earnestly praying for the end of the exile (Dan 9:2). Daniel had been in Babylon since 605 BC, some 66 years, so he was expectant. The angel Gabriel appeared to him, reassured him that the exile would indeed end with Jerusalem being rebuilt but added a whole new period:

> "Seventy weeks (*shabua*, a period of seven) have been decreed for your people and your holy city…" (Dan 9:24a)

Jeremiah's seventy years were multiplied by seven to introduce the most extraordinary predictions of God's plans for Israel and the world:

> 24. "…to finish the transgression, to make an end of sin, to make atonement for iniquity, to bring in everlasting righteousness, to seal up vision and prophecy and to anoint the most holy place.
> 25. "So you are to know and discern that from the issuing of a decree to restore and rebuild Jerusalem until Messiah the Prince there will be seven weeks and sixty-two weeks…" (Dan 9:24b-25)

---

[368] *Dancing in the Dragon's Jaws*, pp. 94-114.

In other words, Daniel's 70 Weeks would see not only the rebuilding of Jerusalem but also the Messiah, the end of Israel's transgression and sin, permanent forgiveness, and the fulfilment of all visions and prophecies.

Messiah the Prince

Daniel is given an exact date for the coming of "Messiah the Prince": "seven weeks and sixty-two weeks", i.e. 483 years, after "'a decree".

As covered in Book 1, there were four decrees to rebuild Jerusalem.[369] Artaxerxes' first decree in 458 BC plus 483 years yields the date of 26 AD,[370] the year in which John baptised Jesus in the Jordan River and pronounced Him Messiah (John 1:29-36), confirmed by the audible voice of the Father (Matt 3:17). Jesus began His ministry, saying:

> *"The time is fulfilled,* and the kingdom of God is at hand; repent and believe in the gospel." (Mark 1:15*)

The time was fulfilled to begin the 70th Week but, Gabriel continued, it would not all go well:

> 26. "Then after the sixty-two weeks the Messiah will be cut off and have nothing, and the people of the prince who is to come will destroy the city and the sanctuary. And its end will come with a flood; even to the end there will be war; desolations are determined.
> 27. "And He[371] will make a firm covenant with *the many* for one week, but in the middle of the week He will put a stop to sacrifice and grain offering..." (Dan 9:26-27a)

After three and half years of ministry, in the middle of the

---

369 Ezra 6:14 lists Cyrus (538 BC), Darius (520 BC), and Artaxerxes (458 and 444 BC).
370 There is no year 0.
371 Some translators and commentators omit the capitalised 'He', wrongly assuming the subject of v. 27 is the future antichrist instead of Messiah the Prince, the primary subject of v. 26 - see Appendix B.

70th Week, Jesus was crucified, offering His blood to make a new covenant with "the many":

> "...for this is My blood of the covenant, which is poured out *for many* for forgiveness of sins." (Matt 26:28*)

He offers this covenant to the whole world while fulfilling all the foreshadowing sacrifices of the old.

It is often not recognised but the crucifixion in 30 AD was the abomination[372] that led to Israel, "the city and the sanctuary" (Dan 9:26), being made desolate by the Roman armies in 70 AD, as the angel explained to Daniel:

> "...and on the wing of *abominations* will come one who *makes desolate*, even until a complete destruction, one that is decreed, is poured out on the one who makes desolate." (Dan 9:27b*)

Fully aware of Daniel's predictions, Jesus had warned the disciples:

> "...when you see Jerusalem surrounded by armies, then recognize that her *desolation* is near... because these are days of vengeance, so that *all things which are written* will be fulfilled." (Luke 21:22)

The 70th Week

As covered in Book 1,[373] the 70th Week's first half was the literal three and a half years when Jesus limited His ministry to the 'lost sheep of the house of Israel' (Matt 15:24) and commanded the Twelve likewise (Matt 10:5-6). The 70th Week's second half, the metaphorical "times, a time, and half a time" was "the times of the Gentiles" (Matt 28:19) which began in 30 AD when He commissioned the Twelve

---

372 As I showed in Book 2 *Slouching Towards Bethlehem*, pp. 265-283, the crucifixion was the fourth "abomination of desolation" in Israel's history with the Antichrist yet to be the sixth and final instance.
373 *Dancing in the Dragon's Jaws*, pp. 113-148.

to proclaim His kingdom to "all the nations" (Matt 28:20).

Contrary to what is often taught, the 70th Week is not the time of the Antichrist and his "Great Tribulation" but is Messiah's Week, Jesus' time to complete His work of redemption.[374] Remember Gabriel's words to Daniel:

> "Seventy weeks have been decreed for *your people* and *your holy city* to finish the transgression, to make an end of sin, to make atonement for iniquity, to bring in everlasting righteousness, to seal up vision and prophecy and to anoint the most holy place." (Dan 9:24*)

I wrote of this:

> ...Israel has yet to "finish the transgression" – they will continue to transgress until the end of the 70th week... [And Jesus] alone was able to make "an end of sin" and "atonement for iniquity" for all who believe (Heb 7:27)... "to bring in everlasting righteousness"... "to seal up vision and prophecy and to anoint the most holy place"... 'in heaven itself' (Heb 9:23-24) for all who trust in Him.[375]

The 70th Week seems to have finished when Israel regained their holy city in 1967 but, as I often point out, we cannot be definitive or dogmatic regarding this timing because Moshe Dayan, Israel's victorious general, handed the Temple Mount back to the Muslim authorities.

What we have established, however, is that we must understand the Old Testament's metaphorical meanings of seven, ten, seventy, and the second half of the 70th Week to understand John's visions, especially Revelation 11, 12, and 13.

We see too that John's three visions of the dragon and the two beasts with seven heads and ten horns reveal God's plan for both Israel and "all the nations" who reject His kingdom.

---

374 Ibid, pp. 101-105. Also in this book's Appendix B.
375 Ibid, pp. 177-179.

Lastly, all of this was foreshadowed in two of His historic actions:

(i) Covenanting with Abram.
(ii) Giving Israel the Land.

Abram & the Ten Horns

At the time of God's promise, Abraham was still called Abram. God called him to cut some sacrificial animals in half:

> 17. It came about when the sun had set, that it was very dark, and behold, there appeared a smoking oven and a flaming torch which passed between these pieces.
> 18. On that day the LORD made a covenant with Abram, saying, "To your descendants I have given this land, from the river of Egypt as far as the great river, the river Euphrates:
> 19. the Kenite and the Kenizzite and the Kadmonite
> 20. and the Hittite and the Perizzite and the Rephaim
> 21. and the Amorite and the Canaanite and the Girgashite and the Jebusite". (Gen 15:17-21)

At first glance, this may seem a comprehensive list of ten city-states in Canaan but there are significant omissions. Where are the Amalekites (Gen 14:7), the Anakim (Deut 1:28), the Philistines (Gen 21:34), the Geshurites (Josh 13:2) and the Girzites (1 Sam 27:8) who were also specifically named to be dispossessed?[376] There were at least fifteen people-groups inhabiting Canaan at the time.

Abraham's list of ten was not to be exhaustive but a sample; the number is a metaphor for *all the nations* inhabiting Canaan. God was revealing His intention in typological form and Paul understood:

---

[376] The Amalekites (1 Sam 15:2-3, 27:8), the Anakim (Deut 9:2, Josh 11:21), the Philistines (Josh 13:2-3), the Geshurites (Josh 13:2-3, 1 Sam 27:8), and the Girzites (1 Sam 27:8).

Threshing Hour

> For the promise to Abraham or to his descendants that he would be *heir of the world* was not through the Law, but through the righteousness of faith. (Rom 4:13*)

This promise is often overlooked today as, for example, in this commentary:

> No express mention of this heirship is made in the Genesis account of Abraham… But since, as Genesis makes clear, God purposed through Abraham and his offspring to work out the destiny of the whole world, it was implicit in the [other] promises to Abraham… The full realization of this awaits the consummation of the Messianic kingdom at Christ's return.[377]

God did indeed promise that "all the nations of the earth", every people-group, would be *blessed* through Abraham and his Seed, Messiah (Gen 22:18, Gal 3:16); Jesus said that He would not return until the gospel reaches them all (Matt 24:14). Jesus also promised that "the meek will inherit the earth" (Matt 5:5).

However, the 'ten nations' promise to Abraham is the commentary's missing 'express mention' of the promise, only seen when we recognise it as typological. As has been demonstrated many times in these studies, typology is the intrinsic, essential basis for understanding the Book of Revelation.

We see then that Abraham and his physical descendants, through Isaac and Jacob, were promised all the land of Canaan inhabited by ten nations but he and his spiritual descendants were also promised all the land of the ten horns, i.e. "all the nations", the whole renewed world. Peter quotes Isaiah 66:22 reaffirming that:

> But according to His promise we are looking for new heavens and a new earth, in which righteousness dwells. (2 Pet 3:13)

---

377 *NASB Study Bible*, Grand Rapids; Zondervan, 1999, p. 1640.

Graeme Carlé

Moses & the Seven Heads

Four hundred and seventy years later, when Moses commissions the Israelites to at last take possession of the Promised Land, he numbers the nations to be dispossessed as only seven:

> "When the LORD your God brings you into the land where you are entering to possess it, and clears away many nations before you, the Hittites and the Girgashites and the Amorites and the Canaanites and the Perizzites and the Hivites and the Jebusites, *seven nations* greater and stronger than you..." (Deut 7:1*)

Paul, speaking in the synagogue in Pisidian Antioch, also describes them as seven:

> "When He had destroyed seven nations in the land of Canaan, He distributed their land as an inheritance..." (Acts 13:19)

So why only seven now?

During the almost five hundred years, inter-Canaanite wars had taken their toll of some (Deut 2:10-12, 20-23) while others - the Kenites (1 Sam 15:6) and the Gibeonites (2 Sam 21:2) - became Israel's allies. However, Moses also leaves out some specifically included by God in His later instructions to Joshua e.g. the Philistines, the Gebalites, the Geshurites, and the Maacathites (Josh 13:2-13).

The "seven nations" are therefore also not to be understood as incidental or literal but as another prophetic and typological sample – the battle for the Promised Land foreshadows the battle for the whole world: "seven nations" prefigure the seven Gentile empires that the nation of Israel has been battling before Messiah finally comes in His power. They are *the seven heads of Revelation* 12:3, 13:1 and 17:3-9.

It is all there for us to see and marvel at the consistency of God's words and plans being outworked in our time and history.

Fulfilling Covenants

In Book 4,[378] I showed how all eight of the Father's 'everlasting covenants' – with Jesus, Adam, Noah, Abraham, the nation of Israel, Levi, David, and us - are still in force. I highlighted Jesus' teaching that He did not come to abolish but to fulfil the Law when He said:

> "Do not think that I came to abolish the Law or the Prophets; I did not come to abolish but to fulfill. For truly I say to you, until heaven and earth pass away, not the smallest letter or stroke shall pass from the Law until all is accomplished." (Matt 5:17-18)

Here we see the last battle to be fought by Jesus will fulfil the Abrahamic and Mosaic covenants to "the smallest letter or stroke" (v. 18).

His most powerful enemies, the dragon, i.e. Satan, and the first beast, i.e. the principality and power of the Gentiles, will be in their ultimate manifestation as the seventh head with the ten horns, i.e. "all the nations".

The second beast, i.e. the spirit of antichrist, will be in its final manifestation as 'the false prophet', the Antichrist, and all three will be leading "all the nations", united by their purpose to take Jerusalem from Israel. Jesus of Nazareth, the true Prophet and the Christ, will be seen to be the Seed of Abraham and the ultimate Prophet like Moses, just as Peter explained to the men of Israel in 30 AD:

> 20. ...[God will] send Jesus, the Christ appointed for you,
> 21. whom heaven must receive until the period of restoration of all things about which God spoke by the mouth of His holy prophets from ancient time.
> 22. *"Moses said,* 'THE LORD GOD WILL RAISE UP FOR YOU A PROPHET *LIKE ME* FROM YOUR BRETHREN; TO HIM YOU SHALL GIVE HEED to everything He says to you...
> 25. "It is you who are the sons of the prophets and of

---

378 *Silencing the Witnesses*, pp. 312-338.

the covenant which God made with your fathers, saying to Abraham, 'AND IN YOUR SEED ALL THE FAMILIES OF THE EARTH SHALL BE BLESSED.'
26. *"For you first, God raised up His Servant and sent Him to bless you by turning every one of you from your wicked ways."* (Acts 3:19-26, capitals identifying quotes)

As mentioned earlier, Revelation reveals that as 'the fullness' of believing Gentiles (Rom 11:25) and believing Jews (Rom 11:26) come into God's kingdom, His opponents, both demonic and human, will also come to the fullness of their opposition.

To summarise, Jesus judging the beast in the time of its seventh head with ten horns signifies that at the Last Trumpet, He will finally, completely, perfectly, justly deal with all of the kingdoms of the earth when they unite in one purpose with the beast to become "the kingdom of the world":

> Then the seventh angel sounded; and there were loud voices in heaven, saying, "The *kingdom of the world* has become the kingdom of our Lord and of His Christ; and He will reign forever and ever." (Rev 11:15*)

Summary of Seven, Ten, and Seventy

(i) The numbers seven and ten are always significant in Revelation, being found throughout the Scriptures as having both a metaphorical and a literal meaning: seven signifies just, complete, or perfect; ten signifies numerous, all, every, the whole, or the fullness.

(ii) When God said He would punish Israel with seven strikes, He was promising them perfect and complete justice. Conversely, the blood of sacrifices being sprinkled seven times signified a just, complete, and perfect atonement.

(iii) The seven heads on the dragon and the first beast are the seven literal Gentile empires[379] who have attacked and are yet to attack Israel, fulfilling the Law's seven strikes. The ten horns are ten kingdoms which symbolise "all the nations" and their leaders who will be judged as well, ensuring there will be justice for all, for the Jew first and then the Gentile.

(iv) Israel's annual Day of Atonement has the same conjunction of numbers, being on the tenth day of the seventh month.

(v) Seventy can have three metaphorical meanings but for our purposes, we focused on the third, i.e. seven times ten. Israel's seventy years in exile in Babylon was for the land to keep ten sabbath years, i.e. for *all* the sabbaths that its people had refused to keep.[380]

(vi) God then multiplied that seventy by seven, creating the timetable for Messiah. This period would see the end of Israel's transgression and sin, permanent forgiveness, and the fulfilment of all visions and prophecies, which necessarily includes both comings of Jesus.

(vii) Daniel's 70th Week is central to understanding Revelation, given that Chapters 11 and 13, and half of 12, are set in its second half. The first 'sixty-nine weeks', i.e. 483 years, ended in 26 AD, the year that Jesus was immersed in the River Jordan. The 70th Week started with Jesus ministering to Israel for three and a half years but when they rejected and crucified

---

379 Egypt, Assyria, Babylon, Medo-Persia, Greece, Rome, and "all the nations".

380 All Sabbaths including the seventh year prefigure the rest we are supposed to enter when we cease working to be righteous and trust instead in Jesus' atoning death on the cross (Col 2:16-17, Heb 4:9-10).

Him in 30 AD, God turned to the Gentiles. The second half of the 70th Week began the metaphorical "times of the Gentiles" which seems to have ended in 1967 when Israel regained Jerusalem.

(viii) The ten horns at the last battle are illustrating God's promise to Abraham that he and his descendants will inherit the whole earth after it has been recreated anew; the seven heads show He will overcome all that the principalities and powers can ever do to stop Him.

(ix) This extraordinary symmetry demonstrates that He will execute perfect justice in all the affairs of nations and their principalities and powers.

Appendix B
3½ Year Tribulation?

The idea of one last three and a half year period of great tribulation comes from a misunderstanding of Daniel's 70th Week prophecy which some believe predicts a seven year reign for the Antichrist. They believe he will be an extraordinary political and/or religious leader who will emerge from the European Union or from the Vatican and make a seven year peace-treaty with Israel, allowing Israel to rebuild the Temple in Jerusalem and reinstitute their sacrificial system. After three and a half years, they believe, he will renege and break the treaty, stopping Israel's sacrifices and unleashing a terrible time of great tribulation for the remaining three and a half years.

My dear friend, Barry Smith, taught this as a well-known End-Times preacher and evangelist in New Zealand and the South Pacific. He used to add this means Jesus cannot return for at least another seven years because the Antichrist has not yet made this seven-year peace treaty with Israel and they have not yet rebuilt the Temple in Jerusalem.

The idea these things will happen comes from a misreading of one word in one verse - the pronoun "he" in Daniel 9:27.[381] This misunderstanding was set in stone for many by Scofield's Reference Bible of 1917[382] which popularised the views of J.N. Darby (1800-1822). Compounding this, many well-known Bible teachers such as Chuck Missler have promoted some incorrect dates calculated by Sir Robert Anderson. I covered this in Book 1[383] but here is a recap.

---
381 See *Dancing in the Dragon's Jaws*, pp. 94-116.
382 C.I. Scofield (1843-1921) popularised the views of J.N. Darby (1800-1882), C. I. *Scofield Reference Notes (1917 Edition)*, www.studylight.org/commentaries/eng/srn/daniel-9.html, 2 Jan, 2022.
383 See *Dancing in the Dragon's Jaws*, Appendix C – Dating Daniel's 70th Week, pp. 192-193.

We need to read Daniel 9:27 in context and resolve three issues:

(i) When was this period?
(ii) What was to be achieved during it?
(iii) What is the significance of it being "a week"?

Dating the 70 Weeks

Let us first establish when the sixty-ninth week of years[384] ended and the seventieth began. Gabriel told Daniel:

> 24. "Seventy weeks have been decreed for your people and your holy city, to finish the transgression, to make an end of sin, to make atonement for iniquity, to bring in everlasting righteousness, to seal up vision and prophecy and to anoint the most holy place.
> 25. "So you are to know and discern that *from the issuing of a decree to restore and rebuild Jerusalem until Messiah the Prince there will be seven weeks and sixty-two weeks...*"
> (Dan 9:24-25*)

The first "seven weeks and sixty-two weeks", i.e. sixty-nine weeks or 483 years, did not begin with Artaxerxes' second decree in 444 BC, as is often taught, but with his first decree in 458 BC. This takes us to 26 AD,[385] when Jesus was baptised in the Jordan and announced as "Messiah the Prince":

> After being baptized, Jesus came up immediately from the water; and behold, the heavens were opened, and he saw the Spirit of God descending as a dove and lighting on Him, and behold, a voice out of the heavens said, *"This is My beloved Son*, in whom I am well-pleased"
> (Matt 3:16-17*)

This is why Jesus began His ministry in 26 AD, saying:

> *"The time is fulfilled,* and the kingdom of God is at hand; repent and believe in the gospel." (Mark 1:15*)

---

384 Israel celebrated Sabbath days and years (Lev 25:8).
385 There being no year 0.

Jesus' baptism began Daniel's 70th Week.

What Was Achieved?

Gabriel told Daniel that this time was to complete six objectives:

> "Seventy weeks have been decreed for your people and your holy city, to finish the transgression, to make an end of sin, to make atonement for iniquity, to bring in everlasting righteousness, to seal up vision and prophecy and to anoint the most holy place." (Dan 9:24)

He added that Jerusalem and the Temple would be rebuilt (v. 25) but more importantly, that after the sixty-ninth week, Messiah would come (v. 25). Astonishingly, however, Messiah would lose everything and be killed (v. 26) and Jerusalem and the Temple would be destroyed again (v. 26). The Temple was rebuilt by 516 BC (Ezra 6:15) and Jerusalem's wall rebuilt by 444 BC (Neh 6:15).

However, *none* of the six stated objectives of v. 24 were accomplished in the first sixty-nine weeks of years, leaving everything to be achieved in the 70th Week.

Gabriel then told Daniel that there would be a covenant made "for one week" and that a remarkable event would occur "in the middle" of it. Here is the text as translated in the *NASB* with the ambiguous pronoun:

> "And *he* will make a firm *covenant* with the many for *one week*, but in the middle of the week *he* will put a stop to sacrifice and grain offering..." (Dan 9:27*)

This has led many to believe that 'he' refers to "the prince who is to come" mentioned in the preceding verse, v. 26, thinking that must be the future Antichrist. However, that verse reads:

> "...*the Messiah* will be cut off and have nothing, and *the people of the prince who is to come* will destroy the city and the sanctuary" (Dan 9:26*)

We do not have to guess at what this means because we know what actually happened - after Jesus was "cut off", crucified in 30 AD, the Romans led by Titus, their general and later emperor, razed "the city", Jerusalem, and "the sanctuary", the Second Temple, in 70 AD. We also know why because Jesus told the disciples:

> "...when you see Jerusalem surrounded by armies, then recognize that her desolation is near... because these are days of vengeance, so that all things which are written will be fulfilled." (Luke 21:20-22)

These were "the days of vengeance" for "cutting off Messiah".

Who then is the 'he' of Daniel 9:27? 'Messiah the Prince', the *primary subject* of the two preceding verses, v. 25 and v. 26. The "prince who is to come" is actually the third subject, after his "people".

Again, we know what actually happened - Jesus ministered to Israel for three and a half years (Luke 13:6-9) and "in the middle of the week", He made "a firm covenant", i.e. the new, eternal covenant, "with the many", i.e. with everyone who will believe, both Jew and Gentile. As He said at the time:

> "...this is My blood of the covenant, which is poured out for *many* for forgiveness of sins." (Matt 26:28*)

This rendered Israel's entire sacrificial system 'obsolete and... ready to disappear' (Heb 8:13), which it did with the razing of the Temple in 70 AD. The 'he' of verse 27 should therefore be capitalised:

> "And *He* will make a firm covenant with the many for one week, but in the middle of the week *He* will put a stop to sacrifice and grain offering..." (Dan 9:27*)

Jesus Did It

We see then that Jesus proclaimed the kingdom to Israel for three and half years (Luke 13:6-9), i.e. the first half of the 70th Week, but then was "cut off and [had] nothing" (Dan 9:26), i.e. crucified. He thereby achieved in 30 AD four of the six objectives of Daniel 9:24 for *all who trust in Him*:

(i) "Make an end of sin" (Gal 6:14).

(ii) "Make atonement for iniquity" (Col 2:13-14).

(iii) "Bring in everlasting righteousness" (2 Cor 5:21).

(iv) His blood was to "anoint the most holy place" (Heb 9:12).

What of the other two, "to seal up vision and prophecy" and "to finish the transgression"?

(v) "To seal up vision and prophecy".

The Hebrew verb, *chatham*, means 'to close up; especially to seal: - make an end, mark, seal (up), stop'.[386] Jesus fulfilled many Messianic prophecies regarding His life, death, and resurrection in the 1st century and will return to fulfill every remaining prophecy and vision regarding the End Times and Judgement Day.

(vi) "To finish the transgression"

The Hebrew noun, *pesha*, means 'a revolt (national, moral or religious): - rebellion, sin, transgression, trespassive',[387] referring to Israel's behaviour. Remember, Gabriel told Daniel:

> "Seventy weeks have been decreed for *your people* and *your holy city*..." (Dan 9:24*)

Israel's revolt/rebellion against Jesus as Messiah was punished by their losing Jerusalem until 1967 which, as I argue in

---

386 *Strong's* H2856.
387 Ibid, H6588.

Book 1,[388] marks the end of "the times of the Gentiles" (Luke 21:24) and the end of the 70thWeek.

What then of the "abomination of desolation"?

> "...and on the wing of abominations will come one who makes desolate, even until *a complete destruction*, one that is decreed, is poured out on the one who makes desolate." (Dan 9:27*)

That abomination was the Crucifixion. Abominations that cause desolation are sins so egregious as to be the last straw for God, so that He judges the perpetrators; the crucifixion was actually the fourth that Israel had committed[389] and triggered the "complete destruction" of Jerusalem, the Temple, and the nation, just as Jesus had warned it would (Luke 21:22).

This means that 'the one who makes desolate' here is not the future Antichrist, as we have been taught, but the unbelieving nation of Israel in 30 AD.

The Mystery of the Half-Week

We see therefore that Jesus' ministered to Israel for the first half of the 70th Week; then "in the middle of the week", He dealt with our sins, introduced the "firm covenant", and rendered the sacrificial system of the Old obsolete. This was all done by 30 AD. What then of the second half of the 70th Week?

Daniel had twice heard the mysterious phrase "a time, times, and half a time" (Dan 7:25, 12:7) but when he asked about 'the end of these wonders' (Dan 12:6), he was told:

> "Go your way, Daniel, for these words are concealed and sealed up until the end time." (Dan 12:9)

In other words, it is a Biblical mystery, "concealed and sealed up" for almost seven hundred years until John saw it as the

---

388 *Dancing in the Dragon's Jaws*, pp. 120-125.
389 Details in *Slouching Towards Bethlehem*, pp. 265-283. The Antichrist's proud boasting (2 Thess 2:3-4) will be the sixth.

centre of the Book of Revelation. It is the period when:

(i) The two witnesses of Revelation 11 are testifying in Jerusalem (Rev 11:3).[390]

(ii) The woman of Revelation 12 is being pursued by the dragon (Rev 12:13-15) but preserved by God (Rev 12:6).[391]

(iii) The two beasts of Revelation 13 are waging war on the saints and overcoming them (Rev 13:5)[392] and marking their followers on the hand and forehead (Rev 13:16-18).[393]

Variously referred to as 'a time, times, and half a time' (Dan 7:25, 12:7; Rev 12:14), '1,260 days' (Rev 11:3, 12:6), '42 months' (Rev 11:2, 13:5), and 'three years and six months' (Luke 4:25, Jas 5:17), it is actually the second half of the 70th Week.

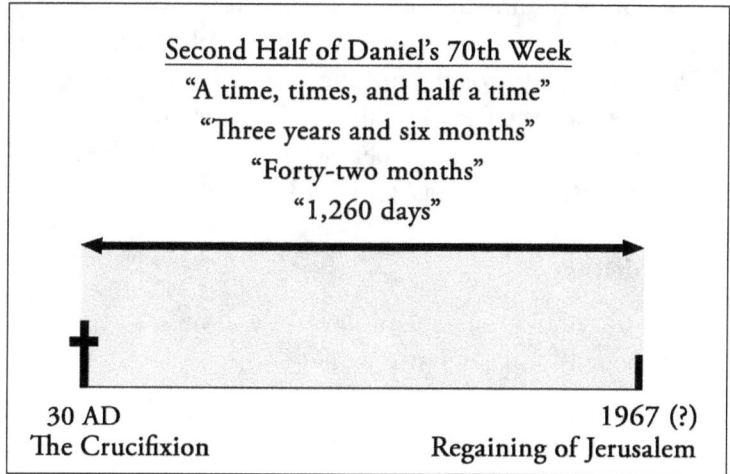

Fig (iii) The second half of Daniel's 70th Week

---

390 See my *Silencing the Witnesses.*
391 See *Dancing in the Dragon's Jaws.*
392 See *Slouching Towards Bethlehem: The Rise of the Antichrists.*
393 See *Gotta Serve Somebody.*

Many have assumed this will be a literal and future time-period but, as I showed in Book 1,[394] this time is a metaphor. It refers to the last 2,000 years, from 30 AD until 1967, during which the Gentiles were allowed to "tread underfoot the holy city" (Luke 21:24, Rev 11:2), i.e. Jerusalem.

From Literal to Metaphorical

This change from a literal time period to a metaphorical one is not as strange as it may appear. When Jesus introduced the New Covenant, all literal observances of the Law's festivals, Sabbaths, food laws, priests, sacrifices, Tabernacle and Temples also became metaphorical and spiritual realities:

(i) Festivals

Under the New Covenant, we are to observe the Passover and Unleavened Bread, not by ridding our homes of unleavened bread but by ridding our bodies of malice and wickedness (1 Cor 5:7-8); we are all to experience a personal Pentecost (Acts 2:38) and Day of Atonement for our sins (Heb 9:11, 24); we are to celebrate the Feast of Tabernacles which prefigures our daily lives in our mortal 'tabernacles', i.e. our bodies, until the Day of Resurrection (2 Cor 5:1-4).

(ii) Sabbaths

We are not under the Sabbath laws but all need to enter the rest provided for us by Jesus' work:

> Therefore no one is to act as your judge in regard to food or drink or in respect to *a festival* or a new moon or *a Sabbath day* - things which are *a mere shadow* of what is to come; but the substance belongs to Christ.
> (Col 2:16-17*)

---

[394] *Dancing in the Dragon's Jaws*, pp. 120-125.

So there remains a Sabbath rest for the people of God. For the one who has entered His rest has himself also *rested from his works*, as God did from His. (Heb 4:9-10*)

(iii) Food laws

The Law's food requirements served their purpose of keeping Israel separated from every other nation but, under the New Covenant, there are no food laws (Mark 7:19, Acts 10:13-16, 1 Tim 4:3-5) except abstaining from eating strangled animals, i.e. not bled (Acts 15:29, Gen 9:4 & 12).

What we can learn from the Law, however, is to not swallow everything we hear (Mark 4:24).

(iv) Priests, sacrifices, and Temples

We no longer need a Levitical priest descended from Aaron because every believer in Jesus has become a 'royal priest' (1 Pet 2:9) as well as part of the new Temple:

> You also, as *living stones*, are being built up as *a spiritual house* for *a holy priesthood*, to offer up *spiritual sacrifices* acceptable to God through Jesus Christ. (1 Pet 2:5*)

These sacrifices include:

> Therefore I urge you, brethren, by the mercies of God, to *present* your bodies *a living and holy sacrifice*, acceptable to God, which is your *spiritual* service of worship. (Rom 12:1*)

> Through Him then, let us continually offer up *a sacrifice of praise* to God, that is, the fruit of lips that give thanks to His name. And do not neglect doing good and sharing, for with *such sacrifices* God is pleased. (Heb 13:15-16*)

With all of these obviously metaphorical rather than literal under the New Covenant, it is not so strange for Daniel's 70th Week's second half to also be metaphorical from that exact time. After all, Daniel describes "a time, times, and half a time" as part of "wonders" (Dan 12:6-7), only to be understood in hindsight through the New Covenant (Dan 12:9). This means we are living at the end of Daniel's 70th Week and God is working with Israel back in their Promised Land.

Messiah's Week

Daniel's 70th Week was not for the Antichrist's supposed seven-year peace-treaty with Israel and to rebuild the Temple – it was for Jesus as the Christ to do His unique work. He worked among the Jews for the literal first half; He has worked among the Gentiles for the second half which is metaphorical and is measured by the status of Jerusalem i.e. the last 2,000 years.

As I spell out in Book 1,[395] there are six Biblical narratives which foreshadow the work of Messiah over seven days and seven years:

(i) Creation

Creation took *seven days*; we are His new Creation - 'if anyone is in Christ, he is *a new creature*' (2 Cor 5:17) – and He is working still.

(ii) Noah's Flood

Noah and his family were given *seven days* to enter the ark before the Flood (Gen 7:1 & 4); we are too, to enter Jesus before the Last Day (1 Pet 3:20-21).

(iii) Jacob's family

Jacob was to work *seven years* for his brides (Gen 29:18-28); our Bridegroom is still working for His.

---

395 *Dancing in the Dragon's Jaws*, pp. 102-106.

(iv) Joseph's provision

Joseph stored grain for *seven years* to save everyone, both Jews and Gentiles, from *seven years* of famine (Gen 41:28-49); Jesus is today giving us the bread to live forever (John 6:51).

(v) The red heifer's ashes

Israel's cleansing from the defilement of death took place on the third and *seventh day*; Jesus cleanses us through His resurrection on the third day and our resurrection on the *Last Day* (John 11:24).[396]

(vi) Solomon's Temple

Solomon built the Temple in *seven years* (1 Kin 6:38), using Jewish and Gentile workers (1 Kin 5:13-16); Jesus is today building us into a temple of living stones (1 Pet 2:5), using Jewish and Gentile workers. All of this means that Jesus may be coming sooner than we thought.

---

[396] See my book *The Red Heifer's Ashes: The Ultimate Messianic Prophecy*..

Appendix C
Seduction to Apostasy

Paul, Peter, and Jude identified several other causes of apostasy - where coercion failed, seduction often succeeded. Professing Christian leaders went astray off both sides of the narrow way to life: some promoted a false spirituality of extreme self-denial, forbidding marriage and enjoyment of food; others practised licentious self-indulgence. Others took over the priesthood of all believers, following 'the way of Cain… the error of Balaam, and… the rebellion of Korah' (Jude v. 11). I will only briefly mention these practices here but details are on our website: www.emmausroad.org.nz

Asceticism

Paul predicted that some would be tempted to a false spirituality based on severe self-denial:

> 1. But the Spirit explicitly says that in later times[397] *some will fall away from the faith,* paying attention to *deceitful spirits* and *doctrines of demons…*
> 3. men who *forbid marriage* and *advocate abstaining from foods* which God has created to be gratefully shared in by those who believe and know the truth. (1 Tim 4:1 & 3*)

By the 4th century, this asceticism was accepted, advocated, and institutionalised by the Desert Fathers and the Catholic Church.[398] The oldest recorded canon on celibacy was agreed at the Synod of Elvira (c. 305 AD), a gathering of bishops in southern Spain:

---

[397] The expression 'later times' (v. 1) is often assumed to mean just before the Lord's return but, as Hebrews 1:2 makes clear, 'these last days' began with Jesus' first coming.
[398] Details on www.emmausroad.org.nz/asceticism.

> It is decided that marriage be altogether prohibited to bishops, priests, and deacons, or to all clerics placed in the ministry, and that they keep away from their wives and not beget children; whoever does this shall be deprived of the honor of the clerical office. (Canon 33)

The *Catholic Encyclopedia* quotes Epiphanius (310-403 AD), Bishop of Salamis in Cyprus:

> Holy Church respects the dignity of the priesthood to such a point that she does not admit to the diaconate, the priesthood, or the episcopate, no nor even to the sub-diaconate, anyone still living in marriage and begetting children. She accepts only him who if married gives up his wife or has lost her by death… (Haer., lix, 4).[399]

In 390 AD, the ecumenical Council of Carthage in North Africa decreed:

> It is fitting that the holy bishops and priests of God… observe perfect continence, so that they may obtain in all simplicity what they are asking from God… It pleases us all that bishop, priest and deacon, guardians of purity, abstain from conjugal intercourse with their wives, so that those who serve at the altar may keep a perfect chastity. (Canon 3)

The *Catholic Encyclopedia* summarises:

> …it may fairly be said that by the time of St. Leo the Great (440–61) the law of celibacy was generally recognized in the West.[400]

The Eastern Orthodox Churches also explicitly forbade marriage to their bishops and archbishops; priests must be married but only before they are ordained.

Paul, however, taught that marriage was the norm for all in financially supported ministry:

---

[399] *Catholic Encyclopedia,* www.newadvent.org/cathen/03481a.htm, 1 Mar, 2022.
[400] Ibid.

> Do we not have *a right* to take along a believing wife, even as the rest of the apostles and the brothers of the Lord and Cephas? Or do only Barnabas and I not have a right to refrain from working? (1 Cor 9:5-6*)

Jesus, John the Baptist, Paul, and Barnabas were unmarried by their own choice and unique calling (1 Cor 9:12). Paul is unequivocal regarding '*the rest* of the apostles' - the Scriptures name twenty-two named and two more are unnamed.[401] They were all married and their wives accompanied them in their ministry travels. He explicitly notes 'the brothers of the Lord', James and Jude (Gal 1:19; Jude 1:1), were married, in contrast to Jesus being unmarried, and confirms that Cephas/Peter was married.

According to the apostate teachers, however, none of the Twelve or 1st century apostles except Paul and Barnabas would have been allowed in ministry!

In the 16th century Reformation, Zwingli and Luther renounced their Catholic priesthood and married. John Calvin also married.

Licentiousness

At the other extreme, Peter warned of apostate prophets and teachers (2 Pet 2:1) who would...:

> ...secretly introduce destructive heresies, even denying the Master who bought them... *Many* will follow their *sensuality*... For speaking out arrogant words of vanity they *entice* by *fleshly desires*, by sensuality... promising them freedom while they themselves are slaves of corruption. (2 Pet 2:1-2, 18-19*)

---

[401] The Twelve (Matt 10:2); Matthias (Acts 1:26); James the Lord's brother (Gal 1:19); Paul and Barnabas (Acts 14:14); Silas and Timothy (1 Thess 2:6, cf. 1:1); Apollos (1 Cor 4:6, 9); Andronicus and Junia (Rom 16:7); Epaphroditus (Phil 2:25). Two unnamed (2 Cor 8:23).

Jude likewise warned his 1st century audience to:

> ...contend earnestly for the faith which was once for all handed down to the saints. For certain persons have crept in unnoticed..., ungodly persons who *turn the grace of our God into licentiousness* and deny our only Master and Lord, Jesus Christ. (Jude v. 3*)

By the 10th century gross immorality was institutionalised, despite many individuals, believers and nonbelievers, denouncing it.

Pope John XII reigned from 955 AD until 963 AD and the *Catholic Encyclopedia* describes him as:

> a coarse, immoral man, whose life was such that the Lateran [the oldest and greatest patriarchal basilica in Rome] was spoken of as a brothel, and the moral corruption in Rome became the subject of general odium.[402]

Nevertheless, he is today still counted as the 130th pope in the line of 'apostolic succession'.[403]

Popes number 145, 147 and 150 were just one man, Benedict IX (r. 1032-1045, 1045, 1047-1048). Selected as no. 145 in 1032, he was deposed for debauchery after three years and replaced by no. 146, Sylvester III. However, within two months he deposed Sylvester to become no. 147 before selling the papacy to no. 148, Gregory VI (r. 1045-1046) who was succeeded by no. 149, Clement II (r. 1046-1047). Benedict was not finished yet though. When Clement died a

---

[402] *Catholic Encyclopedia*, www.newadvent.org/cathen/08426b.htm, 12 Sep, 2022.

[403] This doctrine is held by the Roman Catholic, Eastern Orthodox, Oriental Orthodox, Old Catholic, Moravian, Hussite, Anglican, Church of the East, and Scandinavian Lutheran traditions and requires every bishop to be consecrated in a direct line of succession from the 1st century apostles, despite many of the "successors" being clearly apostate. Other appalling popes include Stephen VI (r. 896-897), Urban VI (r. 1378-1389), Alexander VI (r. 1492-1503), Julius II (r. 1503-1513), and Leo X (r. 1513-1521).

year later, he reinstalled himself to become no. 150!

After eight months, he was deposed by the emperor Henry III and died in 1055.[404] In 1051, Cardinal Peter Damian (1007-1072) described Benedict as a 'demon from hell in the disguise of a priest' and concluded 'that wretch, from the beginning of his pontificate to the end of his life, feasted on immorality.[405] One successor, Pope Victor III (r. 1086-1087), wrote of Benedict's 'rapes, murders, and other unspeakable acts. His life as a pope so vile, so foul, so execrable, that I shudder to think of it'.[406]

Today, the *Catholic Encyclopedia* calls him a 'disgrace to the chair of St. Peter'[407] but in the official list[408] of apostolic successors, the grossly self-indulgent Benedict IX is still there three times.

This was not apostolic succession but institutional apostasy. These false prophets and teachers promised 'freedom while they themselves [were] slaves of corruption' (2 Pet 2:19), as predicted by the last words of the man they think was their first pope!

...

---

404 *Encyclopedia Britannica*, www.britannica.com/biography/Benedict-IX, 24 Oct, 2022.
405 *Catholic Encyclopedia*, www.newadvent.org/cathen/11764a.htm, 12 Sep, 2022.
406 Victor III, third book of *Dialogues*.
407 www.newadvent.org/cathen/02429a.htm, 24 Oct, 2022.
408 Ibid. Official list of popes at www.newadvent.org/cathen/12272b.htm, 12 Sep, 2022.

Bibliography

Books

Alford, Henry. 1976. *Greek Testament Critical Exegetical Commentary,* London: Guardian Press

Bruce, F.F. 1972. *Answers to Questions,* Grand Rapids, MI: Zondervan Publishing House

Carlé, Graeme. 1998. *Because of the Angels: Unveiling 1 Corinthians 11:2-16.* Auckland: Emmaus Road Publishing
- 2001. *The Red Heifer's Ashes: Mysteries of Ancient Israel,* -Auckland, Emmaus Road Publishing
- 2011. *Dancing in the Dragon's Jaws: The Mystery of Israel's Survival,* Auckland: Emmaus Road Publishing
- 2012. *Slouching Towards Bethlehem: The Rise of the Antichrists,* Auckland: Emmaus Road Publishing
- 2014. *Gotta Serve Somebody: The Mystery of the Marks & 666,* Auckland: Emmaus Road Publishing
- 2017. *Silencing the Witnesses: Jerusalem & the Ascent of Secularism,* Auckland: Emmaus Road Publishing

Chilton, David. 1987. *The Days of Vengeance,* Ft. Worth, TX: Dominion Press

Cline, Eric. 2004. *Jerusalem Besieged: From Ancient Canaan to Modern Israel,* Anne Arbor, MI: University of Michigan Press

Durant, Will, *The Story of Philosophy,* 2005. New York; Simon & Schuster

Dwyer, Charles H. H. 2003. *The Rise of Babylon: Sign of the End Times,* Chicago, IL: Moody Publishers

Eckstein, Zvi & Botticini, Maristella. 2012. *The Chosen Few: How Education Shaped Jewish History, 70-1492,* Tel Aviv: Tel Aviv University Press

Félice, G. de. 1851. *History of the Protestants of France: From the Commencement of the Reformation to the Presen Time,* Charleston, SC: Nabu Press

Gabriel, Mark A. 2003. *Islam and the Jews: The Unfinished Battle,* Lake Mary, FL: FrontLine

Haught, James A. 2002. *Holy Horrors: An Illustrated History of Religious Murder and Madness*, Buffalo, NY: Prometheus Books

Kline, Meredith G. 2006. *God, Heaven, and Har Magedon: A Covenantal Tale of Cosmos and Telos*, Eugene, OR: Wipf and Stock Publishers

Koester, Craig R. 2001. *Revelation and the End of All Things*, Grand Rapids, MI: Wm. B. Eerdmans Publishing Co

- 2014. *Revelation, Anchor Yale Bible 38A*. New Haven, CT: Yale University Press

Guy, Laurie. 2004. *Introducing Early Christianity: A Topical Survey of Its Life, Beliefs & Practices*, Downers Grove, IL: InterVarsity Press

- 2009. *Making Sense of the Book of Revelation*, Oxford: Regent's Park College with Smyth & Helwys Publishing
- 2016. *Unlocking Revelation*, Bletchley, UK: Paternoster Press

Jeremiah, David. 2008. *What in the World is Going On? 10 Prophetic Clues You Cannot Afford to Ignore*, Nashville, TN: Thomas Nelson

Kruger, Michael J. 2016. *A Biblical-Theological Introduction to the New Testament: The Gospel Realized*, Charlotte, NC: Crossway

Lane, Tony. 1996. *The Lion Concise Book of Christian Thought*, Oxford; Lion Hudson Plc

Morris, Leon. 1969. *Revelation: An Introduction and Commentary*, London: The Tyndale Press

Mitchell, Margaret. 2020. *Gone With the Wind*, London: Penguin

Perkins, Pheme. 1988. *Reading the New Testament*, New York: Paulist Press

Rees, Lawrence. 2005. *Auschwitz: The Nazis and the Final Solution*, London; BBC Books

Richardson, Joel. 2017. *Mystery Babylon: Unlocking the Bible's Greatest Prophetic Mystery*, Leawood, KS: Winepress Media

Ryrie, Charles Caldwell. 1976. *The Living End*, Old Tappan, NJ: Revell

Taylor, A. J. P. 1975. *From Sarajevo to Potsdam*, Orlando, FA: Harcourt Brace Jovanovich Publishers

Tenney, Merrill C. *Interpreting Revelation*. 1958. London: Picjering & Inglis Ltd

Walvoord, John F. 1962. *Israel in Prophecy*, Grand Rapids, MI: Zondervan
- 1966. *The Revelation of Jesus Christ*, Chicago, IL: Moody Press
Wilcock, Michael. 1975. *The Message of Revelation: I Saw Heaven Opened*, Leicester: Inter-Varsity Press
Wright, N.T. 2011. *Revelation for Everyone*, London: SPCK Publishing
Wuest, Kenneth S. 1973. *Golden Nuggets from the Greek New Testament*, Grand Rapids: Wm. B. Eedermans
York, Michael. 1995. *The Emerging Network: A Sociology of the New Age and Neo-Pagan Movements*, London: Rowman & Littlefield

Books Online

Alford, *Greek Testament Critical Exegetical Commentary*, https://archive.org/details/ GreekTestamentCriticalExegeticalCommentaryByHenry/04. GreekTestament.CritExegComm.v4.Heb.toRevel. Alford.1878./

Aquinas, Thomas. *Summa Theologiae*. https://aquinas101. thomisticinstitute.org/st-iiaiiae-q-11#SSQ11A3THEP1

Augustine of Hippo. *Exposition on Psalm 65*, Pt 2. www.ccel.org/ccel/schaff/npnf108. ii.LXV.html

Calvin, John. *Institutes of the Christian Religion*. www.ccel.org/ccel/calvin/institutes.toc.html

Epiphanius of Salamis. *Panarion*, https://ia801202.us.archive. org/21/items/EpiphaniusPanarionBksIIIII1/Epiphanius%20 -%20_Panarion_%20-%20Bks%20II%20%26%20III%20 -%201.pdf

Eusebius, *Church History*. www.loebclassics.com/view/ LCL153/1926/volume.xml

Hippolytus, *On the Twelve Apostles*. www.ccel.org/ccel/hippolytus

Ireneaus, *Against Heresies*. www.earlychristianwritings.com/irenaeus.html

Jerome, Letter CXXVII. *To Principia*. www.newadvent.org/fathers/3001127.htm

Josephus, Flavius. *The Wars of the Jews.* www.gutenberg.org/files/2850/ 2850-h/2850-h.htm#link62H_4_0001

Tacitus, *Annals.* http://penelope.uchicago.edu/Thayer/E/Roman/Texts/Tacitus/home.html

Articles Online

Chabad website - www.chabad.org/library/article_cdo/aid/4100306/jewish/The-Sanhedrin-The-Jewish-Court-System.htm

Christian Broadcasting Network - www1.cbn.com/ChurchWatch/archive/2009/02/06/pope-benedict-xvi- luther-was-right

Encyclopaedia Britannica - www.britannica.com

German History In Documents and Images - https://ghdi.ghi-dc.org/pdf/eng/English_100.pdf

Tablet - http://tabletmag.com/jewish-news-and-politics/81660/raw-deal

Vatican website - www.vatican.va/content/john-paul-ii/en/speeches/1998/october/documents/hf_jp-ii_spe_19981031_simposio.html

Bible Translations

Authorised (AV) or *King James Version (KJV)*, 1611. Oxford: Oxford University Press

Christian Standard Bible (CSB), 2012. Nashville, TN: B&H Publishing

English Standard Version (ESV), 2001. Wheaton, IL: Crossway

New American Standard (NASB), 1970. La Habra, CA: The Lockman Foundation

New International Version (NIV), 1978. Grand Rapids, MI: Zondervan Bible Publishers

New King James Version (NKJV), 1992. Nashville, TN: Thomas Nelson Publishers

New Revised Standard Version (NRSV), 1989. New York: American Bible Society

Prophecy Study Bible, Gen. ed. Time LaHaye. 2000. Chattanooga, TN: AMG Publishers

Revised Standard Version (RSV), 1971. New York: Collins

Schofield Reference Bible, 1909. Oxford University Press

The Kingdom New Testament (A Contemporary Translation), 2011. N.T. Wright. New York: HarperOne Publishers

The New Oxford Annotated Bible (New Revised Standard Version with the Apocrypha), Augmented 3rd College Edition, 2001. New York: Oxford University Press

The New Testament, 1969. William Barclay. London: Collins

The New Testament (An Expanded Translation), 1961. Kenneth Wuest. Grand Rapids, IL: Wm. B. Eerdmans Publishing Co

The New Testament in Modern English, 1962. J.B. Phillips. London: Harper Collins

Zondervan (NASB) Study Bible, 1999. Grand Rapids, MI: Zondervan

Dictionaries & Encyclopaedia

An Expository Dictionary of New Testament Words, W.E. Vine. 1975. London: Oliphants

Concise Oxford Dictionary, 1985. Oxford University Press

Illustrated Bible Dictionary (also known as *Easton's Bible Dictionary*), 3rd ed. London: T. Nelson & Sons

International Standard Bible Encyclopedia. 1915. Chicago Howard-Severance Co

NAS Exhaustive Concordance of the Bible, 1981. Nashville, TN: Holman

The American Heritage Dictionary of the English Language, 5th Ed. 2011. Boston, MA: Houghton Mifflin

The Exhaustive Concordance of the Bible, James Strong, 1890. New York: Abingdon Press

Theological Dictionary of the New Testament, Kittel & Friedrich, abridged by Geoffrey Bromley. 1990. Grand Rapids, MI: William B. Eerdmans Publishing Co

Theological Wordbook of the Old Testament, Harris et al. 1980. Chicago: Moody Press

The Zondervan Pictorial Encyclopedia of the Bible, ed. Merrill C. Tenney. 1977. Grand Rapids, MI: Zondervan

Newspapers & Magazines

The Daily Express, report on David Lloyd George, British Prime Minister, 17 Sep, 1936

Articles & Pamphlets

Address to the International Symposium on the Inquisition, 31 Oct, 1998.

Article on 'Revelation', *Encarta 96.* 1996. Buffalo, New York: Microsoft

Websites Accessed

www.abarim-publications.com/Meaning/Megiddo.html
www.aish.com/h/pes/f/48969191.html
https://americanvision.org/6370/christians-just-want-jews-slaughtered- and-converted/
https://aquinas101.thomisticinstitute.org/st-iiaiiae-q-11#SSQ11A3THEP1
www.bbc.co.uk/religion/religions/christianity/pope/johnpaulii_1.shtml, 31 Oct, 2022.
https://biblehub.com/commentaries/daniel/9-27. htm
https://bibletopicexpo.wordpress. com/2015/12/02/zechariah-son-of-berechiah-mt-2335/
www1.cbn.com/ChurchWatch/archive/2009/02/06/pope-benedict-xvi- luther-was-right
http://churchandstate.org.uk/2022/06/holy-horrors-christian-persecution- of-anabaptists/
www.chabad.org/library/ article_cdo/aid/107769/jewish/The-Rambam.htm

www.charismamag.com/spirit/spiritual-warfare/49907- 3-end-time-wars-armies-gather-at-armageddon
www.ccel.org/ccel/schaff/npnf102.iv.XX.19. html#iv.XX.19-p6
http://christianactionforisrael.org/un/record.html
www.unwatch.org/site/apps/nlnet/content2. aspx?c=bdKKISNqEmG&b=1314451&ct=1715019
http://christianactionforisrael.org/stillbirth/
www.fas.org/irp/world/para/docs/980223-fatwa.htm
www.cufi.org.uk/opinion-analysis/united-nations-and-bias-against-israel- explained/
https://unwatch.org/database/
www.dw.com/en/lutherans-reconcile-with-mennonites-500-years-after-bloody-persecution/a-5837683
www.emmausroad.org.nz
https://ghdi.ghi-dc.org/ pdf/eng/English_100.pdf
https://israelinstitute.nz/2022/01/new-zealand-votes-to-fund-unprecedented-attack-on-israel/, 27 Jan, 2022.
www.jewfaq.org/marriage.htm#Ceremony
www.jewishencyclopedia.com/articles/1760-ariel
www.jewish-history.com/palestine/period1.html
www.jewishvirtuallibrary.org/background-and- overview-six-day-war
www.jewishvirtuallibrary.org/the-great-revolt-66-70-ce
www.gutenberg.org/files/10890/10890-h/10890-h.htm#a68_32
https://mappinghistory.uoregon.edu/english/EU/EU10-04.html
www.middleeasteye.net/news/43-times-us-has-used-veto-power-against-un-resolutions-israel
www.ncregister.com/commentaries/why- vatican-ii-was-necessary
www.nationalreview.com/magazine/2021/08/02/christians-under-xi/#slide-1
www.ohchr.org/EN/HRBodies/HRC/CoIOPT-Israel/Pages/ Index. aspx
www.oic-oci.org/states/?lan=en
www.opendoorsusa.org/christian-persecution/stories/11christians-killed-every-day-for-their-decision-to-follow-jesus/
www.pewresearch.org/fact- tank/2017/04/05/christians-remain-worlds-largest-religious-group-but- they-are-declining-in-europe/

www.pewresearch. org/fact-tank/2019/05/14/more-than-half-of-countries-are-democratic/
https://pubmed.ncbi.nlm.nih.gov/23511276/
www.revelationrevolution.org/revelation-17-a-preterist-commentary/
https://sacred-texts.com/ cla/sib/sib.pdf
www.scoop.co.nz/stories/PA1704/ S00151/mccullys-diplomatic-blunder-on-israel-damaging.htm
www.sefaria.org/MishnahTaanit.4.6?lang=bi
www.tampabay.com/archive/1993/10/16/lutherans-to-apologize-to-jews/
www.jewishvirtuallibrary.org/declaration-of-the- evangelical-lutheran-church-in-america-to-the-jewish-community
www.theguardian.com/world/2000/mar/13/catholicism.religion
www.tyndale.com/sites/leftbehind/
www.un.org/en/member-states/
www.un.org/press/en/2007/sgsm11053.doc.htm
https://unwatch.org/database/
https://unwatch.org/ database/?showCountry=24246
www.vatican.va/archive/hist_councils/ii_vatican_council/ documents/ vat-ii_decree_19641121_unitatis-redintegratio_en.html
https://winstonchurchill.org/publications/finest-hour/finest-hour-156/ the-truth-about-hitler-1935-hitler-and-his-choice-1937/
www.worlddate.info/ religions/christianity.php
https://worldpopulationreview.com/country-rankings/most-christian- countries

Index

A

'A time, times and half a time'
  metaphorical meaning of
  16, 135, 153, 230-233
Abominations 59, 94-95, 99,
  101, 103, 109, 115, 117
'Abomination of desolation'
  definition of 59, 86, 229-230
  Crucifixion as fourth 216, 230
  five historical occurrences
    59, 91, 182-183, 216, 230
  in Daniel 86, 216, 230
  in Luke 183, 216
  in Mark 182-183
  in Matthew 182-183
  sixth, future and final 182-183
Abraham, the patriarch 14, 59,
  66, 127, 156, 159, 218-219
  covenant of 156, 221, 218-224
  descendants as stars 14, 87, 112
  inheriting land of ten nations
    218-219
Abyss, the
  definition of 130
  emerging from 131-139, 143,
    145-146
Afghanistan 88, 154
Al-Aqsa Mosque 158
al-Bashir, Omar 158
al-Bukhari 45
al-Qaeda 45
al-Quds, Islamic name for the
  Temple Mount 66, 127
Albigensian Crusade 169
Alexander VI, Pope 239
Alexander the Great 29

Anabaptists 171, 176
Antichrist - definition 163, 179-180
  competing regimes of 18-19,
    135, 154
  different Christian perspectives
    99, 139-141
  Muslim fulfillment 19, 160, 181
  the final 10, 16-19, 21, 26, 42,
    80, 99, 163, 178-184, 188,
    196-199, 208, 215-217,
    221, 225-230, 234
Antichrist, the spirit of 10, 16-19,
  21, 26, 153, 163, 173, 196-
  199, 208, 221
  in Christian regimes 167, 173
Antiochus IV Epiphanes 91
Antisemitism 176
  Martin Luther's 171, 176
Apostasy, definition 164
Apostasy, the Great 163-172
  the end of 172-179
Aquinas, Thomas 169
Armageddon - spelling variants
  11, 48, 69
  See Har-Magedon & Megiddo
Assyrian Empire 14, 27, 58, 71,
  73, 87, 139, 187-188, 223
Augustine 115-117, 125-126, 141
Augustus Caesar 17-18, 182

B

Babylonian Empire 14, 16, 27,
  87, 90, 92, 110, 121-122,
  127, 138, 180, 187-188, 214
Bangladesh 154, 157
Bashir, Omar al- 158

Beast, identity of John's first 15, 25
  identity of John's second
    17-19, 26
  Daniel's four 135
  end of 36
  John's composite of Daniel's 36
  wounded head of 2, 25
Benedict IX, Pope 239-240
Benedict XVI, Pope 165, 173,175
Bethel 70
Bethlehem 14, 52, 92, 102, 158
Bruce, F. F. 23
Bruise, prophecy of 198

C
Cathar Crusade 169
Catholicism - see Roman
  Catholicism
Chilton, David 96
Churchill, Winston 190
Conquistadors 169
Crown, Triregnum 173
  See also Diadems
Crusades, the 14, 18, 45, 169,175
  John Paul II apology for 175

D
Dan, the city 70
Daniel, the prophet 27, 182,
    214-215
  dreams of 27, 54, 147-148
Daniel, Book of
  Chapter 1 - 124
  Chapter 2 - 10, 27-36, 149, 151
  Chapter 4 - 109, 126
  Chapter 5 - 111
  Chapter 6 - 28,
  Chapter 7 - 25, 26, 36-38, 131,
    135, 138,147-148, 152-153,
    196-198, 230-231
  Chapter 8 - 24, 28, 59, 138-139
  Chapter 9 - 78-80, 86, 90-91,
    214-217, 180, 183, 214
    217, 225-231, 233
  Chapter 11 - 62
  Chapter 12 - 12, 186, 230, 233
  Jesus' quoting of 30-31, 36-37,
    86-87
David, King 52-57, 68, 70-72,
    83, 90, 92, 111
  covenant of 52, 221
'Days of vengeance' 86, 216, 228
Days of Vengeance, The 96
Dea Roma 15, 17-18, 102, 145
  image on coin 137
Dea Roma et Augustus 17
Devil, the 13, 37, 112
  See also Satan
Diadems, on seven heads 14, 26
Dio Cassius 82
Dispensationalist view 15, 180
Domitian 97
Dragon - see also Devil and Satan
  manifesting in Gentile empires
    14, 17-18
  wounded head of 20-21

E
Eastern Orthodoxy 165, 170, 175
    177, 237, 239
Elijah, the prophet 20, 73,
    132-133, 188
  the mystery of 20, 183
  the spirit of 183
Emperor-worship 114, 154
Encarta 96 12

European Economic Community (EEC) 225
Ezra, the scribe 90, 144, 215, 227

F
Forty two months, metaphorical meaning of 16, 21, 153-154

G
G10 countries 24
Gabriel, Mark 45
Gabriel, the archangel 138-139, 186, 214-217, 226-229
Genocide, Sudanese 158
Gentiles, definition of 29, 80
   kingdoms of 36,
      'the times of the...' 16, 21, 67, 80, 134-135, 144, 150, 153, 216, 229
Germany, Hitler's 132, 135,154, 190-191
Gospel, 'different' 119
   of the kingdom 84, 203-204, 219
'Great Satan', aka USA 159

H
Hadad-rimmon 69-70
Har-Magedon, meaning of 50-51, 69-72
   location of 48-51
Heel, metaphorical meaning of 20, 198
Herod the Great 98, 180
Hirohito, Emperor 19, 132, 135, 154,
Hitler, Adolf 14, 19, 132, 135, 154, 190-191

Holocaust, the 14, 78, 87, 171, 175, 191
Horn, the eleventh 152-154
Horns, the ten, meaning of 24-25, 147-149, 153-155
   Abraham and 218-219
   place on heads 21-23
Huguenot Massacre 169,
Hus, Jan 18, 170, 174
Hussein, King of Jordan 65
Hussein, Saddam 99-100

I
Image of the beast, meaning17-18
Incas 134
   Pizarro's massacre of 169
Inquisition, the 18, 169, 174
Iran 66, 132, 154,
Iran-Iraq War 157
Irenaeus 97
Islam, 45, 102, 132, 154, 155, 181
   impact on UN 154-161, 163
   control of the Holy Place 134, 158-159
Islamic countries 154
Islamic Empire 19
Islamic Jihad in Palestine 65
Islamic Revolutionary Guard 66
Israel, in exile 29, 90-92, 124, 145, 146, 150-151, 180, 214-215, 223
   origin of liberal democracy 31
   relevance to the beast 133-139 143-144
   restoration of 89-93, 150-151, 221-222
   spiritual cf. ethnic Israel 203-204
   target of Islam 154-160

J

Jacob, patriarch 66, 213, 234
'Jacob's Trouble' or Distress 77-81, 89-93
Jehovah's Witnesses 120, 123
Jenkins, Jerry 79
Jeremiah, the prophet 98, 101, 111, 114-115, 213-214
  "70 years" prophecy 90, 213-214
  almond rod vision 40,
  "Jacob's trouble" 77-78, 89-93
  lament for Josiah 70
  threshing metaphor 54
Jeremiah, David 15, 179-180
John the Baptist 55, 112, 238
John Paul I, Pope 173
John Paul II, Pope 173-175
Jordan River 215, 223, 226
Jordan, the Hashemite Kingdom of 65, 152
Josephus, Flavius 81-83
Josiah, king 75, 144, 165
  prefiguring Jesus 71-72, 75
  tragic death of 48, 69-72

K

Khomeini, Ayatollah 132, 159
Kim Il Sung 19, 132
King, meanings of 23-24
Kingdom of God, 30-31, 149, 215, 226
  as leaven 31
  in Son of Man 36-38
  as the Stone 29-31, 149
  future coming of 203-204
  hiddenness of 31-32, 95-96, 198, 202
  mysteries of 95-96
  offered to all 215-216
  source of liberal democracy 31

L

LaHaye, Tim 78-79
Left Behind series 79
Leviathan 131
Liberal democracy 19, 31, 204-205
Lloyd-George, David 190-191
Luther, Martin 18, 99, 165, 170-171, 175, 238
  antisemitism of 170-171, 176
  Catholic vindication of 175
Lutheran Church 171, 176,

M

Mahdi, the 45, 160, 163, 183-184
Mao Zedong 19, 135
Maori 204
Martyrs Christian 168
Medo-Persian Empire 14-16, 26, 27-28, 38, 90, 92-93, 131, 138-139, 145, 223
Meggido 62
Millennium, the 9, 62, 149, 208
Moses, the prophet 39, 64, 132-133, 143, 150, 210, 212, 221
  Law of 71-72, 130, 210
  link to the seven heads 220
  miracles of 41-43
  Song of 54
  staff 40-41
  Tabernacle of 54
Moses Maimonides 64
Muhammad 102, 154, 159
  prophecy of 45, 102
Mussolini, Benito 19, 132, 135, 154

Mystery, definition of 95-96
   of "a time, times and half a
   time" 135, 153-154, 216-218,
   230-233
   of Babylon 94-108
   of Christ Himself 201
   of the crucifixion 198, 202
   of Daniel's 70th Week 230
   of Elijah 20, 183

N
Nebuchadnezzar, dreams of
   27-36, 54, 126, 147, 149
   self-glorifying of 109, 126, 129
Nehemiah 144
Nero, Emperor 139-141, 150
Nero Decree of Hitler's 191
New Zealand 31-32, 120, 160, 225
   actions in UN 158-160
   Maori renaissance 204

O
Orthodox Churches 165, 172,
   175, 239
   beginning of 170
   number of followers 172
   on marriage 177-178, 237
   use of coercion 170
Orthodox Jewish rabbis 72, 132,
   176

P
Palestine, Mandate of 65
   UN member 154, 158
Parable of
   faithful steward 172
   fig tree 203-204

   kingdom 95-96
   leaven 31
   wedding feast 81
Passover, Festival of 15, 39, 46
   Jesus' fulfillment 197, 232
   Josephus's reference 82
   Josiah's 71
Pergamum 17-18
Persecution of believers 16, 87-89
   by the church 18, 164-174
Pilate, Pontius 168
Pizarro, Francisco 169
Pol Pot 19, 132, 154
Popes - Alexander VI 239
   Benedict IX 239-240
   Benedict XVI 165, 173-175
   Clement II 239
   Gregory VI 239
   John XII 239
   John Paul I 173
   John Paul II 173-175
   Julius II 239
   Leo I 237
   Leo X 239
   Paul VI 173-174
   Stephen VI 239
   Sylvester III 239
   Urban VI 239
   Victor III 240
Population, Jewish 1st century 83
Preterist view 94, 96-97, 102
Prince, Derek 188
Principalities and powers
   definitions 15, 142, 195
   of the Gentiles 15, 25, 38, 45,
      143, 195
   of the State 131-139, 142, 145
Protestant Churches
   antisemitism of 170-171, 176
   apologies to Anabaptists 176

apologies to Jews 176
beginning of 18
number of followers 172
rejection of coercion 18-19, 176
use of coercion 18-19, 170-172

Q
Quds Force 66

R
Ratzinger, Cardinal 165, 173-174
Red, meaning of 133
Rees, Lawrence, author 189-190
Reformation, the 165, 170-172
Richardson, Joel 100
Roman Catholic Church
  antichrist spirit 18
  apologies, general 174
  apologies to Jews 175-176
  apologies to Muslims 174-175
  apology to Orthodox 175
  apologies to Protestants 174
  as Babylon 9, 99-104, 122
  as the Great Apostasy 164-170
  asceticism 177-178, 236-238
  beginning of 18, 167-170
  end of the Apostasy 172-179
  licentiousness in 238-240
  number of followers 172
  on marriage 177-178, 236-238
  rejection of coercion 172-176
  use of coercion 167-172
Roman emperors
  Augustus 17-18, 182
  Constantine 167
  Domitian 97
  Gratian 167
  Hadrian 83
  Henry III 240
  Maximus 168
  Nero 139-141, 150
  Titus 81-82, 228
  Theodosius I 167
  Valentinian II 167
  Vespasian 82, 137, 140, 182
Russia 14, 19, 159
  pogroms 14
  Stalin's time 132, 135, 154

S
Satan, enemy of God 9, 11, 103
  authority of 37, 113, 137-138
  boast of 50, 181
  'bruising of head' 20-21
  dragon 13-14
  dwelling place of 17-18
  fall of 20-21, 112-113, 181
  false wonders of 40-43, 180
  Great Satan 159
  King of Babylon 110-113
  King of Tyre 112
  last battle of 61-62, 159
  origin of 112-113
  political machinations of 14, 45-47, 87-88
  seeking worship 17-18, 181
  throne of 17-18
Sea, metaphorical meaning of 131
  Mediterranean 135
Serpent of old, metaphor for Satan 13-14, 20-21, 112-113
Servetus, Michael 171, 176
Six Day War 65, 152
Snake. See serpent.
Solomon, King 35, 48, 111, 127, 235
  apostasy of 71
  Temple of 54, 180, 235
  wisdom of 10, 32, 95, 123-124

Spanish Inquisition of 169, 174
Stalin, Joseph 19, 132, 135, 154
Sudanese genocide 157-158

T
Tacitus, Cornelius 15
Temple Mount, the 62-63, 134, 136, 152, 158
  Islamic claim 19, 181-184
  UN claim 152, 158-160
Third Reich, the 189-191
Titus, Roman general, later emperor 81-82, 150, 228
Totalitarianism 19, 100

U
United Nations, the 35,
  as the seventh head 149, 152-162
  plaque 60

V
Vengeance, the days of 150, 216, 228
Vespasian 82, 132, 137, 140, 182

W
Wound, fatal 21, 25, 210
  See also Bruise
Wright, N. T. 24, 58, 140-142
Wycliffe, John 18, 99, 170

Other Books by Graeme Carlé

Available from:

Emmaus Road Publishing
PO Box 38-823
Howick
Auckland 2014
New Zealand

Website: www.emmausroad.org.nz

Books & eBooks
Amazon
Barnes & Noble
Kindle
Kobo
Koorong
Nook
and more...

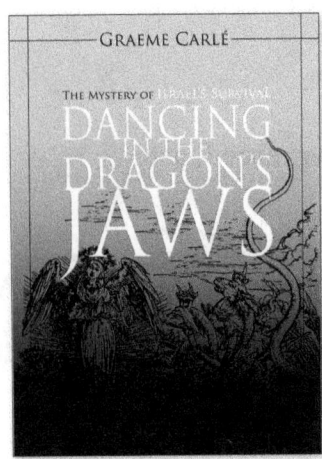

Book 1 in the Revelation series

Dancing in the Dragon's Jaws
The Mystery of Israel's Survival

Graeme Carlé

Why is the Book of Revelation so misunderstood?
Wasn't its whole point to give revelation? Well, in typically Jewish manner, yes and no.
 The Book of Revelation was written as an apocalypse, a Jewish literary genre which also includes the extraordinary Books of Daniel and Zechariah. Profound truths were concealed from outsiders and opponents using elaborate symbolism, to be understood only by those properly taught – as Jesus explains in Matthew 13:10-13.
 The apostle John's original 1st century audience, having been led by Jewish Christians, would have readily understood his imagery from Jewish history. His plagues echo the ten plagues of Israel's exodus; his seven trumpets resonate of the Old Testament battle for Jericho.
 Many think the keys to unlocking the Book of Revelation are lost. Not so. We still have Old Testament history and, for those who know where to look, full explanations of its symbols in the New Testament. What we need is the humility to learn from the 1st century Jewish believers the mysteries of the woman, the Messiah, the dragon, the comings of Elijah, and 'the times of the Gentiles'. From these we can understand God's continuing purpose for Israel.

ISBN 978-09582746-5-4

Book 2 in the Revelation series

Slouching Towards Bethlehem
The Rise of the Antichrists

Graeme Carlé

The lost keys of Revelation?

It is often thought today that the keys to understanding the Book of Revelation have been lost and are irretrievable – but they're not. They were just buried under centuries of rubble created by the Gentile church's foolish attempts to distance itself from its Jewish foundations. If, like any archaeologist, we dig carefully we can rediscover them.

In *Dancing in the Dragon's Jaws*, we found one key to understanding Revelation chapter 12 is the metaphorical "time, times, and half a time" and we unlocked the last 4,000 years of Jewish history.

This book, *Slouching Towards Bethlehem*, unlocks Revelation chapter 13 and the last 2,000 years of the Christian era, with startling results. Not only can we now understand the forces shaping history and the deaths of some 270 million in 20th century genocides but we can also project the future of Israel and the Middle East.

ISBN 978-0-9582746-8-5

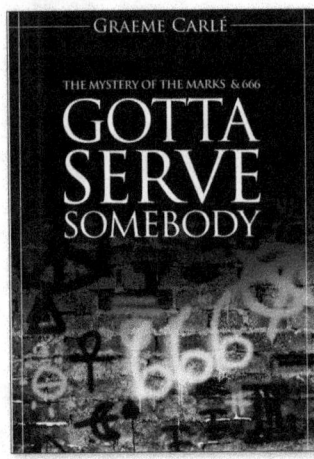

Book 3 in the Revelation series

Gotta Serve Somebody
The Mystery of the Marks & 666

Graeme Carlé

Are you confused about the mark of the beast?

You're not alone. The Mark and the number 666 have been controversial for centuries. Scholars and laymen alike have offered numerous interpretations, calculations and wild guesses but most predictions have failed to materialize. Some say we just have to wait.

In this book, Graeme uses the keys recovered in the first two of his series (*Dancing in the Dragon's Jaws* and *Slouching Towards Bethlehem*) to unlock the symbols and 'times' of the infamous and misunderstood mark in human history.

Instead of waiting for a world government or a global banking system that may never eventuate, Graeme believes and shows that The Mark is already here - and has been for the 2,000 years! We've just not recognized it.

It's actually the beast's *counterpart* of marks that God Himself placed on the forehead and hand of His people at the exodus and in the wilderness, with a numbering system of names as described in the Book of Numbers. We don't need a profound theological education or esoteric enlightenment but we do need a basic grasp of Jewish History and the Old Testament, as understood by 1st Century Jewish believers in Jesus of Nazareth.

ISBN 978-0-9582746-9-2

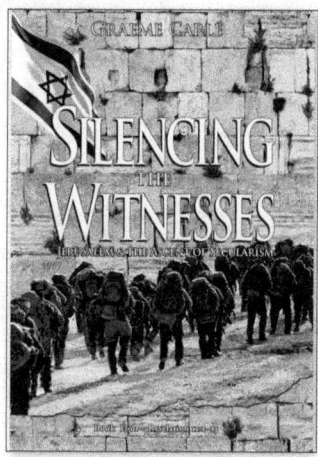

Book 4 in the Revelation series

Silencing the Witnesses
Jerusalem & the Ascent of Secularism

Graeme Carlé

Moses and Elijah back from the dead?

The most popular interpretation of Revelation 11 today is *literal* – that Moses and Elijah are soon to reappear in the streets of Jerusalem as witnesses, to preach for three and a half years, then be killed by a metaphorical beast (a man called the Antichrist) before being resurrected again after three and a half days.

The most common academic view today, however, is that these are all *metaphorical* images, referring to the church being persecuted initially by the Romans, today by the whole world, but ultimately vindicated.

In this book, Graeme takes the metaphorical approach but from a Jewish perspective. The Early Church was, after all, led by Jewish disciples and/or Gentiles taught by Jewish disciples. He shows how the two witnesses would have been understood by John's 1st Century audience to be the Law and the Prophets, making essential connections with Jesus' parable of the rich man and Lazarus, and with Paul's two Jerusalem's in Galatians 4.

In doing so, Graeme surveys the effects of the Law over 4,000 years of Jewish history, how it still applies to every Jew not under the New Covenant, and how it is relevant for all of us today.

ISBN 978-0-9941058-2-0

Back in 7
The Seals, Trumpets & Bowls

Graeme Carlé

Do you know the "signs of the times"?

Jesus is coming back and the Scriptures give us twenty-two "signs of the times" of His return but ten have already happened in the last 50-100 years - did you recognise them? Ten more are happening today around us, leaving only two to come and one is the actual, visible return of Christ. We all need to catch up.

To understand Revelation, Graeme seeks answers to questions few even think to ask: where in the Old Testament did John find all of his images and metaphors, and what did they mean there? Why does God choose the signs that He does? Why seals, trumpets, and bowls? What else would John's 1st century audience, who were either Jewish or taught by Jewish apostles, have already known and readily recognised? This book offers the answers.

We are usually presented with one of four perspectives of Revelation - Preterist, Historicist, Futurist, or Idealist - but as Graeme points out, all four are partly right, which is why each has adherents, but none are completely right, which is why there are three other perspectives. His 1st Century Jewish Teenage Approach resolves the debates, showing where each view is wrong and where each is right.

ISBN 978-1-7385820-2-0

Eating Sacred Cows
A Closer Look at Tithing

Graeme Carlé

To tithe or not to tithe?

Tithing is one of the most misunderstood and abused aspects of modern day religion, and there are fine Christian leaders on both sides of the issue. Images of tele-evangelists and pastors living extravagant lifestyles can fuel resentment and mockery, but the defence is often that God's 'prosperity' ideal is being upheld (at least for the receiver of tithes). But what of the givers?

Many Christians testify how God has blessed them for tithing, but many others are disappointed, often too ashamed to speak openly in case they are 'letting God down'. Sermons on tithing almost always quote Malachi's rebuke of ancient Israel, "You are cursed for you are robbing God! Bring the whole tithe into the storehouse…" (Malachi 3:8–9). But what exactly did Malachi mean? Doesn't God still want us to tithe? Well, not in the way we are usually taught today.

Citing Biblical texts about tithing that are rarely, if ever, referred to by those teaching tithing to fund the church, Graeme shows instead how God wants us to receive a revelation of His goodness as we take time off to enjoy annual holidays. He also wants us to be generous, giving freely to those in need rather than tying up our resources in unnecessary church assets. Find out for yourself how to stand firm in your freedom and enjoy being generous!

This newly revised version expands the original by 50%.

ISBN 978-0-9941058-1-3

The Red Heifer's Ashes
Mysteries of Ancient Israel

Graeme Carlé

Israel's best-kept secret

This 3,500-year-old ritual is considered by Orthodox rabbis to be the greatest mystery of the Law of Moses. It is also essential to the rebuilding of the Temple in Jerusalem for which many today are hoping, including many Christian end-time preachers, and only became possible when Israel regained the Temple Mount in 1967. The ashes were to sanctify water sprinkled on worshippers to cleanse them from the defilement of death and that would include today's builders.

In all of Jewish history, only nine red heifers needed to be offered with the last of the ninth's ashes either disappearing when the Second Temple was razed in 70 AD or, as some historical sources indicate, running out at the beginning of the 4th century. However, in the 12th century, one of Israel's greatest sages Moses Maimonides taught that Messiah will come to offer the tenth. Many therefore believe we are living in that time.

The ritual, however, provides a truly astonishing revelation of Jesus of Nazareth as Messiah, who He was, why He had to die and be raised on the third day, and will return on the Last Day. This book unfolds the meaning of every detail as the reader follows a supernatural path through the whole of the Old Testament, just as the two disciples did on the road to Emmaus.

ISBN 0-473-08128-8

Born of the Spirit
A Study Guide for New Believers

Graeme Carlé

Growing in God

Jesus said that "it is enough for the disciple that he become like his teacher" (Matt 10:25) and that is always to be our goal - to become like Jesus. The question is, how can we be discipled by Jesus Himself, to be and to do what He wants, rather than limited by the teachings of any particular denomination?

For example, some do not practice water baptism and communion; others assume you become a Christian when you are sprinkled as baby; others know very little about the Holy Spirit and His gifts for us all; others do not understand that there is only one church and everyone who believes in Jesus belongs to it.

This interactive Bible study is for anyone who wants to develop their personal spirituality by checking the foundations of what Jude the Lord's youngest brother called 'the faith which was once for all delivered to the saints' (Jude 3). Avoiding all denominational allegiances, find out for yourself how God wants us to love, live and learn.

ISBN 978-0-9941058-1-3

Because of the Angels
Unveiling 1 Corinthians 11:2-16

Graeme Carlé

Lost in Translation

This text has been completely lost to the church today, dismissed as Paul's 1st century cultural baggage regarding veils and hairstyles. Ironically, our response was actually our 20th century cultural baggage because it had become unfashionable for women to wear hats and men to keep their hair short.

We then ended up in the right practice of discarding hats and veils and not worrying about hair length but for the wrong reason, while those concerned for the integrity of the Scriptures often retained hats, veils, and hair length for the right reason but with the wrong understanding of the text.

Paul was divinely inspired to write it, as Peter explained:

> …our beloved brother Paul, according to the wisdom given him, wrote to you, as also in all his letters… in which are some things hard to understand, which the untaught and unstable distort, as they do also the rest of the Scriptures, to their own destruction. (2 Pet 3:15-16)

We have to humble ourselves and learn what Paul was trying to teach the Greeks 'according to the wisdom given him'. The key to understanding this passage is recognising its 1st century Jewishness: Paul was using Old Testament metaphors of 'head' and 'covering' and New Testament revelations of the fall of Satan and spiritual warfare.

ISBN 0-473-04955-4

www.ingramcontent.com/pod-product-compliance
Lightning Source LLC
Chambersburg PA
CBHW070650120526
44590CB00013BA/898